The Argument of the *Tractatus*

SUNY Series in Logic and Language

John T. Kearns, Editor

The Argument of the *Tractatus*

*Its relevance to contemporary theories of
logic, language, mind and philosophical truth*

Richard M. McDonough

State University of New York Press

To Nancy Gerth and Bruce Goldberg

Published by
State University of New York Press, Albany

For information, address State University of New York
Press, State University Plaza, Albany, N.Y., 12246

Library of Congress Cataloging in Publication Data

McDonough, Richard M., 1950–
  The argument of the Tractatus.

  (SUNY series in logic and language)
  Bibliography: p. 297
  Includes index.
    1. Wittgenstein, Ludwig, 1889–1951. Tractatus logico-philosphcus.
  2. Logic, Symbolic and mathematical. 3. Language—Philosophy.
  I. Title. II. Series.
  B3376.W563T7343   1985   192   85–9916
  ISBN 0–88706–152–4
  ISBN 0–88706–153–2 (pbk.)

10 9 8 7 6 5 4 3 2 1

This is an art
Which does mend nature—
Change it rather; but
The art itself is nature.

Shakespeare,
The Winter's Tale

Contents

Acknowledgments

It is with great pleasure that I am finally able to thank some of the persons who have contributed in so many ways to the success of this project.

First, I must thank my family and friends, especially my parents, Walter and Marilyn McDonough, who made it easier by believing in me all these years.

I have been privileged to have studied under such fine philosophers and teachers as Kurt Baier, Richard Gale, Sydney Shoemaker, David Lyons, Nicholas Sturgeon, Oswaldo Chateaubriand and Hector Castaneda. Two of my early teachers, Wilfred Sellers and Norman Malcolm, were of special importance to me. Not only have I learned a great deal from them, but their patient understanding and support was an essential factor in my early years of study. In addition, I am extremely grateful to Peter Strawson, Robert Fogelin, Robert Stecker, John N. Williams, James Breslauer, Antonio Chu, Carl Straub, Sanford Freedman, Thomas Tracy, Ho Hua Chew, John Greenwood, Terry Dartnall, Wayne Patterson, and last, but certainly not least, Tan Yoo Guan who have taken an interest in my work and offered valuable comments and encouragement.

Two persons, Nancy Gerth and Bruce Goldberg, must be singled out for special thanks. Without their contributions, extending over more than a decade, this book would not have been completed in anything like its present form. There is simply no way I can adequately express my thanks to these two remarkable persons and philosophers.

What I have learned from all of these people has had an immeasurable effect on my overall conception of the problems of philosophy. Of course, any errors contained in this manuscript must be mine alone. But if it were not for the advice afforded by these people, there would certainly be more of them.

In the United States we are extremely fortunate to have the generous support of our government in both the sciences and the humanities. I am thankful both to the National Science Foundation, which provided me with a graduate fellowship for the years 1971–74, during which time I first conceived this project; and the National Endowment for the Humanities which provided the post-doctoral research grant for the year 1980–81, during which time I was able to complete the first real draft of the whole project.

Finally, I cannot forget Miss Sylvia Hatch of Bates College who did enormous amounts of typing, often under difficult deadlines, in order that I could complete the manuscript on time; and Mr. Benjamin Wong, a research scholar at the National University of Singapore, and John N. Williams for their excellent proofreading of the manuscript.

Introduction: The Program

Tautologies and the Logical Structure of Language and the World

Despite the fact that a number of powerful interpretations of Wittgenstein's *Tractatus-logico-philosophicus* have been advanced since its first appearance in 1918, there are signs that there are themes in the book, and fundamental ones at that, which remain to be clarified. There are a series of remarks in the *Tractatus* which concern the fundamental nature of logic, and on the basis of that the connection of logic with the essences of both language and the world. These remarks have either been rather casually treated by commentators, or not at all. Perhaps, the single most important of these remarks is the one which Wittgenstein called his 'fundamental idea': "My fundamental idea is that the logical constants are not representatives . . ." (*TLP* 4.0312). Black, drawing on Wittgenstein's *Notebooks,* explains Wittgenstein's conception of a fundamental idea as a "flash of insight which illuminates a tangle of philosophical problems."[1] It ought to be possible to employ the fundamental idea in key deductions of other important views. Commentators have not, however, employed the idea in that way.

Significantly, other passages which are connected with the 'fundamental idea' tend to be passed over by the commentators. Wittgenstein states a variation on this fundamental idea, or *Grundegedanke,* at 5.4 of the *Tractatus:* "At this point it becomes manifest that there are no 'logical objects' or 'logical constants' (in Frege's and Russell's sense)." At 5.47, the seventh comment in 5.4, he writes, "One could say that the sole logical constant was what all propositions, by their very nature, had in common with one another. But that is the general propositional form." The claims that there is really only one logical constant and that it is the general propositional form are striking. The fact that they are connected

1

with the fundamental idea make them even more in need of explanation. And the remark at 5.47 is only one in a series of remarks in the *Tractatus* which, when taken together and in connection with the fundamental idea, can be fitted into an argument of central importance for the understanding of the *Tractatus*.

In addition to his fundamental idea Wittgenstein states his 'fundamental principle':

> 5.551 Our fundamental principle is that whenever a question can be decided by logic it can be decided without more ado. . . .

The context of this remark has to do with the connection between logic and ontology.

> 5.552 The experience that we need in order to understand logic is not that something or other is the state of things, but that something *is:* that, however, is not an experience.
>
> Logic is prior to every experience—that something is so. It is prior to the question "How?," not prior to the question "What?"
>
> 5.5521 And if this were not so how could we apply logic? We might put it in this way: if there would be a logic even if there were no world, how then could there be a logic given that there is a world?

At 5.552 and 5.5521 Wittgenstein indicates that logic somehow presupposes that a world exists. (This is echoed at 6.124 where, for instance, it is said that the propositions of logic describe the scaffolding of the world and presuppose that names have meaning.) These remarks also suggest that logic is connected in some intimate way with the specific nature of the world. When these remarks are taken in conjunction with this fundamental principle which precedes them, it appears reasonable to suppose that it is Wittgenstein's view not merely that there is some intimate connection between logic and the nature of the world but also that it is in principle possible for us to decide on certain ontological matters "without more ado" (5.551). Specifically, it is reasonable to consider whether Wittgenstein believes that there is some type of argument or procedure for settling logical and some (or all) ontological matters "all at once"

(5.47). Unfortunately, Wittgenstein gives no indication here what form this argument or procedure might take.

The theme is, however, repeated in a more promising form in the 6.12's:

> 6.12 The fact that the propositions of logic are tautologies shows the formal—logical—properties of language and the world.
>
> The fact that a tautology is yielded by *this particular way* of connecting its constitutents characterizes the logic of its constituents.
>
> If propositions are to yield a tautology when they are connected in a certain way they must have certain structural properties. So yielding a tautology when combined in this way shows that they possess these structural properties.

Here, the vague suggestion of a connection between "logic" and the world is replaced by the formulation that the fact that there is some specific set of tautologies determines something about the nature of language and something about the nature of the world. *That* such and such are the tautologies is a proposition with a truth value, a proposition which can perhaps be used as a premise in an argument for conclusions about language and the world. But 6.12 is difficult to interpret, in part due to the problematic notion of 'showing' which is involved. What does Wittgenstein mean by saying that the fact that certain expressions are tautologies *shows* such and such?

In his comment on 6.12 Black writes, "It is fair to say that according to Wittgenstein certain kinds of inferences (in a loose sense of that word) from logic to ontology are possible though it is very hard to see what such inferences would be."[2] (Black neglects to say that such "inferences" are supposed to be possible from logic to the structure of propositions as well.) The important point is that Black regards the claim that the tautologies *show* something, to be at least consistent with the view that some sort of *inference* from the tautologies to that something is possible, and here he is correct. Black makes a brief attempt to sketch one form such inferences might take, but he himself finds his attempt unsatisfactory.[3]

Stenius also dismisses the program of 6.12 too quickly. In reference to the view that "tautology or contradiction 'shows' the logical properties of the world" Stenius writes: "Now Wittgenstein seems to think that this applies to 'tautologies' and 'contradictions' in the truth functional sense and this a closer examination shows to be a confused idea."[4] Stenius' only direct support for this claim is given in a brief footnote to the passage. Whether or not Black and Stenius are wrong in their evaluations of Wittgenstein's program, their treatment of this passage (6.12) is hasty, and they are two of the most serious commentators. The fact that a plausible way of reconstructing these inferences from logic to ontology and to the structure of propositions has not been found, does not imply that one does not exist.

If we assume provisionally that the remark at 6.12 is the statement that there is some set of inferences from the fact that such and such are the tautologies, to views concerning the nature of language and the world, perhaps it can still be doubted just how extensive, and how significant, this set of linguistic and ontological theses really is. The remark at 6.12 is immediately preceded by 6.113:

> 6.113 It is the peculiar work of logical propositions that one can recognize that they are true from the symbol alone, and this fact contains in itself the whole philosophy of logic. . . .

But perhaps it can even be questioned how extensive is the domain of "the whole philosophy of logic." Surely, the description of the general propositional form is a part of the philosophy of logic. And in his comments on 5.47, quoted earlier in the present section, Wittgenstein writes that the "general propositional form is the essence of a proposition" (5.471) and that to "give the essence of a proposition is to give . . . essence of the world" (5.4711). A similar theme is found in the *Notebooks*.

> My *whole* task consists in explaining the nature of the proposition. That is to say in giving the nature of all facts, whose picture the proposition *is*.
>
> In giving the nature of all being.
>
> (And here being does not stand for existence—in that case it would be nonsensical.) (*NB*, p. 39)

Again and again Wittgenstein comes back to the view that the nature or general form of a proposition has broad ontological consequences, and that, therefore, the philosophy of logic must determine the essence of the world.

The program stated at 6.12 is a bold one. If by "the formal properties of language" Wittgenstein means the general logical features of propositions, the program would appear to be very difficult to bring to completion. For what connection could there be between the fact that '$p \ v \sim p$' is a tautology and such logical features of propositions as that genuine propositions are contingent, or that they are structured arrangements of signs which stand for objects? Nevertheless, this is the task which the interpreter of the *Tractatus* must face. Every general logical feature of genuine propositions must be, in some sense, derivable from the fact that certain expressions are tautologies.

But the second part of Wittgenstein's claim at 6.12 is even more bold than the first. The tautologies are alleged to show the form of *the world*. Of course, the idea that there is some connection between the tautologies and ontology is not uncommon. Recently, Dummett and others have focused again on the question whether and to what degree the law of the excluded middle, or perhaps the law of bivalence, carries a commitment to an ontological realism. But Wittgenstein's view is more radical than these. It does not merely claim that the tautologies are connected with these general ontological positions, but that the tautologies involve commitments to *specific* theses both about the structure of language and about the "scaffolding of the world." (6.124)

Following Black, I interpret 6.12 and 6.124 to suggest the possibility of some sort of inferences from the tautologies to the nature of language and the world. The thesis that there is some intimate connection between logic and the natures of langauge and the world is repeated over and over again in the *Tractatus*. This thesis is especially interesting because it unifies an interrelated set of propositions which concern the fundamental ideas and principles of the *Tractatus* and which tend to be passed over by the commentators. But, in addition, the question of whether the propositions of logic can somehow be the basis for an argument to specific ontological and linguistic conclusions is a sustained theme throughout Wittgenstein's writings. In the *Philosophical Investigations* at paragraphs 352 and 356, *On Certainty* at paragraphs 199 and 200, and Part IV of the *Remarks on the Foundations of Mathematics* Wittgenstein considers the question whether there is some "queer argument" (*PI* 352) or relationship which connects the tautologies to a set of ontological and linguistic views. One difference between the context of the allusions to this argument in Wittgenstein's later writings and in the *Tractatus* is that in the later writings

Wittgenstein's attitude to the argument seems to have become critical. It is in fact the case that the recurrent controversy over the relationship between Wittgenstein's earlier and later writings can be resolved by focusing attention on the attempt of the *Tractatus* to base ontological and linguistic theses on the tautologies.

Not only is there a set of remarks in the *Tractatus* which center around logic, the philosophy of logic and the connection between these and ontology, a set some of whose members are explicitly cited as the fundamental ideas of the *Tractatus*. In addition, the question whether there can be such an argument from logic and the philosophy of logic to ontology is a theme of sustained interest throughout Wittgenstein's writings. Unfortunately, the commentators have elected to pass over these facts in silence. For these reasons alone it appears worthwhile to develop a fresh interpretation of the *Tractatus,* an interpretation based upon the entire text.

A Sketch of Wittgenstein's Strategy

The view of the *Tractatus* is that a tautology is a book whose subject matters are the general forms of language and of the world. That "book" is written in a language which needs to be deciphered: ". . . logic is not a field in which *we* express what we wish with the help of signs, but rather one in which the nature of the absolutely necessary signs speaks for itself" (6.124). Learning this language, the a priori language of logic, or learning to hear the absolutely necessary signs "speak for themselves" is the only strictly fundamental method for deriving the system of ontological and linguistic propositions of the *Tractatus*.

The problem is to find a way to tap the ontological and linguistic information contained in the tautologies. To do this one must develop the proper interpretation of the tautologies, the logical propositions. It should be no surprise that the key idea in the interpretation of the logical propositions is the fundamental idea which concerns the nature of the logical constants.

Wittgenstein's fundamental idea is that the logical constants are not representatives, that they do not stand for objects. This idea is used in an argument that the tautologies are themselves not representational, that they are not about anything in the world. But, of course, they are about something. They have a meaning in some sense (6.124) and they have a truth value. It is argued on this basis that what the logical propositions are about is not external, but is internal to their symbols. The tautological symbol has a kind of self-referential property (see 6.113 and 6.127). It is about some aspect of its own structure. But what is this aspect of its own structure which it is about?

In the specification of that which is relevant to the truth value of a tautology like "It is raining or it is not raining," no reference need be made to any specific features of the particular propositions involved. "It is raining or not raining" is not about the weather. This is why a tautology can be represented by an expression like '$p \lor \sim p$' which contains only propositional variables. So what a tautology appears to be about is something which pertains to propositions in general. It turns out that that which is internal to the tautological symbol and which the tautologies are about, is nothing other than the general propositional form. At this point a method must be developed to extract the hidden linguistic and ontological content from the general propositional form so characterized. This is, the general propositional form is not given to us simpliciter, but within the context of the tautology. It is given with a great deal of logical structure around it. And the general propositional form stands in an intimate relation to this logical structure. It is not possible here to indicate what this relation is, but the key idea is in Wittgenstein's striking remark at 5.47 that the general propositional form is *the sole logical constant*. (See Chapter III, sections 1–3).

The "whole task" (*NB*, p. 39) of the *Tractatus* consists in determining precisely what is and what is not implicit in the general propositional form. This may seem to be too strong a claim since the general form of a proposition is expressed as "This is how things stand" (*"Es verhält sich so und so,"* 4.5). But that is only the expression in which the general form of a proposition is summed up. In fact, the general form of a proposition consists in everything which Wittgenstein says about genuine propositions in general in the *Tractatus:* that propositions are about something external to their symbol (2.173), that propositions represent objects to be in *the same relation* in which the names of those objects are themselves put in the propositional symbol (2.15 and 2.151), and so on. If the general form of a proposition is so rich in ontological and linguistic content that a determination of this content can be called the "whole task" of the *Tractatus,* and if the argument, which is based on the

fundamental idea and the associated interpretation of the tautologies, serves
to determine this content, then that argument deserves to be called "The
argument of the *Tractatus*."

The Historical Objections to Wittgenstein's Program

There are both historical and conceptual reasons why philosophers
have not made serious attempts to carry out Wittgenstein's program. The
historical objections are considered in the present section. By the historical
objections I mean that set of objections which is based on the view that
since Wittgenstein only says that the tautologies *show* the logical form of
language and the world, there cannot be any worthwhile philosophical
account of that connection. After all, doesn't Wittgenstein hold that what
is shown cannot be put into words, is nonsensical, is mystical, so that any
attempt to put the connection into some precise form is doomed to failure?
Those who hold this opinion regard the fact that the tautologies *show*
such and such as the admission that we have come to the point where
logic and language simply fail us. In this way the attempt to reconstruct
Wittgenstein's program is prevented from even getting off the ground.

This idea that though there might be some sort of connection between
logic or mathematics on the one hand and ontology on the other, but
that the connection cannot be expressed in precise language, goes as far
back as Russell's 1918 lectures on logical atomism. Russell himself writes
that his eight lectures, *Lectures on Logical Aromism,* "are very largely
concerned with explaining certain ideas which I learnt from my friend and
former pupil Ludwig Wittgenstein."[5] Russell writes at the very beginning
of these lectures that the philosophy of logical atomism "is one which has
forced itself upon me in the course of thinking about the philosophy of
mathematics, although I should find it very hard to say exactly how far
there is a definite logical connection between the two."[6] Wittgenstein's
remark that tautologies show the logical form of language and the world
may have been taken in a similar vein: that there is not necessarily any
"definite logical connection" between logic or the philosophy of logic and
these ontological and linguistic views.

Second, the logical positivists were among the first to take an interest
in the *Tractatus,* and they tended to either ignore or reject the program
of 6.12. The positivists were suspicious of the view that the tautologies

could show anything about the structure of language which is even remotely like the logical form of language presented in the *Tractatus*. This is, in part, because many of the positivists embraced a proposal theory of the structure of language.[7] They regarded language as a system of signs governed by rules where there are no a priori limitations on the kinds of linguistic rule systems which can be instituted; certainly no a priori limitations of the stringent sort presented in the *Tractatus*. If one does admit to a substantive a priori limitation on the structure of language, then one is close to admitting a place where metaphysics can find a foothold. Thus the rejection of the view that tautologies show the logical form of language is an important part of the positivist rejection of the ontology of the *Tractatus*, and the development of a proposal theory is essential to their own anti-metaphysical concerns. The positivists rejected the idea that there must be any single logical form to language and thus they never took seriously Wittgenstein's claim that the tautologies could involve commitments to such a single logical form.

But the positivists' most damaging influence was their more basic suspicion of the doctrine of showing itself. Since "what is shown cannot be said" (4.1212), and since "what cannot be put into words . . . is what is mystical" (6.522), the positivists inferred that the doctrines of showing and all associated doctrines are mystical doctrines. They associated the program of 6.12 with the mysticism of the *Tractatus* and not with the sober attempt to describe or propose the logical syntax of the language(s) of science.[8]

The association of Wittgenstein's doctrine of showing with mysticism and "nonsense" has led to the rejection of the kind of program sketched at 6.12. This is perhaps the most common of the misunderstandings of the *Tractatus*. For it means that one does not understand the program of 6.12 to be consistent with the existence of inferences from logic to ontology. The tendency is to put showing, mysticism, and nonsense in a sphere which is completely removed from the sphere of logic, sense, and the language of natural science. But this interpretation is far too simple.

In the first place, there is not one category of showing and the shown in the *Tractatus* but several, and each has a different status as regards expressibility and connection with fact-stating language. When at 6.522 Wittgenstein says that the mystical is what cannot be put into words but instead "makes itself manifest," the verb is *zeigen sich*. But at 4.1212, for example, when Wittgenstein says that what is shown cannot be said, the verb is simply *zeigen*. The difference is considerable and might be put in this way: Wittgenstein distinguishes between that which is shown by symbols or a symbolic system and that which shows itself, that is, shows itself without any connection with symbols. It is only the latter which is identified with the mystical. But the former is intimately bound up with fact-stating language. That is, all propositions which say something, all the propositions of natural science, also show something. Specifically, all genuine propositions show their sense (4.022). Though a great many distinctions remain to be made in this connection, this much is clear. There is a sense of "showing" which is not only identified as a mystical notion but must be involved in any account of propositions which say something.

Perhaps it will be said that though the charge of mysticism is misguided, still Wittgenstein does hold some strong negative views about the possibility of philosophical propositions and philosophical communication:

> 6.54 My propositions serve as elucidations in the following way: anyone who understands me eventually recognizes them as nonsensical, when he has used them—as steps—to climb up beyond them. (He must, so to speak, throw away the ladder after he has climbed up it.)
>
> He must transcend these propositions, and then he will see the world aright.

And this is one of the most famous doctrines of the *Tractatus*.

With regard to the doctrine that philosophical propositions are nonsense, it must be pointed out that "sense" in the *Tractatus* is a technical term. To say that a proposition has sense is to say that it is about objects in the world, that it is contingent, and such things. To say that a proposition is nonsense is to say that it is not that sort of proposition. The category of "nonsense" in the *Tractatus* is fundamentally a category not of criticism but of differentiation. Wittgenstein's notion of nonsense does not bear any simple relationship to the notion of nonsense in ordinary usage. The view that the philosophical propositions are nonsense in this technical meaning does not imply that they are absurd or worthless.[9]

Similarly, his remark that one must throw away the ladder after one has climbed it has persuaded his interpreters to not climb it at all. His claim that tautologies *show* the logical form of language and the world is not inconsistent with the existence of a demonstration of the logical form of language and the world. It is not inconsistent with the existence of the "ladder." Wittgenstein only requires that after one climbs the ladder and produces the inferences from logic to ontology, one must "throw it away." One must "transcend" the demonstration. Everything depends, therefore, on one's reading of "transcend." On one reading, the view that one must transcend these philosophical propositions and demonstrations only means that after one produces them one must make certain qualifying remarks concerning their natures. One must give an account of the notion of an "elucidation" which distinguishes elucidations from fact-stating propositions. This does not mean that philosophical propositions and demonstrations are not useful or illuminating, and it certainly does not mean that one should not build the ladder or climb it.

The discussion in the present section does not exhaust the significance of Wittgenstein's views that philosophical propositions are nonsense, that one must throw away the ladder after one has climbed it, and related doctrines. (A fuller treatment of these views is undertaken in Chapter VII.) My aim has only been to indicate that those objections which are designed to prevent the program of 6.12 from even getting off the ground are based on oversimple interpretations of the relevant passages of the *Tractatus*. Of course, in order to defend the feasibility of the program of 6.12 one could simply admit that even if Wittgenstein did think his own program nonsense in the ordinary sense, he was wrong in that evaluation of his program. In this case one would have to claim to belong not to the interpreters of Wittgenstein but to the ranks of those who have corrected his work. It has been my aim to show here that even if we adhere to Wittgenstein's intentions as these are expressed in the text, the relevant doctrines do not support the strong negative views concerning the possibility of philosophical language which have been hastily claimed for them. The attempt to reconstruct, along rigorous lines, the remark that the tautologies show the logical form of language and the world ought not to be rejected on the grounds that even Wittgenstein admits that such a program is "nonsensical" and "mystical." The text simply does not warrant placing such an interpretation on these terms and doctrines.

A Conceptual Objection to Wittgenstein's Program

If it is admitted that it is Wittgenstein's program to base a derivation of certain specific ontological and linguistic theses on the tautologies, this does not guarantee that the program is coherent. There seems to be an obvious conceptual objection to the program. If there cannot be more in the conclusions than there is in the premises, and if there are only empty logical propositions in the premises, then there cannot be substantive ontological and linguistic views in the conclusions. However, though Black characterizes Wittgenstein's view as the view that the inferences are from "logic to ontology" Wittgenstein nowhere endorses this sort of loose formulation.

The language at 6.12 is to the effect that the fact that certain expressions are tautologies shows the logical form of language and the world. Whereas 'p v $\sim p$' is a tautology, the expression "'p v $\sim p$' is a tautology" is not itself obviously a tautology, and it is expressions of this latter sort which figure as premises in the argument. But even if this expression is a tautology, there are other sorts of premises in the argument as well. In particular, the argument contains premises of a philosophical nature which are involved in an interpretation of the nature of the tautologies, premises such as Wittgenstein's 'fundamental idea'. The argument can by no means be characterized as simply involving inferences from logic to ontology. It would be better characterized as involving inferences from the fact that certain expressions are tautologies, plus a certain interpretation of the nature of the tautologies, to the ontological and linguistic theses which constitute the system of the *Tractatus*. An argument so characterized cannot be said to run up against the obvious sort of conceptual objections. There may be objections which can be brought up against the argument, but these must await its detailed formulation in the subsequent chapters.

The Scope of the Present Interpretation

In the early chapters the fundamental ideas concerning the logical constants are employed in order to develop the account of the logical propositions. On the basis of this, as described earlier, the basic features of the system of the *Tractatus* are demonstrated. These include, for example, the views that the genuine proposition is contingent, that it is about a subject matter external to its symbol, that this subject matter is substance (unalterable and subsistent), that the genuine propositional symbol involves a picture of what it is about, and so forth. This is completed by the conclusion of Chapter IV.

Several issues are selected for more intensive treatment. In Chapters V and VI the theory of meaning for genuine propositions is developed in considerable detail. This includes an account of the perceptible propositional sign in Chapter V, and an account of the thought, the actual meaning component of the proposition, in Chapter VI. The result of this interpretation is that Wittgenstein's notion of the thought is considerably more important and more sophisticated than previously imagined. Its connection with Brentano's notion of the 'mental' is developed. And it is shown to be intimately connected with certain views which are just beginning to be developed in the contemporary theory of meaning.

In Chapter VII Wittgenstein's account of philosophical propositions and philosophical systems is developed. Wittgenstein's views of these matters are shown to be much more positive than has been been imagined. It is argued that Wittgenstein is a holist with regard to philosophical propositions and systems, and that his seemingly negative views about them can be explained in these terms. This is significant for two reasons. First, it is of considerable historical interest since it can be shown that Wittgenstein's account on these matters has both undeniable similarities and undeniable differences with holistic accounts of philosophical truth in the tradition of German idealism. Second, the question whether atomistic or holistic conceptions of language are true has recently acquired a central status in the philosophy of language and Wittgenstein's view makes a contribution to these current debates.

Finally, Wittgenstein's accounts of communication for both genuine and philosophical propositions are considered in Chapter VIII. Once again, Wittgenstein's views turn out to clarify contemporary discussions, in this case most notably in the field of psycholinguistics. The key concepts and views which are presupposed in important parts of this field are isolated and clarified. Though it is not the purpose of the present work to prove or refute these current views, the clearer grasp of Wittgenstein's more sophisticated account of the process of communication shows where the real conceptual problems for this field are located.

The Status of the Present Interpretation

It is worth emphasizing that the philosophical arguments and con-clusions developed in the present book are merely presented as an inter-pretation, or reconstruction, of the *Tractatus*. The present book is neutral with regard to the truth of these views. It is the point of view of this author both that almost none of the particular views of the *Tractatus* can be accepted just as they stand, and that the basic presumptions of the whole system can be brought into question. The author of the *Tractatus* is operating under a very definite way of looking at things, a way of looking which is so common that it can easily go unnoticed. However, any attempt to take up this critical task in the present work would be of limited value. The tasks of criticism, and of replacement by a more adequate view, if these are to be done properly, must be the sole theme of a work devoted solely to those purposes. For this reason this book is to be followed by a sequel called *The Truth of the Argument of the Tractatus* in which these tasks are undertaken.

It might be wondered why, if it is admitted at the outset that Wittgenstein's views must be modified, it is so important to expend so much energy comprehending them. But if this is a good reason for giving less attention to the *Tractatus,* then the other great works of philosophy from Aristotle's *Metaphysics* to Kant's *Critique* must suffer a similar verdict. The fact is that the *Tractatus* is, like these other works, one of the greatest and most unique intellectual accomplishments to be produced in philosophy, and that this is so is made clearer on the present interpretation. Second, the fact that the views of the *Tractatus* cannot be accepted in their present form does not mean that they are unconnected with the final truth on the matter. A more complete and penetrating formulation of the views of the *Tractatus* cannot but facilitate a more sure grasp of the truth. And third, whether right or wrong, the views of the *Tractatus* bear a special relation to our time. Though some may take it for granted that the views of the *Tractatus* are dated, it is nonetheless true that certain views of the *Tractatus* are held but acknowledged by contemporary philosophers and psycholinguists. (This is argued, most notably in Chapters VI and VIII of the present work, in connection with Wittgenstein's views on the nature of meaning and of communication.) A clearer vision of the views of the

Tractatus will illuminate our own context all the more clearly. Whether the views of the *Tractatus* are correct or not, a clearer understanding of them is, for these reasons, a necessary *preparation* if the truth about logic, meaning, mind and reality is to be established.

CHAPTER I

Negation, Negative Facts and Wittgenstein's 'Fundamental Idea'

One of the dominant themes in Wittgenstein's *Notebooks* concerns "the mystery of negation: This is not how things are and yet we can say how things are not" (*NB*, p. 30). There is a logical and an ontological dimension to this mystery. The logical question is: "How does the proposition '$\sim p$' really contradict the proposition 'p'?"(*NB*, p. 30). The ontological question is whether, when '$\sim p$' is true, it corresponds to a negative fact. Wittgenstein reflects his concern with the ontological question in many places in the *Notebooks;* for instance, he writes that "the *dualism* of positive and negative facts. . .gives me no peace" (*NB*, p. 33).

Russell deals with the problem of negative facts in his "Lecture on Logical Atomism."[1] He describes the "Lectures" as containing "certain ideas which I learnt from my friend and former pupil Ludwig Wittgenstein."[2] But I shall argue that though Russell "inclines" toward admitting negative facts,[3] it is fundamental to Wittgenstein's conception that there cannot be negative facts. (Obviously certain distinctions must be made in this connection, since Wittgenstein does give a use to the expression "negative fact" in the *Tractatus;* see *TLP* 2.06.) Furthermore, I argue that according to Wittgenstein's view an incorrect answer to the ontological question precludes giving the correct answer to the logical question.

However, the significance of the present chapter goes beyond the presentation of Wittgenstein's solutions to the problems of negation. It turns out that Wittgenstein's solution to these problems requires the insight which is embodied in the 'fundamental idea' (4.032) of the *Tractatus.* Black, quoting from Wittgenstein's *Notebooks,* explains a 'fundamental idea' as a "flash of insight which illuminates a tangle of philosophical problems."[4]

16

But commentators have not appealed to the fundamental idea for the solution of any philosophical problems except in vague ways. Thus, part of the real significance of the present interpretation is that it enables one to see just how the fundamental idea has a precise role in the solution of a significant philosophical problem. And that idea has other applications as well. The present chapter includes one of these—the *Grundgedanke* based definition of the logical constants in general. These applications afford uncommon insight into the ontological views of the *Tractatus,* and into their logical foundations.

I.1   Russell's Distinction Between Negative and Molecular Propositions

It is useful to consider Russell's discussion of negative facts prior to considering Wittgenstein's view, despite the fact that Russell's discussion of these issues is indeterminate and sometimes just confused. In order to resolve the problem it is necessary to introduce ideas and techniques which go beyond Russell's.

Russell asks, "How are we really to interpret '$\sim p$'?"[5] But before he goes on to state his own view, and in order to set up a contrast with his view, Russell describes the theory put forward by one of his students, Mr. Demos:

> When we assert '$\sim p$' we are really asserting that there is some proposition 'q' which is true and is incompatible with 'p' . . .
>
> As e.g. if I say 'This chalk is not red' I shall be meaning to assert that there is some proposition which in this case would be the proposition 'This is white' which would be incompatible with 'It is red', and that you use the general negative forms because you do not happen to know what the actual proposition is that is true and is incompatible with 'p'.[6]

The motivation behind Demos's view is to avoid an account of the negative proposition which would commit one to the positing of negative facts. In order to do this, Demos presents an account in which the negative proposition is relegated to a subsidiary role, and is even theoretically eliminable.

Demos assumes that by eliminating the need for the negative prop-osition, one also eliminates the need to posit negative facts. (This is, of course, an important assumption and need not be regarded as obvious.) But the important point about Demos's view is that both '*p*' and '~*p*' are supposed to assert the existence of a positive fact.[7] In effect, Demos presents not a dualism of positive and negative facts, but a dualism of positive and positive facts. His theory is "dualistic" in the sense that for Demos both '*p*' and '~*p*' assert the existence of a fact.

Russell's objection to Demos's view is that in it distinct propositions are simply asserted to be logically incompatible, and no further account of the incompatibility is possible. One might infer from this that Russell's solution to the problem of negation must involve the development of some account on which '*p*' and '~*p*' are (in some sense) not distinct propositions! This does conform to Wittgenstein's resolution of the problem, but it turns out the same cannot be said for Russell.

Russell objects to Demos's view and at the same time reaffirms his commitment to the existence of negative facts. About Demos's view, he writes: "it makes incompatibility a fundamental and objective fact which is not so much simpler than allowing negative facts."[8] That is, though propositions of the forms '$R_1(a_1 . . . a_n)$' and '$R_2(b_1 . . . b_n)$' are not in general incompatible, there are simply, on Demos's view, some such cases of logical incompatibility for which no further explanation is possible.[9]

Russell states that he is "still inclined to admit negative facts."[10] But, with characteristic honesty, he admits that the notion of negative facts is troubling:

> One has a certain repugnance to negative facts, the same sort of repugnance that makes you wish not to have a fact '*p* v *q*' going about the world. You have the feeling that there are only positive facts, and that negative propositions have somehow or other got to be expressions of positive facts.[11]

But despite this repugnance, Russell inclines toward admitting negative facts and against admitting molecular facts. Although Russell does not make this point fully explicit, his objection to admitting molecular facts seems to be based on the recognition that the truth or falsity of a molecular proposition like '*p* or *q*' is dependent solely upon the truth or falsity of the component propositions.[12] That is to say, the truth value of '*p* or *q*' does "not depend upon a single objective fact which is disjunctive but depends upon two facts one of which corresponds to '*p*' and the other to '*q*'."[13] Thus, '*p* or *q*' does not appear to be about a single fact which is disjunctive, but seems to be only a way of making a particular compound assertion involving two (possible) facts.

Furthermore, Russell seems to connect this with the view that in '*p* or *q*' the '*or*' does not stand for something in the world. Immediately after making the point that '*p* or *q*' does not depend upon a "single objective fact which is disjunctive," Russell goes on to state:

> You must not look about the real world for an object which you can call 'or' and say, "Now look at this. This is 'or'."[14]

Though it is unclear what is premise and what is conclusion here, one interpretation of Russell's argument would be that since '*p* or *q*' is not about a single disjunctive fact, the constituent '*or*' does not add any content to the compound assertion, that is, it does not stand for an object. The logical constant, '*or*', is not involved in the construction of an altogether new proposition about an altogether new fact. Instead, the logical constant only has the function of marking which particular compound assertion involving '*p*' and '*q*' is being made. The only possible facts which are involved in '*p* v *q*' are those involved in '*p*' and in '*q*', not some distinct and *emergent* fact expressed by '*p* or *q*'.

Russell's remark that '*or*' does not stand for an object is reminiscent of the 'fundamental idea' of the *Tractatus:*

> 4.0312 . . . My fundamental idea is that the logical constants are not representatives; . . .

However, there seems to be one significant difference between Russell's view and Wittgenstein's 'fundamental idea.' Russell appears to except '*not*' from the claim that the logical constants do not represent something. Russell seems to argue that since there are no disjunctive facts, it follows that '*or*' does not represent something. But he does believe that there are negative facts. This at least suggests that he thinks '*not*' does represent something, and there is some support for this in the text.

And Russell does strongly suggest that '*not*' stands for something. He states that "the meaning of disjunction will be entirely explained by its truth table."[15] But when asked how he would define a negative fact, he answers, "You could not give a general definition of it if it is right that negativeness is an ultimate."[16] Russell does not appeal to a truth table in order to explain the meaning of negation, suggesting that in this case only, the meaning of this logical constant is not "entirely explained" by the truth table, that is, that it alone among the logical constants has some "ultimate" content—"negativeness."

Russell does not make his view explicit on the connection between the fact that '∼' does or does not stand for something and the existence of negative facts. He does not explicitly state either of the following views: *(S1)* If *'not'* does stand for something then when '∼*p*' is true, it is made true by a negative fact, and *(S2)* If *'not'* does not stand for something, then when '∼*p*' is true, it is not made true by a negative fact. But he does seem to argue that if *'p or q'* does not stand for a single disjunctive fact, then *'or'* does not stand for something. If one takes the contrapositive of this and substitutes *'not'* for *'or'* and '∼*p*' for *'p or q'*, and 'negative fact' for 'single disjunctive fact,' one gets *S1*. Whether Russell would assent to *S2* or not is not so clear. But, it turns out that Wittgenstein accepts *S2*. And since he holds that none of the logical constants are representatives, he does not accept the existence of any molecular facts (including negative facts).

We have reached some tentative conclusions about Russell's view of the matter. First, no account of the relationship between *'p'* and '∼*p*', which, as in Demos's view posits "fundamental objective incompatibilities," can be acceptable. Second, Russell's remarks suggest that in order to avoid such a view the positive and negative propositions must, in some sense, not be distinct propositions. Third, though Russell himself inclines toward admitting negative facts, it is a reluctant inclination. Russell seems to find himself forced to choose between Demos's fundamental and objective incompatibilities and negative facts. But neither feels totally acceptable, and this is a symptom that some third way is needed. Finally, Russell does make some connection between these issues and an idea which is very like Wittgenstein's fundamental idea. But exactly how the fundamental idea fits in is not made clear. Before these issues are resolved, the notion of negative facts must itself be clarified.

I.2   An Account of the Notion of a Negative Fact

Russell first raises the question whether there are negative facts in this form:

> Are there negative facts? Are there such facts as you might call the fact that Socrates is not alive?[17]

But this is not, even on Russell's own view, a sufficient explanation of the notion of negative facts. In the question session which followed his lecture he engages in the following dialogue:

> ————: If you had a formal test whether one has a positive or a negative proposition would it not follow that you would know whether there were negative facts or not?

> Mr. Russell: No I think not. In the perfect logical language that I sketched in theory it would always be obvious at once whether a proposition was positive or negative. But it would not bear on how you were to interpret negative propositions.

> ————: Would the existence of negative facts ever be anything other than a mere definition?

> Mr. Russell: Yes, I think it would. It seems to me that the business of metaphysics is to describe the world, and it is in my opinion a real definite question whether to mention negative facts or not.[18]

But if the existence of the true negative proposition, *even* given the promised perfect logical language, does not guarantee the existence of the negative fact, then the notion of a negative fact is empty unless some other criterion can be given. Some account must be given of what it would mean to say that it is "a real definite question" and part of the "the business of metaphysics" whether there are negative facts or not.

Russell does little to provide a clear account of negative facts. But without such an account he cannot distinguish his view from Demos's. For if the existence of the true negative proposition does not guarantee that there are negative facts, then the existence of the true positive proposition does not guarantee the existence of a positive fact. So when Demos states that '~p' is proxy for another proposition 'q' which is incompatible with '*p*', Russell has no basis for saying that what '*q*' refers to is not a negative fact after all. Russell's objection to Demos seems actually to be an objection to the analysis of '$\sim p$' in terms of another positive *proposition* '*q*'. The objection seems to be that Demos attempts to do away with the negative form of the proposition. But in Russell's own view that is irrelevant to the ontological question which is supposed to be at issue; at least it is irrelevant in the absence of a clear account of the relation of the negative proposition to the negative fact.

But if we contradict Wittgenstein's fundamental idea (and follow Russell's suggestion that '*not*' stands for something "ultimate," something which is not captured in the ordinary truth table definition of '$\sim$'), then there is in principle a clear distinction between positive and negative facts.[19] For if '$R(a_1. . .a_n)$' is the positive proposition, and $a_1. . .a_n$ are the n objects which are referred to by the proposition, then the corresponding negative proposition refers to $n+1$ objects where a_{n+1} is the logical object referred to by '*not*'.[20]

This account can be generalized: If '$x_1. . .x_n$' is the positive proposition and '$x'_1. . .x'_n$' are the signs which are components of the proposition, then the negative proposition is '$\sim x_1. . .x_n$' where there is some $[x_i. . x_k]$ ⊆ $[x_1. . .x_n]$ and '$\sim$' combines with '$x_i. . x_k$' such that the references of '$x_i. . .x_k$' are distinct from their references in the positive proposition. The result of this is that the negative proposition '$\sim x_1. . .x_n$' is made true by the existence of a fact distinct from that fact which makes '$x_1. . .x_n$' true. It is a distinct fact because it has distinct constituents.

On this view the function of '*not*' is to combine with none or more (none if $['x'_i. . .'x'_j] = \emptyset$) of the signs of the positive proposition such that the resulting negative proposition represents a distinct complex from that represented by the positive proposition. The case in which $['x'_i. . .'x'_k]$ = $\emptyset$ is the limiting case in which '*not*' itself stands for an object which is one of the objects in the fact referred to by the negative proposition.

According to this account both '*p*' and '$\sim p$' assert the existence of a fact. If '*p*' = 'aR_1b' then '*p*' is true if the possible fact that a is R_1 to b exists. Similarly '$\sim p$' = '$\sim aR_1b$'. But the '$\sim$', for example, combines with 'R_1' to form the complex '$\sim R_1$', and '$\sim R_1$' stands for some relation other than R_1, say the relation R_2. Thus, if '$\sim p$' is true it is because the possible fact that a is R_2 to b exists.

But there are problems for this notion of negative facts. If *PF* is the positive fact, and *NF* the negative fact, then the existence of *PF* makes

'p' true and the existence of NF makes '$\sim p$' true. But the existence of PF also makes '$\sim p$' false, and that of NF makes 'p' false. Russell points out that two propositions correspond to each fact,[21] but it is also true in his view that there are at least two *possible* facts relevant to the truth of each proposition. But the relationship between a proposition and the fact which makes it false is obscure. If 'p' is 'aR_1b' then '$\sim p$' is, for example, equivalent to 'aR_2b' where 'aR_2b' is made true by a complex distinct from, but incompatible with, that which makes 'aR_1b' true. But on the face of it 'p' only mentions a, b and R_1. It does not mention R_2, a constituent of the fact which makes it false. It does not appear to make the additional claim that a is not R_2 to b.

If there are positive and negative facts, that is, if the existence of one complex makes 'p' true and the existence of a distinct complex makes '$\sim p$' false, then the proposition 'p' does not make a single assertion, but rather, two assertions: The proposition 'p' asserts that (1) a certain positive fact obtains, and (2) a certain negative fact does not obtain. But note that if 'p' = 'aR_1b' and 'p' = $_{df}$ 'aR_1b obtains and aR_2b does not obtain', then one runs up against the same "fundamental objective incompatibility" that one encountered between 'p' and '$\sim p$' on Demos's theory.[22] For what is the logical relationship between the two assertions made by 'p' ('aR_1b obtains' and 'aR_2b does not obtain')? If it is supposed to be a logical incompatibility, then Russell is in the same position as Demos. Russell is quick to point out that Demos's view involves these fundamental objective incompatibilities, but he does not notice that they are present in his own view as well. This is partially because Russell retains the negative form, '$\sim p$', in a significant position, whereas Demos analyzes '$\sim p$' into some obviously distinct proposition 'q'. Demos's theory wears its problems on its sleeve. Russell's view involves exactly the same problems, but they are relocated to a less noticeable position.

In both Demos's and Russell's views one simply comes to the point at which distinct propositions are arbitrarily stated to be logically incompatible. This is because in both Russell's and Demos's views the function of '*not*' is to combine with none or more of the signs in the positive proposition, such that the references of some of the signs in the resulting negative proposition are distinct from their references in the positive proposition. In a clear sense, for *both* Russell and Demos the '*not*' sign makes a contribution to the content or sense, of the proposition. The result of this is that the positive proposition is made true by the existence of one fact, and the negative proposition is made true by the existence of a distinct fact.

Demos and Russell quibble over whether it is a positive or a negative fact which makes '~*p*' true, but the important point, the source of the "fundamental objective incompatibilities," is that it is a distinct fact from that which makes '*p*' true. Both Russell and Demos agree that '*p*' and '~*p*' are made true by *the existence of distinct facts*. And *that* is the real source of the problem. If '*p*' is made true by the existence of one fact, and '~*p*' is made true by the existence of a distinct fact, then there is no way in which one can avoid positing the problematic fundamental objective incompatibilities.

The theories of Russell and Demos really differ only as to where, and how well concealed, is the presupposition of the fundamental incompatibilities. The quibble over whether the fact which makes, '~*p*' true is positive or negative is an evasion of the real problem. With the real issue firmly in view it is possible to present Wittgenstein's solution to the problem.

I.3   Wittgenstein and the Dualism of Positive and Negative Facts

In the *Notebooks* Wittgenstein writes:

It is the *dualism*, positive and negative facts, which gives me no peace. For such a dualism can't exist. But how to get away from it. (*NB*, p. 33)

On the same page, he writes:

The question is really this: Are there facts besides the positive ones? (For it is difficult not to confuse what is not the case with what is the case instead of it.) (*NB*, p. 33)

This is a key remark. Both Russell and Demos "confuse what is not the case with what is the case instead of it." Both hold that '~*p*' is true when some fact is the case instead of the fact which would be the case if '*p*' were true. And this is the most basic reason why their views, intended by each to be antithetical to the other, are really quite similar. Both hold views that '*p*' is made true by one fact, and '$\sim p$' by *another*, and that the two distinct facts are, for some unexplained reason, not logically independent of each other.

Demos provides a dualism of positive-positive and Russell one of positive-negative facts. Fundamentally it is *dualisms* to which Wittgenstein is opposed, for such dualisms (and not simply the "negative facts" view) cause the fundamental confusion. The particular dualism of positive and negative facts is singled out by Wittgenstein for the most attention, because the difficulties with Demos's dualism of positive-positive facts are in plain view.

The quotation from the *Notebooks,* with which this chapter began, expressed "the mystery of negation" as the fact that "we can say how things are not." Now we can see, at least, how this is *not* accomplished: We do not say that something is not by saying that something else is the case which is incompatible with it.

The problem with *any* dualistic theory is that it treats '$\sim p$' as an *affirmative* proposition. It is affirmative, according to such theories, in the sense that it is regarded as affirming the existence of a fact. Even though Russell emphasizes the negative form, '$\sim p$', he understands this proposition as affirming the existence of a negative fact. But on Wittgenstein's view, '$\sim p$' can only deny that a fact obtains, and it cannot do this indirectly by *means of* an affirmation that some other (incompatible) fact is the case. Wittgenstein writes, "The negative proposition excludes reality' (*NB*, p. 39). It does not "include" any reality incompatible with that affirmed by the positive proposition. Negation is as fundamental an operation as affirmation.

The important insight can be expressed by analogy (which turns out, on Wittgenstein's final view, not to be an analogy at all). To affirm that an object is red, one pictures the object as red and affirms that which the picture shows. To deny that the object is red, one does not picture its being blue or gold. One does not picture what "is the case instead of it." Rather, to deny that the object is red, one draws a picture of its being red, and then one denies that which the picture shows, that is, one "excludes" the "reality" presented by the picture.

It is of great importance that, in a straightforward sense, both Russell and Demos regard '*not*' as contributing to the *representational content* of the proposition. In the particular example presented earlier, if '*p*' = '*aF*', then in '$\sim p$' the '$\sim$' combines with the predicate, with the result that a new predicate is produced, '$\sim F$', which refers to a distinct property from that referred to by 'F'. The second step in their program, after assimilating '*not*' into the content of the proposition, is to regard '$\sim p$' as the *affirmation* of this "negative content."

The essence of Wittgenstein's view is that negation does not enter into the representational content of the proposition. This means that, in a sense to be defined shortly, 'p' and '$\sim p$' must have *the same* representational content and differ only in what one might call the attitude of the proposition to the content. That is, the possible fact which is represented by 'p' and by '$\sim p$' is the same possible fact, and the difference between 'p' and '$\sim p$' is in their "attitude" to its existence. There is *only one* possible fact relevant to the truth values of both 'p' and '$\sim p$', and where 'p' "includes" its existence, '$\sim p$' "excludes" the existence of one and the same fact. It is in this way only that the dualism, with its accompanying "fundamental objective incompatibilities," is avoided.

Though the notion of '*sense*' involved in the *Tractatus* is a complicated one, the simplest way to express Wittgenstein's insight is to say that 'p' and '$\sim p$' must have the same sense. This may seem to be incompatible with the text, for at 5.2341 Wittgenstein writes that "Negation reverses the sense of a proposition." Thus, 'p' and '$\sim p$' must have opposite senses. But this only means that one must distinguish between two different, but related, notions of the sense of a proposition. I shall designate the different notions, *sense*$_1$ and *sense*$_2$. It turns out that in order to explain how 'p' and '$\sim p$' have opposite *sense*$_2$s, they must have the same *sense*$_1$s.

According to Stenius, Wittgenstein's remark at 5.2341

> expresses his rejection of an idea which he felt a strong temptation to hold. This is the thought that there must be some "neutral kernel" which is common in affirmative and negative propositions and which is given direction by being affirmed or denied.[23]

But Wittgenstein does hold that there is something in common between 'p' and '$\sim p$'. Stenius argues that there is no "neutral kernel" which is common to 'p' and '$\sim p$' by arguing that the "kernel" is not undirected. But this is a confusion. From the fact that the kernel is not neutral in some respect it does not follow that it (my *sense*$_1$) is not common to the positive and the negative proposition. That is, from the fact that the sense is "directed," it does not follow that '*p*' and '∼*p*' do not contain the same sentence radical, or *sense₁*, and that '∼' "reverses the direction" of that radical.

In order to make this more concrete, let us consider the way in which the kernel is said to have a "direction." Stenius writes:

> The sentence radical already has a direction: it shows things standing in one way and not in the opposite way.[24]

It is true that the *sense₁* of '*p*' and of '∼*p*' each has a direction in this sense. But still, they have the same direction. If '*p*' represents *a* being *R* to *b*, then so too does '∼*p*'. On any other view one must run up against a dualism. Note that Stenius implicitly endorses such a dualism himself when he speaks of '∼*p*' representing things standing "in the opposite way," that is, the way opposite to the way '*p*' represents them standing. Stenius confuses that which is not the case with that which would be the case if things stood in some "opposite" way.

'*p*' and '∼*p*' each represent things standing in the same way. In this sense they each have the same *sense₁*. In addition, one can speak of the *sense₂* of a proposition. There are only two possible *sense₂s* of a proposition, depending on whether the proposition is positive or negative. Furthermore, two propositions cannot have opposite *sense₂s* unless they have the same *sense₁*. This is so, since if '*p*' and '*q*' have different *sense₁s,* they represent different states of affairs and so are logically independent of one another.

When Wittgenstein writes that negation "reverses the sense of a proposition" he is speaking of its *sense₂*. It seems to me that the notion of the *sense₁* of a proposition is involved at 4.064:

> 4.064 Every proposition must *already* have a sense: it cannot be given a sense by affirmation. Indeed, its sense is just what is affirmed. And the same applies to negation, etc.

Since "its sense is just what is affirmed," or negated, the positive and negative proposition have the same sense. The fact that the "direction" of the *sense₁* is reversed by negation does not at all imply that '∼*p*' does not contain the same *sense₁* as '*p*'. One cannot argue, as Stenius does, that because the sense is directed, it is not common to '*p*' and '∼*p*'.

To specify the $sense_1$ of a proposition is to specify that which is relevant to its truth value. To say that 'p' and '$\sim p$' have the same $sense_1$ is to say that the same possible fact is relevant to their truth value, that is, it is to say that there is no dualism of facts involved. Given that one has specified the $sense_1$ of the proposition, one must go on to specify its $sense_2$. That is, one must specify whether the proposition "includes" or "excludes" the existence of the possible fact indicated by the $sense_1$.

Though Anscombe does not explicitly give the same account of sense as the one presented here, it does seem to me that she is on the same track when she writes:

> The picture theory of the proposition is that the proposition in the positive sense says: "This is how things are" and in the negative sense says: "This is how things aren't"—the '*this*' in both cases is being the same. . . .[25]

That is, that which the propositions represents, the '*this*', is the same (my $sense_1$), but 'p' and '$\sim p$' take opposite attitudes to that same '*this*'. They have opposite $sense_2s$.

Though it may be debatable whether these two notions of sense are actually the vehicle which Wittgenstein chose to express his view in the *Tractatus*, it is important that the substantive idea involved is not lost in a mere terminological debate. Whether one wishes to express this by saying that the '*this*' is in both cases the same, or that 'p' and '$\sim p$' have the same $sense_1$, or that they contain the same picture, is immaterial.

The questions with which we began were a logical and an ontological question concerning the interpretation of the negative proposition. The most important interpretation of the logical question in the *Notebooks* is the following:

> It is NOT ENOUGH to point to '$\sim p$''s lying outside 'p'. It will only be possible to derive all the properties of '$\sim p$' if '$\sim p$' is introduced *essentially as the negative of* 'p'.
>
> But how to do that? (*NB*, p 57)

Russell and Demos can both say that '$\sim p$' "lies outside" 'p'. They can both claim *that* 'p' is incompatible with '$\sim p$'—there was never any doubt about that. But they cannot explain why '$\sim p$' is "essentially the negative of 'p'." In their views 'p' and '$\sim p$' are, in effect, propositions with distinct senses. Their incompatibility is a brute fact for which there is no explanation. But in Wittgenstein's view, that which 'p' asserts is essentially connected with that which '$\sim p$' asserts in the sense that they have the same $sense_1$. One and the same possible fact is at stake in 'p' and '$\sim p$'. But 'p' affirms that that fact obtains and '$\sim p$' denies that *that same fact* obtains. It is because there is only one possible fact which is relevant to both 'p' and '$\sim p$' that they can be "essentially" incompatible with each other. What the one affirms is exactly what they other denies. That '$\sim p$' is essentially the negative of 'p' presupposes that 'p' and '$\sim p$' have the same $sense_1$.

There are two ways in which an account of the negative proposition can be dualistic, one logical or propositional, and the other ontological. First, one's account involves a propositional dualism if 'p' and '$\sim p$' are conceived as being distinct propositions. They are distinct propositions if the function of '$\sim$' is conceived after the fashion suggested in the preceeding account (that is, '$\sim$' combines with none or more . . .). Second, one's account involves an ontological dualism if the possible fact which is relevant to the truth value of 'p' is a distinct possible fact from that which is relevant to the truth value of '$\sim p$'. (Alternatively, one could say that the account is ontologically dualistic if there are two possible facts relevant to the truth value of 'p', that is, one which makes it true and a distinct one which makes it false.)

As we have seen in section 1.1, Russell raises the obvious objection to Demos's view. On that view 'p' and '$\sim p$' are really distinct propositions which are simply claimed, without further explanation, to be logically incompatible. One is faced with "fundamental objective incompatibilities." Russell himself suggests, even if not in a direct fashion, that in order to escape this commitment to fundamental objective incompatibilities, 'p' and '$\sim p$' must, in some sense, not be distinct propositions.

We can now see the way in which in Wittgenstein's view 'p' and '$\sim p$' are not distinct propositions. They are not distinct in the sense that they have the same $sense_1$, and thus avoid the postulation of distinct, but logically incompatible, propositions and states of affairs. In another sense, of course, they are distinct propositions: they have opposite $sense_2$s. The reality included by one is "excluded" by the other.

That 'p' and '$\sim p$' have the same $sense_1$ is the key to understanding how it is that '$\sim p$' contradicts the proposition 'p', for it enables one to escape the propositional dualisms of Demos and Russell. The same insight enables one to avoid the ontological dualism, the view which confuses what is not the case with what is the case instead of it. The solutions to both sorts of dualism, propositional and ontological, constitute the essence of Wittgenstein's basic response to Demos and Russell. However, this response requires a modification of certain common views about the *Tractatus*. These modifications are considered in the following section.

I.4   Negative Facts and the Tractatus

At 2.06 Wittgenstein defines the non-existence of a state of affairs as a negative-fact:

2.06   The existence or non-existence of states of affairs is reality.

(We also call the existence of states of affairs a positive fact and their non-existence a negative fact.)

But according to the preceding interpretation Wittgenstein does not accept negative facts, and in the *Notebooks* the dualism of positive and negative facts is said to "give me no peace . . . [for] such a dualism can't exist." Is the preceding interpretation wrong? Did Wittgenstein change his mind in the transition from the *Notebooks* to the *Tractatus?*

In order to resolve the prima facie contradiction one must distinguish two different senses of negative facts. At 2.06 Wittgenstein gives one definition of a negative fact which I call a *negative fact*₁.

A negative fact$_1$ is the *non-existence* of a state of affairs.

The sense in which Wittgenstein, in both the *Notebooks* and the *Tractatus*, rejects negative facts, is embodied in my definition of a negative fact$_2$:

A negative fact$_2$ is the *existence* of a state of affairs, i.e., a state of affairs which exists instead of that which is affirmed to exist by the positive proposition.

Only *negative fact*₂*s* involve the dangerous dualism, and the confusion of that which is not the case with that which is the case instead of it. According to the *Tractatus,* '$\sim p$' asserts the non-existence of a state of affairs, a *negative fact*₁. Wittgenstein does not hold that '~p' asserts the existence of any state of affairs, positive or negative. There is all the difference in the world between saying that '~p' asserts the non-existence of a state of affairs, and saying that it asserts the existence of a (negative) state of affairs.

A good way to put Wittgenstein's view is this: At 2.061 Wittgenstein writes, "states of affairs are independent of one another." If there are *negative facts*₂ then this could not be true, that is, the state of affairs whose existence would make 'p' true is not logically independent of that state of affairs whose existence would make '~p' true. But on Wittgenstein's view, which calls the non-existence of a state of affairs a "negative fact," we have, not one state of affairs which is logically dependent on another, but the non-mysterious view that the existence of a state of affairs is incompatible with *its own* non-existence.

By defining the non-existence of a state of affairs as a negative fact, Wittgenstein encourages the mistaken view that he had abandoned his earlier *(Notebooks)* view that there could not be negative facts. And if he had abandoned his earlier opposition to negative facts, then he would also have abandoned his earlier opposition to dualistic theories like Russell's and Demos's. But one must keep clear the distinctions between the two definitions of a negative fact, and their very different relationships to dualistic theories. Rather than signifying an abandonment of his earlier opposition to dualistic theories, Wittgenstein's definition of a negative fact, as the non-existence of a state of affairs, shows that he had not altered the view of the *Notebooks*. One might put it this way: If by saying that there are negative facts one only means that some states of affairs do not exist, then Wittgenstein has not altered his views and embraced an ontological dualism.

In the *Tractatus,* to speak of negative facts (my *negative fact*₁) is only a way of speaking. Wittgenstein introduces the notion of a *negative fact*₁ as a mere definition ("We also call. . . ."). Such a definition might be introduced for convenience's sake, so that one might speak of "the facts" as that which "makes" propositions true or false. But the notion of a *negative fact*₁ involves no ontological dualism.

That Wittgenstein's notion of a *negative fact*₁ is a mere definition for convenience's sake is also shown by the fact that the definition of a negative fact is given in 2.06, and 2.06 is the sixth comment on proposition number 2 in the *Tractatus:*

2 What is the case—a fact—is the existence of states of affairs.

This is Wittgenstein's basic definition of a fact. It is the notion of "fact" which is relevant in the statement of his substantive ontological views. It follows from this definition that the non-existence of a state of affairs is not a fact. To say that there are negative facts, in the *Tractatus,* is only to say that some negative propositions are true.

Recall that Russell says that even if one were in the possession of the perfect logical language, and has a formal test whether a proposition is genuinely negative, it would not follow that one knows whether there are negative facts or not. Russell says that this would not follow, because the question whether there are negative facts "is a real definite question" and part of "the business of metaphysics." This is a vague way of saying that demonstrating the existence of negative propositions does not settle the question whether there are *negative facts*$_2$ since what is called for in metaphysics is an interpretation of the nature of the negative proposition, that is, an answer to the question: What sort of things do they assert? If one is to say that there are, in a substantive sense, negative facts, then negative propositions must assert the existence of something. Showing that they do assert the existence of something would be of great interest to metaphysics. But if the negative proposition is interpreted to assert the non-existence of a fact, and then this is *defined* as a negative fact, no positive answer has been given to the *metaphysical* question whether negative facts exist.

Commentators have not, in general, appreciated the problem of negative facts faced by Wittgenstein. Black, for instance, never takes seriously any notion of a negative fact other than that of a *negative fact*$_1$. This means that the dualism which gave Wittgenstein "no peace" is never confronted by Black, and his ire gets directed against the harmless, non-dualistic, notion of a *negative fact*$_1$. Black casually dismisses the notion of a *negative fact*$_2$: "It would be preposterous to say that the objects *a* and *b* are combined—but in a negative way."[26] Black is right that it would be preposterous, but it has been said. The whole problem, when dealing with "the mystery of negation" is to not find oneself *forced* to say something "preposterous." Both Russell and Demos present views in which, in a sense, objects "are combined—in a negative way." The case is clearer in Russell though it applies to Demos as well. For Russell the objects referred to by a genuine negative proposition are combined in some way which is bound up with the "ultimate" nature of negation. The objects are negatively combined in the sense that, as in any dualistic theory, their being so combined is *incompatible* with the existence of the fact which would make the positive proposition true.[27]

I.5 Wittgenstein's 'Fundamental Idea'

The substance of Wittgenstein's alternative to the logical and ontological dualisms of Russell and Demos is now clear. The key which is needed to avoid these dualisms is the insight that '*p*' and '~*p*' have the same *sense*₁. But the important question remains concerning the relationship between their views and the fundamental ideas of the *Tractatus*.

It is possible, using views present only in the *Tractatus*, including the 'fundamental idea', to present an argument which has the desired conclusions. Furthermore, one form this argument takes emphasizes certain views which are also present in the *Notebooks*. Though this argument is not the simplest argument which one can construct using the fundamental ideas of the *Tractatus*, it is not without interest, for it seems to correspond to the actual gensis of Wittgenstein's final view. The *Notebooks* argument is presented first. But in order to state the argument of the *Tractatus* in its simplest, and most fundamental form, it is ultimately necessary to replace the *Notebooks* argument by a simpler argument, an argument in which the fundamental idea plays a more significant role.

The following series of remarks, some taken from the *Notebooks* and some present in both the *Notebooks* and the *Tractatus*, suggest the first premise of the *Notebooks* argument:

> The fact that in a certain sense the logical form of *p* is present even if *p* is not the case shows symbolically through the fact that '*p*' occurs in '~p'. (*NB*, p. 21)

Later in the *Notebooks*, he adds:

> Must the sign of the negative proposition be constructed by means of the sign for the positive one? (I believe so.) (*NB*, p. 32)

This point is not confined to the *Notebooks*. The following remark occurs both in the *Notebooks* (p. 33) and the *Tractatus:*

> 5.512 '∼p' is true if 'p' is false. Therefore, in the proposition '∼p' when it is true, 'p' is a false proposition. How then can the stroke make it agree with reality?

Obviously the significance of the remarks in the *Notebooks* is not fully clear to Wittgenstein at that point (though he apparently eventually felt he had achieved enough clarity about the basic idea to justify its inclusion in the *Tractatus*.) But it is clear that this simple observation about the symbolism struck Wittgenstein and suggested to him that in order that two propositions contradict each other, they must share something. In order that two propositions are "logical opposites," they must have something in common.

Wittgenstein does not here characterize this common element as the sense of the proposition, but it obvious that he is getting close to some such formulation. There is in the *Notebooks* one statement, explicitly associated with the preceding observation about the symbolism, which is almost identical to the conclusion we seek:

> If the positive proposition does not *have* to occur in the negative mustn't the protopicture of the positive proposition occur in the negative one? (*NB*, p. 33)

Substitute "sense₁" for "proto-picture" and one has the desired conclusion. This observation about the symbolism is an early way of getting at the view that '*p*' and '∼*p*' must have the same sense₁. But in order to translate that observation into the view that '*p*' and '∼*p*' must have the same *sense*₁, one must add premises which guarantee that (1) that which is shared in common between the two propositions (that is, the symbol of the positive proposition itself) is relevant to the determination of the sense₁ of the proposition, and (2) that which is different in the two propositions (the inclusion of the '∼' sign in the negative proposition) does not enter into the sense₁ of the proposition.

Black restates the view of the *Tractatus* which insures that the first requirement is satisfied. He writes that "the principle of sense as a function of a reference occupies a central position . . . in Wittgenstein's exposition of the essence of language."[28] However, Black's formulation of this view must be qualified. First, for Wittgenstein, sense is always primarily the sense of a proposition. Second, and more important, the sense of a proposition is not determined solely by the reference. *'aRb'* and *'bRa'* have, in general, different senses, but the same references. The *order* of the referents is relevant. And third, on Wittgenstein's final view, though the relation expressed by the proposition is not expressed by a term in the proposition, the relation that the terms are in is relevant to the sense as well. Though the referents and order are the same in the two propositions, if *'a'* is put in the relation *R* to *'b'* this expresses a different sense than is expressed by putting *'a'* in the relation *R'* to *'b'*. But fortunately these complications can be ignored, since according to the preceding observation about the symbolism, the order and relation in the positive and negative propositions are identical. That is, since the negative proposition is constructed by means of the positive proposition, the order, the relation involved, and so forth, are the same.

The view of the *Tractatus* which is needed in order to satisfy the second condition, that that which is different in the positive and negative propositions does not affect the sense$_1$ of the proposition, is the 'fundamental idea.' That which is different in *'p'* and *'~p'* is that the latter proposition contains a negation sign. But given that sense$_1$ is a function of reference, the negation sign does not affect the sense$_1$ of the proposition if the negation sign does not have a reference.

My formulation of the *Notebooks* argument is as follows:

1. The sign for the negative proposition must be constructed by means of the sign for the positive proposition.

∴ 2. Except for the '~' sign, the referring expressions (and their order, etc.) are identical in *'p'* and *'~p'*. (1)

3. Other things being equal, and they are equal, the sense$_1$ of a proposition is a function of the references of its constituent terms.

4. The logical constants, including '~', do not refer to an object. (fundamental idea)

∴ 5. *'p'* and *'~p'* have the same sense$_1$. (2, 3, 4)

But the historical argument, as stated thus far, is not quite complete. That the sense$_1$ of the positive and negative propositions is the same is a necessary condition for the view that that which the negative proposition denies is exactly that which the positive proposition affirms, but it is not a sufficient condition. In addition, it must be the case that it is the complete sense$_1$ of the proposition which is affirmed and denied in the respective propositions. That this is Wittgenstein's view is also expressed in some very interesting remarks in the *Notebooks*. For example, Wittgenstein writes:

> It is as if the logical constants projected the picture of the elementary propositions on to reality—which may then accord or not accord with this projection.

> Although all logical constants must already occur in the simple proposition, its own peculiar proto-picture *must* surely occur in it whole and undivided. (*NB*, p. 39)

Again, substitute "sense$_1$" for "proto-picture" and Wittgenstein is seen to be saying that the sense$_1$ of a proposition occurs in the proposition *whole and undivided*. The logical constants project this sense$_1$, whole and undivided, onto reality.

So, two more steps must be added to the preceding five step argument if the historical argument is to be complete. The argument concludes:

6. The sense$_1$ of the proposition, whole and undivided, is affirmed or negated.

∴ 7. '$\sim p$' denies exactly what 'p' affirms, and vice versa. (5, 6)

If, therefore, 'p' affirms the existence of a fact, '$\sim p$' can only deny its existence. This explains why '$\sim p$' is "essentially" the negative of 'p', and why '$\sim p$' does not affirm the existence of a fact which is incompatible with the fact whose existence is affirmed by 'p'.

This seven line argument employs views which are to be found in the *Tractatus*, and it has the virtue that in it the fundamental idea is employed in the solution of a fundamental problem, one which "gave me no peace." But from the standpoint of the philosopher who wishes to construct a philosophical systems which "sets the standard of simplicity" (5.4541), the argument leaves much to be desired. That is, this argument may very well build on certain remarks emphasized in the *Notebooks* in which Wittgenstein sought to avoid the "great dualism," but it is too complicated in itself to provide the foundation for a system which must meet the stringent requirements of 5.4541.

In particular, lines 1 and 3, the first two premises in the argument, are not obvious at all. Demos, for instance, would not agree that the sign for the negative proposition *must* be constructed by means of the sign for the positive one. This is the sort of thing that needs to be proved. For it is not obvious that this alleged feature of the symbolism is not simply a feature of one particular artificial language. Similar remarks apply to the second premise—that other things being equal, sense is a function of reference. Black is right that this is a view of the *Tractatus,* but it too stands in need of proof. And finally, the feeling that the preceding seven line arguments is not the simplest presentation of Wittgenstein's foundation may derive from the fact that in it the fundamental idea is lost in a group of premises, some of which seem as important as *it* is in the argument. The fundamental idea ought to be more prominently featured in the final version of the argument.

In order to further simplify the argument, one must look carefully at the fundamental idea itself. The fundamental idea is expressed at 4.0312 of the *Tractatus.* The entirety of 4.0312 is as follows:

> 4.0312 The possibility of propositions is based on the principle that objects have signs as their representatives.
>
> My fundamental idea is that the 'logical constants' are not representatives; that there can be no representatives of the *logic* of facts.

I am going to understand the 'fundamental idea' to be the proposition expressed before the semicolon in the second line (simply "the logical constants are not representatives"). The proposition which follows the semicolon is more abstract and general, and—I believe—is actually a derivative theorem in the *Tractatus.* Furthermore, in the original text, the semicolon is replaced by a period—the latter proposition is not explicitly identified as a 'fundamental idea.'

As Fogelin points out, despite the fact that Wittgenstein says the logical constants do not represent anything, he does refer to the meaning *(Bedeutung)* of the logical constants at 5.541 and to the *Bedeutung* "of a logical schema" at 5.13.[29] Fogelin concludes that "in general he uses the verb *bedeuten* freely throughout the *Tractatus* without giving the slightest indication that he is following Frege's technical conventions governing this term."[30] Though logical constants do not represent, they do have *Bedeutung,* or meaning, in some sense. And surely this is correct. *'Not'* does not mean the same as *'and'.* If we are to understand the fundamental idea everything depends upon determining in what specific senses the logical constants do and in what sense they do not have meaning.

In 4.0312 the logical constants are contrasted with another kind of symbol. The possibility of propositions is said to depend upon the *"Prinzip der Vertretung von Gegenstanden durch Zeichen"*—literally, the principle of the representation of objects through signs. In 4.0312 the logical constants are contrasted with that kind of sign. That is, the juxtaposition of ideas in 4.0312 suggests that there are two kinds of signs, those that do, and those—the logical constants—that do not, represent objects. Taken in context then, it seems to me that the meaning of the fundamental idea is that the logical constants are not included among the kinds of signs which enter into the determination of the representational content of the proposition. I propose that the deep meaning of the fundamental idea is that though there are signs which contribute to the representational content of the proposition, there are other signs, the logical ones, which have a completely different role. This is very different from simply saying that Wittgenstein's fundamental idea is that the logical constants do not refer to an object.

This interpretation of the fundamental idea is suggested in the *Notebooks* when Wittgenstein writes, "Negation refers to the *finished* sense of the negated proposition and not to its way of presenting." (*NB*, p. 25). That is, negation does not enter into the way of presenting, or representing, which constitutes the $sense_1$ of the proposition. Negation, affirmation, and the logical constants in general presuppose that the $sense_1$ of the proposition is "finished." Therefore they have to do only with combining these propositions with finished $sense_1$s into compounds, in which there is no gain or loss of representational content.

If this is the case, then the product of any logical operation on a proposition is another proposition with the same representational content. If the $sense_1$ of a proposition is its projection of that which is relevant to its truth value (that which is represented by the proposition) then 'p' and '$\sim p$' must have the same $sense_1$.

'p' and '$\sim p$' have the same sense$_1$. But they have opposite truth conditions. This is not because they represent different possible facts. They both represent the same possible fact, but this single possible fact is relevant to the truth values of 'p' and '$\sim p$' in opposite ways. This is where the meaning (or *Bedeutung*) of the logical constants comes in. There is only one possible fact which is relevant to both 'p' and '$\sim p$', but if this fact exists, the *affirmative* proposition is true, and if it does not exist, the negative proposition is true. Affirmation and negation do not have any role in determining which state of affairs is *relevant* to their truth values, but with the existence and non-existence of that which is represented by a proposition.

In this way one can account for the sense in which affirmation and negation do, and the sense they do not, have meaning. They do not contribute to the representational content of the proposition; their role is to determine the way in which that which is relevant to the truth value of the proposition determines the truth value of the proposition.

Given this way of reading the fundamental idea, it is possible to state a much simpler argument that 'p' and '$\sim p$' have the same sense, and that '$\sim p$' only denies that which 'p' affirms and vice versa:

1. The sense$_1$ of a proposition is its projection, or representation of that which is relevant to its truth value. (def.: "sense$_1$ of a proposition")

2. The logical constants do not enter into the representational content, or sense$_1$, of a proposition. (fundamental idea)

∴ 3. The positive and negative proposition have the same sense$_1$, the same representational content. (1, 2)

4. It is the sense$_1$ of the proposition, whole and undivided, which is affirmed or negated.

∴ 5. The negative proposition denies exactly that which the positive proposition affirms, and vice versa. (3, 4)

The advantages of this simplified argument over the earlier one are clear. In the present argument the fundamental idea bears the lion's share of the weight in the argument. In the earlier argument the two premises, that sense$_1$ is a function of reference and that the negative proposition is constructed by means of the positive proposition, were at least as crucial as the fundamental idea itself. In eliminating these two premises, one eliminates the necessity of assuming two very substantive propositions—the sort of propositions that stand in need of proof.

By contrast, the only two premises in the simplified argument, other than the new formulation of the fundamental idea, seem considerably less substantive. The first premise seems to be a definition. Line 4 may or may not be definitionally true, but since it is also present in the *Notebooks* argument, nothing has been lost by virtue of its inclusion here.

The crux of the more simplified argument lies in the reinterpretation of the fundamental idea. It is not merely that the logical constants do not refer, but that they do not contribute to the representational content of the proposition at all. On this basis, one can give a *Grundegedanke*-based definition of the logical constants in general: The logical constants signify those operations on propositions which do not result in propositions with a new sense₁, that is, they do not result in propositions with an altered representational content.

It might be objected that '$p \supset q$' has a different sense than does '$p \lor q$' and that, therefore, the logical constants do have a role in determining the sense of a proposition. Black makes such a claim in his remarks on 4.44–4.442:

> But this is not to say that such symbols as '$\lor$' and '$\supset$' are otiose, for these and the other logical symbols contribute to the sense of the compound in which they occur, and $p \lor q$ has quite a distinct sense from that of $p \supset q$.[31]

Black does, of course, have a point. It is true that the logical constants are not "otiose." But to admit that they have a *"Bedeutung"* in some sense is not to admit that they enter into the sense₁ of the propositions in which they occur.

Recall Russell's objection to admitting "disjunctive facts." He says that '$p \lor q$' is not about "a single objective fact which is disjunctive." The whole point is that Russell's intuition is not to regard a disjunctive proposition as representing a single possible fact. Rather, there are two possible facts relevant to the truth value of '$p \lor q$' and they are the possible facts relevant to 'p' and to 'q.' Just as '$p \lor q$' is not properly regarded as about a "single" possible fact, so too it is best not to regard it as having a single unitary sense₁. Rather than regard '$p \lor q$' as having a single unitary sense$_1$, it is less misleading to regard it as a mere logical compound of two propositions, each with a sense. The force of saying that 'p v q' is not about a "single objective fact which is disjunctive" is the same as saying that the logical constants do not enter into the representational content of the proposition.

It would be foolish to regard the logical constants as not making any contribution to the meaning of the proposition in which they occur. But the force of Wittgenstein's fundamental idea is that a logical compound of propositions is not a proposition which has a sense$_1$ that is over and above the sense$_1$ of its component propositions. It is a mere combination of propositions, each with a sense$_1$, without the emergence of any new sense$_1$. Rather than entering into the representational content of the proposition, the logical constants have to do with the determination of the way in which that which the proposition represents is relevant to its truth value.

It is, therefore, misleading to speak of a molecular proposition as having a sense$_1$, for this suggests that there are three sense$_1$'s involved in the proposition 'p v q'—namely, the sense$_1$ of 'p', the sense$_1$ of 'q' and the sense$_1$ of 'p v q'. But the only senses there are the senses of the nonmolecular propositions. The molecular propositions are merely logical combinations of those propositions with a sense$_1$. That they do not contribute to the sense$_1$ of the proposition is the significance of Wittgenstein's suggestions at 5.4611: "Signs for logical operations are punctuation marks." The comparison of logical constants to punctuation marks is a very powerful way of expressing nothing other than the fundamental idea. For no one would think that the period at the end of a sentence itself contributes to the sense$_1$, or representational content, of the sentence. Rather, the period only indicates that the specification of the representational content *has been completed.* And the comma which divides a sentence into parts does not itself contribute to the representational content of the sentence, but rather, it indicates how the various parts of the sentence are united in determining the whole sentence.

It is not the notion of *sense* which is misleading when it is applied to molecular propositions, but rather it is the notion of *the* sense of a molecular proposition. 'p v q' does not have *a* sense, but is a logical compound of two propositions, each with a sense. Speaking of *the sense* of the molecular, or negative, proposition is what misleads one into looking, for example, for disjunctive facts. (It also leads one away from a proper comprehension of the fundamental idea.)

Naturally one can define a notion of the sense of a molecular proposition, and it is obviously convenient to do so. But any such stipulation must be advanced with the clear recognition that the move from speaking of the sense of an elementary proposition, to speaking of the sense of a molecular proposition, is not an innocent one at all. Since, as Fogelin has pointed out, the logical constants do have a *"Bedeutung"* in some sense, it is all to easy to regard the molecular proposition as having an emergent sense. Thus, in any such definition of the sense of a molecular proposition one must be very careful to make it clear that there is no representational content in the molecular proposition that is not in its component propositions.

The significance of Wittgenstein's fundamental idea is that the result of a logical operation on propositions with a sense is not a new proposition with an emergent sense, but is only a particular combination of the propositions, each with a sense. In the case of particular interest in the present chapter, '$\sim p$' has the same sense as 'p', and thus, '$\sim p$' only denies that which 'p' affirms. It does not affirm the existence of some other fact, either positive or negative. There is no dualism of facts in Wittgenstein's view.

This completes Wittgenstein's resolution of the problems of negation. It is not claimed here that his solutions are wholly complete or correct, but they are a vast improvement over Russell's confused views. Wittgenstein's solutions are a clear contribution to thought about negation and negative facts. They deserve, and have not yet received, adequate attention.[32]

CHAPTER II

The Logical Propositions

According to 6.12 of the *Tractatus,* the tautologies show the logical form of language and the world. The argument of the *Tractatus* is an argument which is based on the propositions of logic—the tautologies—and in which the definitive views of the *Tractatus* are demonstrated. In order to carry out the demonstration, the proper interpretation of the tautologies must be developed. It should be no surprise that the proper interpretation of the logical constants, expressed in the fundamental idea, plays a key role in the proper interpretation of the propositions of logic. This account of the nature of the logical propositions is the true point of entry into the philosophical system of the *Tractatus.*

II.1 The Unique Status of the Propositions of Logic

Wittgenstein writes in the *Tractatus* that the propositions of logic must be assigned a "unique status among all propositions" (6.112). But his remarks on the nature of the logical propositions are sketchy and obscure, even for the *Tractatus.* The core of Wittgenstein's account of the propositions of logic occurs in the 6.1's. At 6.1 Wittgenstein describes the propositions of logic as "tautologies." But how is their tautological character to be understood? At 6.11 he gives a hint as to the answer: "Therefore, the propositions of logic say nothing. (They are the analytic propositions)." If '*A*' is a tautology, then '*A*' "says nothing." At 4.46 the tautologies are defined as propositions which are "true for all the truth possibilities of the elementary propositions." But why should a tautology, so defined, be a proposition which "says nothing?"

Perhaps Wittgenstein identifies "what can be said" with the propositions of natural science. Then it might appear that the tautologies "say nothing" in that they are simply not propositions of natural science. The danger of this approach is that some less than fundamental feature of the propositions of natural science may be taken as definitive of what it is for a proposition to say something. Some of the positivists, for example, erred in their interpretation of the *Tractatus* in just this respect, in regarding verifiability to be definitive of what it is to say something. But this is not the key notion in Wittgenstein's account. There is no way to attain clarity and certainty about Wittgenstein's views other than by demonstrating them from the fundamental ideas of the *Tractatus*.

Wittgenstein does seem to regard it as a *datum* that the propositions of logic have a different status from those of natural science. At 6.113 he writes, "Indeed, the logical proposition acquires all the characteristics of a proposition of natural science and this is a sure sign that it has been construed wrongly." But if the propositions of logic do not, like the propositions of natural science, "say something," then what do they do? For they do, at least, have a truth value. A positive account of the nature of the logical propositions is needed. Answering that they "have no representational relation to reality" (4.461) may be correct, but it raises more questions than it answers. If "reality" does not determine the truth value of the logical propositions, what, if anything, *does* determine their truth value?

Wittgenstein's remark at 6.11 that the propositions of logic are the "analytic" propositions, is also uninformative. For this is the only mention of analyticity in the *Tractatus,* and it is not defined there. Commentators have been rather cavalier in their treatment of 6.11. Black, for instance, writes, "The context suggests that he was simply using 'analytic propositions' as a synonym for 'propositions which say nothing.' "[1] But if the context is taken to include 6.113 (the third comment on 6.11), then Wittgenstein's notion of analyticity cannot be treated so lightly. For there he writes that "one can recognize that they are true from the symbol alone and this fact contains in itself *the whole philosophy of logic*" (emphasis added).

If the context of 6.11 is also taken to include the 6.12's, then the necessity of confronting Wittgenstein's notion of analyticity becomes even more urgent. Wittgenstein tells us in the 6.12's that *nevertheless* they "represent *(darstellen)* the scaffolding of the world" (6.124). In the same remark he continues this theme:

This contains the decisive point. We have said that some things are arbitrary in the symbols that we use and that some things are not. In logic it is only the latter that express, but that means that logic is not a field in which *we* express what we want with the help of the signs but rather one in which the nature of the absolutely necessary signs speaks for itself.

These tautologies which "say nothing" do express a great deal in some sense. The complete account of the logical propositions must be based on the fundamental ideas of the *Tractatus*. Such an account turns out to be more fruitful than it at first sight appears, even to the point of containing "the whole philosophy of logic."

A sketch of Wittgenstein's account is this: the "unique status" of the logical propositions is that they are not about anything external to their symbol. They are "formal" truths (or falsehoods) in the sense that that which is relevant to the determination of their truth value is internal to the symbol. The argument that this is so involves the fundamental idea. Though other premises are needed in order to complete the argument, the suggestion of a link between the view that the logical constants have no representational content, and the view that the logical propositions are about nothing external to their symbol, is not unexpected. That the truth "conditions" of the logical propositions are internal to their symbols is obviously akin to the "fact," mentioned at 6.113, that one can recognize the truth value of the logical propositions from the symbol alone. This "fact" contains "the whole philosophy of logic" in the sense that that which is internal to the symbol of the logical propositions and is relevant to their truth value is the general form of the non-logical propositions. A link is forged between the logical propositions and the general form of the non-logical propositions. It is then possible to "read off" the general logical features of the non-logical propositions, that is, produce arguments that they have certain general logical features.

Russell considers views in his "lectures" which are sometimes similar, sometimes dissimilar to Wittgenstein's views. Despite a certain imprecision and occasional inconsistency in Russell's discussion, it once again is convenient to consider Russell's views prior to confronting the sparse text of the *Tractatus*.

II.2   Russell's Account of the Logical Propositions

Russell is, in the "Lectures," not very clear on how one is to understand logical propositions. He begins by suggesting that every logical proposition consists wholly and solely of variables:

> Suppose I say: "xRy implies that x belongs to the domain of R," that would be a proposition of logic and one that contains only variables. You might think it contains such words as "belong" and "domain," but that is an error. It is only the habit of using ordinary language that makes those words appear. That is a proposition of logic. It does not mention any particular thing at all.[2]

The propositions of logic contain only variables and do not mention any particular thing. Perhaps Russell feels that the latter claim follows from the former.

But no sooner has Russell said this than he writes:

> It is not a very easy thing to see what are the constituents of a logical proposition. When one takes "Socrates loves Plato," "Socrates" is a constituent, "loves" is a constituent, and "Plato" is a constituent. Then you turn "Socrates" into x, "loves" into R and "Plato" into y. x and R and y are nothing, and they are not constituents, so it seems that the propositions of logic are entirely devoid of constituents. I do not think that that can quite be true. But then the only other thing you can seem to say is that the form is a constituent, that propositions of a certain form are always true: that may be the right analysis though I very much doubt whether it is.[3]

Russell does not here pretend to be very clear about the nature of the logical propositions. He suggests that since the propositions of logic contain only variables, either they have no constituents or their only constituents are the forms of propositions. But what does he mean by a "constituent" of a proposition?

Russell explains the notion of a constituent of a proposition in the succeeding lecture: "Every constituent has got to be there as one of the things in the world. . . ."[4] This suggests that a constituent of a proposition is one of the things in the world which the proposition is about. It is this use which Russell has in mind when he asks whether Romulus "himself" is a constituent of the proposition "Romulus exists," and answers that he is not: "If Romulus himself entered into our statement it would be plain that the statement that he did not exist would be nonsense. . . ."[5] This odd terminology, in which the things in the world which the proposition is about are the constituents of the proposition, is in keeping with the remark in the second lecture that "the components of the fact which makes a proposition true or false, as the case may be, are the meanings of the symbols which we must understand in order to understand the proposition."[6] The constituents of a proposition are the meanings of the terms in the proposition, and these are identified with the components of the possible fact which the proposition is about. Thus, when Russell asks about the constituents of the logical proposition, at least one of his questions is an ontological one: What things "in the world" are logical propositions about?

Russell also uses "constituent" in another way when he refers to the words or symbols "Socrates," "loves" and "Plato" as the constituents of the proposition.[7] This latter use is more in keeping with the ordinary one in which a constituent of something is one of the parts which actually make it up.

Which use does he have in mind when he asks about the constituents of the logical proposition? It seems likely that he has both uses in mind. Russell asks both (1) What are the components of the symbols of the logical propositions? and (2) What sorts of things in the world are the logical propositions about? In subsequent sections, I shall use the question "what are the *constituents* of the logical proposition?" when the ontological question is at issue, and the question "what are the *components* of the logical proposition?" when the make up of the propositional symbol itself is at issue.

When Russell states that "x, R and y are nothing," he is concerned with the ontological question. These variables are symbols and so are not "nothing," if the make up of the logical symbol is at issue. But if the ontological question is at issue, then they seem to be nothing in the sense that variables are not likely to be understood as standing for something "in the world." In this sense we can say that the variables have no representational content.

When Russell asks what the constituents of the logical propositions are, he is really asking what are the parts of the facts which determine the truth value of the logical propositions. But Russell is in a quandary.

His view that the propositions of logic consist solely of variables suggests that the logical propositions do not mention any particular thing. This itself suggests, and Russell himself tentatively mentions the view that the logical propositions have no constituents, that is, are not about anything at all in the world. But he is not certain about this suggestion.[8]

Russell at this point is still drawn to the view that all propositions must be about some sort of fact in the world—that all propositions, logical or otherwise, must have *constituents* of some kind. So he suggests that the constituents of logical propositions are the forms of propositions. Though this might suggest that the logical propositions are not about something in the world, Russell reminds us time and again of his "realistic bias:"

> I think one might describe philosophical logic . . . as an inventory
> . . . a "zoo" containing all the different forms that facts may have.
> . . . In accordance with the sort of realistic bias that I should put into
> all study of metaphysics, I should always wish to be engaged in the
> investigation of some actual fact or set of facts, and it seems to me
> that that is so in logic just as much as it is in zoology. In logic you
> are concerned with the forms of facts, with getting hold of the different
> sorts of facts, different *logical* sorts of facts, that there are in the world.[9]

Russell's remarks that logical propositions merely express "form" or "connection" suggests that the difference between logic and the natural sciences is a qualitative difference. But by stressing his "realistic bias," by comparing logic to zoology, and by stressing that he is interested in getting clear about the "different logical sorts of facts" which are "in the world," he indicates that the difference is merely one of the degree of generality involved. Perhaps the degree of generality at which logic begins, and the natural sciences end, is reached when one encounters categories so general that they transcend the uses of any particular science like zoology. The category of a subject having a property is not confined to any particular science like zoology. Here is a general structure to the world which is employed by many (perhaps all) sciences. Perhaps that is the level of generality relevant to the "zoo" of philosophical logic.

For Russell the logical proposition " '*xRy*' implies that '*x* belongs to the domain of *R*' " is about the form of a proposition, for instance, the form of the proposition 'Socrates loves Plato'. But in what sense are logical propositions *about* forms of propositions? Is the variable a name of a form or does this assimilate logical propositions too much to the non-logical propositions? It is at this point that Russell seems to rely on the unclarity in his notion of the form of a proposition to enable him to (1) distinguish logical propositions from non-logical ones—that is, logical propositions merely about "forms" of propositions or facts. At the same time, (2) logical propositions *are* about facts of some sort, that is, very general facts.

That Russell is unclear, even about what it means to say that logical propositions are about forms, is evidenced by the fact that he immediately reformulates this view as the view that they are "propositions of a certain form" such that they are "always true." But the fact that a logical proposition has a certain form as a constituent does not imply that it is of that form. A proposition about the subject-predicate form need not itself be of the subject-predicate form. The notion of form has not been clarified by Russell and is being used in an intuitive and uncritical sense. A more sophisticated account of the notion of the form of a proposition is required.

Russell concludes his discussion of the logical propositions with the admission that he is not clear as to their nature:

> [The] propositions of logic. . .have a certain peculiar quality which marks them out from other propositions and enables us to know them a priori. But what exactly that characteristic is I am not able to tell you. . . . I always have to make this apology but the world really is rather puzzling and I cannot help it.[10]

But the one position which dominates Russell's discussion is that the logical propositions are about facts in some sense. They are about something which is "there in the world." This contrasts with Wittgenstein's view in the *Tractatus.*

It is an important part of the *Tractatus* that a non-logical proposition is a "picture." At 2.173 a picture is said to "represent its subject from a position outside it." Non-logical propositions are representations in that sense. They have "constituents" in the sense that they are about something in the world (something external to their symbol). When Wittgenstein writes at 4.0312 that "there can be no representatives of the logic of facts," he is saying that logical propositions are not pictures, that is, are not representations of a subject matter "from a point of view outside it."

In the *Tractatus* the "aboutness" of logical propositions is not the sort of aboutness involved in representations.

It is worthwhile to sum up Russell's four suggestions and to indicate in outline the general lines of Wittgenstein's alternative. Russell considers each of *S1–S4*, but is completely comfortable with only the first two of these suggestions:

> *S1*   Logical propositions contain only variables.

> *S2*   Logical propositions do not mention any particular thing, that is, their constituents are not any particular things.

> *S3*   Logical propositions are about the forms of proposition, that is, their constituents are the forms of propositions.

> *S4*   Logical propositions are true by virtue of their form.

(1) Wittgenstein rejects *S1* but not for the trivial reason that logical propositions contain logical *constants* like '*or*' and '*not*'. It is important to Wittgenstein's view that the logical propositions contain genuine propositions and not variables. For Wittgenstein, an expression like 'p v $\sim p$', where 'p' is a variable, is not a bona fide logical proposition, but is only a schema which means that if one consistently substitutes a genuine proposition 'P' for 'p,' the result is a logical proposition. For Wittgenstein, all the bona fide tautologies are expressions like 'P v $\sim P$' where 'P' is a genuine proposition. Expressions like 'p v $\sim p$', 'p' a variable, are only schemas used to refer in an indeterminate way to actual tautologies. It turns out to be *very important* in Wittgenstein's view that the genuine tautologies contain genuine propositions (even if, as we shall see, the component genuine propositions do not function normally in that context).

(2) Though Wittgenstein rejects *S1* he accepts *S2*. Though a genuine proposition which does mention some "particular thing" is contained in a tautology, the tautology itself does not mention any particular thing ("It is either raining or not raining" is not about the weather, see 4.461). This is connected with my claim that in Wittgenstein's view, it is a very important fact that tautologies contain genuine propositions which do not, in that context, function as genuine propositions. Russell's reason for accepting *S2* appears to be that he accepts *S1*. But Wittgenstein rejects *S1* and accepts *S2*.

Why then does Wittgenstein accept *S2*? More importantly, what is the significance of the fact that there are expressions which contain propositions which mention particular things, but which do not themselves mention those things? Employing the metaphor that the component propositions "cancel" each other does not answer the question. For what special properties do expressions have, in which all component propositions "cancel" each other out? For when they cancel, *what*, if anything, is relevant to the determination of their truth value?

(3) Wittgenstein rejects *S3* since he rejects the view that the logical propositions have any constituents at all. He does hold that logical propositions are about the general form of a proposition, but the latter is not a constituent, not something "there in the world."

(4) Wittgenstein does not accept *S4* as it stands, but he does accept something like it. Furthermore, his notion of analyticity is explicable in some such terms. As a first approximation, Wittgenstein holds that a proposition is analytic if and only if it is true by virtue of its own form, where the form of a proposition is understood in terms of that which is internal to the symbol.

With this background let us turn to a more detailed consideration of Wittgenstein's view.

II.3 What Tautologies Express

In order to determine what sort of thing the logical propositions express, one must first determine what sort of expressions are the bona fide logical propositions. At 6.1 Wittgenstein identifies the propositions of logic with the tautologies. A *"tautology"* is defined as an expression which is true for all the true possibilities of its component propositions (4.46). It is, of course, by no means obvious that all propositions of logic are tautologies in this sense. Nevertheless, Wittgenstein believes that the tautologies have a priority over other sorts of logical propositions, and he even believes that the others are, in some sense, reducible to tautologies.

Wittgenstein does not count expressions like '$(x)(x=x)$' or '$p \lor \sim p$', where 'p' is a variable, as a tautology. In what follows I shall use small letters, 'p', 'q', and so forth, to stand for variables, and capitals 'P', 'Q', and so forth, to stand for genuine propositions. From the definition of a tautology at 4.46, it follows that neither of these expressions is a tautology in the strict sense. Both are composed of variables; neither has component propositions. '$(x)(x=x)$' contains variables which are not even propositional variables. Wittgenstein counts only tautologies in the truth-functional sense as tautologies. Even though '$p \lor \sim p$' is an expression in the truth-functional language, it too contains variables and not genuine propositions, and is therefore not a bona fide tautology.[11]

What is it that the tautologies, so defined, express? The tautology '$P \lor \sim P$' seems to express something about its particular component proposition 'P'. The ordinary language translation makes this explicit: "Either the proposition 'P' or its negation is true." The particular proposition 'P' appears to be the subject of the ordinary language expression. But in the ordinary language expression, the symbol 'P' is used to mention a particular proposition. This is altogether different than in the expression '$P \lor \sim P$' where a particular proposition is used, not mentioned. Though the ordinary language translation may suggest that a particular proposition is the subject matter of '$P \lor \sim P$' this is not so.

If '$P \lor \sim P$' is not about the particular component proposition involved, then what is it about? The proposition '$P \lor Q$', not a tautology, is about the particular subject matters of 'P' and 'Q'—cabbages and kings, for instance. But '$P \lor \sim P$' is *not* about the subject matters of its component propositions! "It is raining or not raining" is not about the weather. From the definition of a tautology, it follows that the truth values of its component propositions drop out as irrelevant to the truth value of the tautology. But to specify that which a proposition is about is to specify that which is relevant to the determination of its truth value. So that which is relevant to the truth value of the tautology does not involve anything which distinguishes 'P' from any other propositions. This is quite important. Wittgenstein distinguishes between essential and accidental features of propositional symbols, ". . . in general, what is essential in a symbol is what all symbols that can serve the same purpose have in common" (3.341). Though some particular proposition or other must occur in the tautology, none of its particular features are essential to the tautological symbol. Since the particular features of 'P' are not essential to the tautology, any distinct proposition, 'Q' for instance, would serve just as well in its place. i.e., '$Q \lor \sim Q$' expresses the same thing as '$P \lor \sim P$'.

For these reasons it is convenient to employ the schema '$p \lor \sim p$', 'p' being a variable, to characterize that which the tautology is about. Though some particular proposition or other must actually occur in the tautology, the truth "conditions" of the tautology abstract from that which $\mathcal{V}$ distinguishes 'P v $\sim P$' from 'Q v $\sim Q$'. That which determines the truth value of 'P v $\sim P$' is the same as that which determines the truth value of 'Q v $\sim Q$'. Though a genuine tautology must contain some particular proposition or other, that which is relevant in the specification of its truth conditions is something which that particular proposition shares with all genuine propositions. 'P v $\sim P$' may appear to be about the particular proposition 'P', or it may appear to be about that which its component propositions are about, but since any proposition can be consistently substituted for 'P' with the result that the new expression is still a tautology, the tautology is in some sense about something shared by propositions in general.

Though it is not strictly correct to call an expression which contains variables like 'p v $\sim p$' a tautology, such an expression does capture that which a tautology is about better than one like 'P v $\sim P$', since in the former expression the abstraction from the particularity of the proposition involved is made explicit. It is just this fact which inclines Russell to regard the tautology as composed of variables. But 'p v $\sim p$', can be called a tautology only in the derivative sense that a bona fide tautology is obtained by consistently substituting any genuine proposition for the variable throughout the expression.

Since that which is relevant to the truth value of the tautologies is something shared by 'P v $\sim P$', 'Q v $\sim Q$', and so forth, it might be tempting to *define* this something-in-common-to-all-propositions as the general form of a proposition. That is, the general form of a proposition is that which is "left over" when abstraction is made from the particular subject matter of the genuine propositions involved. But such a stipulative definition could only serve to confuse the issue. For the real questions are: Is there something "left over" in such a case, and if so, what character, or status, does it have? The proper procedure is first to determine the status of what is "left over" and then introduce an expression like "the general form of a proposition" to capture the notion which has been developed independently.

Wittgenstein does state at 6.124 that "the propositions of logic . . . have no subject matter." They have no subject matter at all, either of a particular or of a general sort. But this view must be demonstrated, not slipped in under the cover of a "stipulative definition." Recall that in Russell's uncritical use of "form or connection" it is not, apparently, ruled out that a proposition which asserts only "form or connection" has some highly general subject matter in the world.

At this point it is safest to say that that which 'P v $\sim P$' is about is something which pertains to propositions in general. Whether this is the general form of a proposition, or whether this is some highly general content "possessed" by all propositions is not yet clear, since the form-content distinction itself has not yet been clarified.

But given that 'p v $\sim p$' expresses something about all propositions, what does it express about them? If one appeals to the ordinary expression for 'p v $\sim p$', it would seem that it expresses something about the truth possibilities of propositions. But this points to a major disanalogy between the ordinary expression of the tautology and its representation in the symbolic language. No predicate words appear in the symbolic expression. Of course, something very important may be gained by this "loss" of the predicate in the translation into symbolic language. For if the ordinary language expression is taken as a guide, it appears that in the excluded middle a property designated by "is true" is predicated of a complex subject which is itself referred to by the expression "either a proposition or its negation." Again, taking the ordinary language expression as a guide, one might hypothesize that logical propositions involve a reference to peculiar logical properties and relations.

One might even go further and postulate that the logical propositions are descriptions of a kind of logical space in which propositions exist. Just as for Kant propositions of geometry describe space, and therefore derivatively apply to objects which are in that space, so too logical propositions might be thought to describe a kind of logical space and apply derivatively to the propositions which are in that space.

According to Wittgenstein, both views about the logical propositions are incorrect. At 6.111 Wittgenstein rejects the view that there are logical properties or objects referred to by '*true*' and '*false*'. He writes there that the view that there are such properties makes the propositions of logic "appear to have content" and that they make the logical propositions too much like the propositions of natural science. Similarly, the view that the logical propositions describe a logical space, a kind of entity, in which propositions exist, is also wrong. Though Wittgenstein does have a notion of logical space, any analogy with some notion of physical space cannot be taken too far. For such an analogy would mean that the logical propositions do have both an independent subject matter and "constituents" of some sort. Wittgenstein's rejection of all such views is implicit in such views as that the propositions of logic "say nothing" (6.11) and that one can "do without logical propositions" (6.122).

At this point the only thing one can say for sure is that what tautologies express is something about the truth possibilities of propositions in general, where this is understood to involve no ontological commitments. To answer these ontological questions, and other more interesting questions about the tautologies, it is necessary to answer the question of how the tautologies express what they express.

II.4   How Tautologies Express

The tautologies are about the truth possibilities of propositions in general, but they do not "say" anything. What is the nature of a type of symbol which expresses something but does not "say" anything?

To answer this question one must focus on the kinds of symbols which are present in the tautologies. There are two sorts of symbols present in the tautologies—genuine propositions and logical constants. It has already been pointed out that in the tautology genuine propositions are used, not mentioned, but that it is also the peculiarity of the tautology that it is not about the subject matter of its component propositions. This is the first appearance of the fact that in the tautologies genuine propositions appear, but do not function as genuine propositions normally do. In tautologies they function instead as *exemplars,* in some sense, of propositions in general.

The only symbols present in the tautology are the logical constants. What is the role of the logical constants? If the logical constants represent some peculiarly logical relations, then expressions like 'P v ∼P' would seem to express something about a relation between propositions in general and their negations. Perhaps the tautologies would then be conceived as describing a kind of space, a logical space, which consists in a system of necessary relations between propositions.

But it is Wittgenstein's 'fundamental idea' that "the logical constants are not representatives," that is, the logical constants do not contribute to the representational content of the proposition in which they occur. Since the only other symbols present in the tautology are genuine propositions, and since their representational content drops out as irrelevant to the truth value of the logical proposition, the tautology has no representational content at all.

In order to get clearer about this view let us consider the tautology,[11] "Either it is raining or it is not raining." The tautology is not about the subject matter of the component propositions. Despite the fact that a particular proposition with a particular subject matter is present in the tautology, the tautology actually seems to express something about the truth possibilities of propositions in general. Now, if the logical constants have some representational content, then the tautology could still possess some representational content. But if the logical constants have no representational content, then *a logical proposition is not a proposition in which a subject matter is described or represented at all.*

In a proposition like "Socrates is wise," a subject matter is said to *be* qualified in some way. The way in which it is said to be is dependent upon the representing term involved, in this case *'wise'*. But in the logical propositions there is no representing term which is being applied to a subject matter. There could be only if the logical constants were conceived as representations of something (like logical properties of logical objects). Thus, *in the logical proposition there is no predicate.* That is, nothing is said to *be* in a certain way, that is, to be as represented. The logical proposition does not contain any verb.

Although nothing has been demonstrated concerning propositions which do represent (it has not yet even been proved that there *are* such propositions), it is useful to contrast the nature of the tautology as conceived by Wittgenstein with that of propositions which do represent. At 4.063 Wittgenstein writes that, "the verb of a proposition is not 'is true' or 'is false' as Frege thought: rather, that which 'is true' must already contain the verb." But the representational content of the genuine proposition involved is not essential to the tautological symbol. That proposition does contain a verb, but it is not essential to the tautology. The tautology could only contain a verb if the other symbols essentially involved had some representational content.[12]

In a proposition like 'P v Q', the propositional symbols 'P' and 'Q' are used to mention their respective subject matters. And the truth value of 'P v Q' is determined by the state of these mentioned entities. But 'P v $\sim P$' is not just another disjunction. Tautologies are not just more propositions. In the tautologies that which is mentioned—the subject matter of the component propositions—is not relevant to the truth value of the tautology. But though that which is represented by the symbol drops out as irrelevant to the truth value of the tautology, that which is presented with, or is internal to, the symbol comes to the fore. That is, in a tautology, that which is presented with the symbol is the sole determiner of the truth value of the tautology. Put another way, in 'P v Q', symbols are the means by which a certain subject matter is represented. Whereas in 'P v$\sim$$P$' it is the *means* by which something is represented, the symbols themselves, which are what the tautology is about.

We must distinguish between two types of symbols. In the *Tractatus* this distinction is of the greatest possible importance. Representational symbols are true (or false) by virtue of something which is external to the propositional symbol. Presentational symbols are true (or false) by virtue of that which is presented with the symbol itself. (Wittgenstein's remark at 6.113 that "it is a very important fact that the truth of a tautology is *recognizable from the symbol alone*" [my emphasis] is explicable in these terms.)

It is representational symbols which have "constituents" in Russell's sense. They are about something which is "there in the world" in that they are about something external to the symbol. Russell cannot avoid the view that all propositions, even logical ones, are representational symbols. Instead, he tends toward the view that the logical propositions are representations of something *very general.*

Similarly, Wittgenstein's objection to Frege (whether his portrayal of Frege is correct or not) is that for Frege there is no distinction between propositions whose truth conditions are presented with (or are internal to) the symbol, and those whose truth conditions involve something independent of the symbol. For Frege, *all* propositions, logical and non-logical, are interpreted as representing a subject as having one of the two properties '*true*' or '*false*'. Logical propositions are interpreted by Frege as describing the range of possible logical properties of some object external to the symbol. According to Wittgenstein, Frege is like Russell in holding the view that the logical propositions have "constituents," (though Frege and Russell may disagree about what sorts of things these constituents are).

When Wittgenstein writes at 6.127 that "every tautology shows itself that it is a tautology," he is saying that that which is relevant to the truth value of the tautology is presented with the symbol, and that there are no logical objects and properties, or any objects and properties, independent of the symbol at all. This is the real significance of Wittgenstein's view that in the tautologies there is no verb, and therefore no *representation* of something's *being* a certain way.

A hint of the distinction between presentational and representational symbols has surfaced in the commentaries. Black writes:

> Wittgenstein has previously stressed the autonomy of logical propositions: their validity is determined solely by their symbolic expression, without appeal to anything external.[13]

The presentational symbols are those whose "truth conditions" are internal to (presented with) the symbol itself. The representational symbols are those which are about something external to their symbol.

Tautologies are presentational symbols, but not everything which is presented with their symbols is relevant to their truth value. Though tautologies must contain particular propositions with a particular representational content, the particular features of the propositions involved are not essential to the tautological symbol. Only the most general features of the particular propositions are relevant to the truth value of the tautology. Thus, that which makes a tautology true conforms to two conditions: (1) it must be that which is presented with the symbol of the tautology, and (2) it consists only in the most general features of propositions, in those features which are common to *all* propositions.

In order to capture some of these distinctions one can make the following definitions. To specify that which a proposition *shows* is to specify that which is presented with the symbol and is relevant to the determination of the truth value of the proposition. Thus, *accidental* features of the symbol, for instance, that it is composed of ink, are not something shown by the symbol. Second, a proposition *says* something if the specification of that which is relevant in the determination of its truth conditions involves the specification of something external to its symbol, that is, the specification of "constituents." Third, a proposition is said to have a *'sense'* if it says something. Thus, logical propositions say nothing, and have no sense. This is so since in the specification of that which is relevant to the truth value of the tautology, no reference is made to anything external to the symbol of the tautology. *Everything* which is relevant to the truth value of a tautology is presented with its symbol. Thus, tautologies "show that they say nothing" (4.461).

There has been much confusion concerning the notions of 'showing' and 'saying' in the *Tractatus*. But insofar as one is referring to that which *propositions* say or show, what is involved is nothing other than the distinction between that which is presented with the symbol in a proposition, and that which is represented by means of a symbol. A proposition shows something insofar as it presents with the symbol something which is relevant to its truth value. It says something insofar as it is a representation of something external to its symbol. Any particular proposition can both show something and say something. (In the normal case, the non-logical propositions, that which is shown by or presented with the symbol is the means whereby the symbol represents something external to itself.)

A tautology does have truth conditions in a sense, since it has a truth value which is determined by that which is presented with its symbol. But what is it that is presented with the symbol in a tautology which determines its truth value? That is, to specify the truth conditions of a non-logical proposition is to specify that possible fact which, if it exists or does not exist, determines that the proposition is true or false. But what is it that is to the tautology as a possible fact is to a non-logical proposition?

That which is presented with the symbol in a tautology is nothing but a particular logical combination of propositional symbols, where everything which distinguishes one proposition from another drops out as irrelevant to the truth value of the tautology. This is appropriately called "the general form of a proposition."

The argument, up to the present point is:

1. A tautology is a proposition which is true no matter what the truth values of its component propositions are. (4.46, def: "tautology")

∴ 2. In a tautology the truth values of the component propositions are irrelevant to the truth value of the tautology, that is, are not essential to the symbol of the tautology. (1)

3. To specify the representational content of a proposition is to specify those entities in the world, and their states, which are relevant to its truth value. (def: "representational content of a proposition")

∴ 4. In a tautology the representational content of the component propositions is irrelevant to the truth value of the tautology. (2, 3)

5. The tautologies are expressions (like '$P \vee \sim P$') which contain only propositions and logical constants. (premise based upon the structure of the symbolic language)

∴ 6. All that is present in the symbol of the tautology are: (a) the component propositions where abstraction has been made from the particular representational content which distinguishes one proposition from another, and (b) the logical constants. (4,5)

7. But the logical constants do not enter into the representational content of the proposition in which they occur. (4.0312, Wittgenstein's 'fundamental idea')

∴ 8. A tautology is not a representational symbol, that is, its truth value is not determined by virtue of the fact that something has been correctly represented. (6, 7)

∴ 9. A tautology is a presentational, not a representational, symbol, that is, the truth value of the tautology is determined by that which is presented with the symbol. (1, 6, 8)

10. The role of the logical constants is only to mark out the way in which that which is represented by the proposition is relevant to its truth value. (See Chapter I, section on the definition of the logical constants in general.)

∴ 11. That which is actually presented with the symbol in the tautology, which is relevant to its truth conditions, are only genuine propositions combined in such a way that everything drops out as irrelevant to the truth value of the symbol. (6, 9, 10)

12. That which is presented with the symbol in a tautology, which is relevant to its truth conditions, and which is common to all propositions, is called "the general form of a proposition." (def: "general form of proposition")

13. That which is shown by a symbol is that which is presented with the symbol and is relevant to its truth value. (def: "showing")

∴ 14. The tautology shows the general form of a proposition. (11, 12, 13)

The basic strategy of this argument is simple. It is first argued that though the tautologies may seem to express something about the subject matter of their component propositions, in fact they express something about propositions in general. In the second stage of the argument, the fundamental idea is employed in order to reach the conclusion that though the tautologies are about propositions in general, they are not representations of propositions in general. That is why it is so important to Wittgenstein that the logical propositions do not consist of variables. A variable is a proxy, a representation of propositions which are not themselves present in the symbol. In Wittgenstein's view a genuine proposition is actually present in the tautological symbol, but since its particular representational content drops out as irrelevant to the truth value of the tautology, it functions as an exemplar, or presentation, of genuine propositions in general.

One must, therefore, distinguish two different senses in which a proposition is "about" something. Non-logical propositions are about₁ a subject matter by virtue of *representing* it, that is, "from a position outside it." Logical propositions are about₂ propositions in general insofar as they present with their symbol something about propositions in general.

Unfortunately Wittgenstein's notion of saying has sometimes been identified with the positivist notions of verifiability or empirical content, and his notion of showing has been understood to involve some sort of non-empirical, mystical (even "nonsensical") dimension. The real distinction between symbols which "say" and symbols which only "show" is the distinction between representational and presentational symbols.

The third stage of the argument tells us what it is that is actually presented by these presentational symbols. The tautologies present the general form of a proposition with their symbol. The primary goal of the present chapter is to determine the nature of the tautologies. But in the long run, the fact that what the tautologies present with their symbol is the general form of a proposition is of even greater significance. For it means that understanding the nature of the tautologies is the key to understanding the nature of the non-logical propositions. Their nature, that is, their general form, is somehow implicit in that which the tautological symbols contain internal to themselves. If one can find a way to "read off" the features implicit in the general form of a proposition, then, as Wittgenstein suggests at 6.113, the understanding of the logical propositions is the key to "the whole philosophy of logic." This progress is carried out in the subsequent chapters.

Wittgenstein's basic answer to Russell's questions are clear. The *components* of the tautological symbol, that is, the parts of the symbol itself, are not variables, but are the symbols of particular genuine propositions combined in such a way that their particular features drop out as irrelevant to the truth value of the tautology. Secondly, the tautologies have no constituents at all in Russell's sense of the term. The tautologies are not about something *external* to their symbol at all, however general. The difference between logical and non-logical propositions does not have to do with the degree of generality of the facts involved.

Given the distinction between components and constituents, there is an interesting way of putting the difference between logical and non-logical propositions. Non-logical propositions use components in order to represent their constituents, and are made true or false by virtue of something about those constituents. Logical propositions are made true by virtue of their components (strictly speaking, by the most general features of their components). And it is in these terms that Wittgenstein's notion of analyticity is to be explicated. A proposition is analytic if it is true by virtue of that which is presented with its symbol, that is, by virtue of its components (not like non-logical propositions whose truth values are determined by the state of their constituents).

This distinction between representational and presentational symbols is of tremendous importance in the *Tractatus*. It is not surprising, therefore, that the second major application of the 'fundamental idea' is in the argument that the tautologies are not representational but are presentational symbols.

II.5 Sign and Symbol

Wittgenstein makes a distinction between sign and symbol which is quite important in interpreting the preceding results. At 3.31 Wittgenstein writes that "any part of a proposition that characterizes its sense . . . [is called] an expression (or a symbol)." At 6.126 he states that in a logical "calculation" one does not "bother about sense or meaning . . . [but uses] only *rules that deal with signs*" (Wittgenstein's emphasis). The contrast seems to be that the sign is merely a syntactic entity; it is taken in abstraction from sense or meaning. It also seems clear that the symbol is not equivalent to the sign plus the rules for the use of those signs.

In general, we call "formal" those considerations which pertain to the signifying entities themselves, as opposed to that which is signified by those entities. But we have drawn a distinction between sign and symbol, and thus there are two notions of form, one of which pertains to signs and the other to symbols.

First, insofar as one is concerned with mere signs, one can speak of the syntax of a language as the form of that language, and regard the list of the syntactical rules for the use of the propositional sign to be the form of the proposition. This is similar to the standard positivist treatment of propositions. For example, Carnap writes:

> We will call "formal" such considerations or assertions concerning a linguistic expression as are without sense or meaning.[14]

But the symbol is itself an entity (as it turns out a compound one), and the symbol is normally about something external to itself. One can also, therefore, distinguish between the form and the content of the symbol. I call the $form_2$ of a proposition that which is internal to, or presented with, the symbol of the proposition which is relevant to its truth value. (The tautologies could, therefore, be called $formal_2$ truths.)

The preceding interpretation of the logical propositions is concerned with the tautological *symbol*. It did not abstract from "sense or meaning." It asked, for instance: What does the tautology express? How does it express it? In Wittgenstein's view the symbol cannot be reduced to signs, that is, the notion of $form_2$ cannot be reduced to that of $form_1$.[15]

The second important dimension of the sign-symbol distinction is stated at 3.32: "A sign is what can be perceived of a symbol." Only the sign of a symbol is perceptible. There is a component of the symbol which is in some sense imperceptible. In order to understand Wittgenstein's remark at 3.32, it must be recognized that it is a comment, however indirect, on proposition number 3 of the *Tractatus:* "A logical picture of facts is a thought." The symbol involves an imperceptible component in the sense that the symbol is a complex of a sign and a thought, and thoughts are imperceptible.

Signs are perceptible entities. Thoughts are imperceptible entities which are paired with them. One is concerned with the $form_1$ (or syntax) of language insofar as one abstracts from "sense or meaning" and considers only the perceptible entity, the sign, and the rules for its use. If one does not abstract from sense or meaning, then one is concerned with symbols, and to be concerned with symbols is to be concerned with the signs *plus the thoughts which are paired with them*. The thought is the meaning component of the symbol.

The $form_1$ of propositions, or language, is not the key notion of form in the *Tractatus*. $Formal_1$ treatments of language have to do with mere signs and the rules for their use, but not with symbols, not with the proposition insofar as it *means* something. The phenomenon of signs in use is, so to speak, the epiphenomenon of meaning, that is, it is merely one of the phenomenal manifestation of a thought.

The significance of these views in the context of the present chapter is this. First, the meaning component of the symbol is the thought. Thoughts are normally about something external to themselves. But since the tautology is a presentational symbol, and since the symbol is not considered in abstraction from "sense or meaning," the tautology is true by virtue of that which is presented with or is internal to the thoughts themselves. It is the thought paired with the signs which presents with itself that which is relevant to the truth value of the tautology.

Second, since we already know that anything which distinguishes one proposition from another drops out as irrelevant to the truth value of the tautology, it is also true that anything which distinguishes one thought from another drops out. Tautologies are true by virtue of the structure of thoughts in general.

Obviously, Wittgenstein's view is psychologistic *in a sense*. He may seem to deny this at 4.1121, but this is not so.

4.1121 Psychology is no more closely related to philosophy than any other natural science. Theory of knowledge is the philosophy of psychology.

Does not my study of sign language correspond to the study of thought processes, which philosophers used to consider so essential to the philosophy of logic? Only in most cases they got entangled with unessential psychological investigations, and with my method too there is an analogous risk.

By saying that most philosophers have gotten tangled in unessential psychological investigations, he is saying that no considerations discovered by the *science* of psychology are relevant to the philosophy of logic. His view is not psychologistic in the sense in which a view is psychologistic if it depends on any *contingent* "laws of thinking." Wittgenstein's view does not in any way make the laws of logic dependent on how people happen to think. Wittgenstein's view involves the idea of the universal (non-contingent) structure of thought.

In subsequent chapters the notion of the general structure of thought is rendered more concrete. In the following section Wittgenstein's account of the *a priori* is explained in terms of the ideas developed above.

II.6 The Autonomy of Logic

The very first remark in the *Notebook* is that logic "must take care of itself" and, Wittgenstein adds, "This is an extremely profound and important insight" (*NB*, p. 2). The view that logic must take care of itself is associated with the way in which Wittgenstein accounts for the *a priori* status of logical truth, and the accounts of both of these views are implicit in the account of the tautologies as presentational symbols.

Wittgenstein does not wish to appeal to a notion of self-evidence in his account of the a priori status of logical truth. "Self-evidence, which Russell talked about so much, can become dispensable in logic only because language itself prevents every logical mistake" (5.4731). Nor, as Black points out, does Wittgenstein wish to adopt a conventionalistic account of the truth of the logical propositions.[16] Since these constitute the standard range of alternatives, Wittgenstein's challenge is a difficult one: How can one account for their a priori status without appealing either to the notions of self-evidence or human convention?

Black discusses the view that "logic must take care of itself" under the title "The Autonomy of Logic." Yet Black misses the key notions in Wittgenstein's account of the autonomy of logic. His interpretation is a characteristic example of the way in which the views of the logical positivists are read backward into the *Tractatus,* with the result that the unique view of the *Tractatus* is overlooked.

According to Black, rather than appealing to a notion of self-evidence in his account of logical truth, Wittgenstein employs the notion of a calculation:

> The correct method for recognizing the validity of complex logical propositions is calculation (6.233, 6.2331). The construction of tautologies by means of a systematic truth table procedure can be regarded as an instance of such 'calculations'—an instance of the way in which a well-designed notation renders superfluous any supposed need to appeal to a psychological criterion like self-evidence.[17]

Something akin to the notion of a presentational symbol here surfaces in Black's commentary. But Black explains that the validity of a tautology is determined by that which is "internal" to the symbolism in the sense that its validity can be decided by appeal only to the rules or "procedures" which are internal to a "well-designed notation." In short, Black explains Wittgenstein's account of the a priori status of the logical propositions in terms of *formal*$_1$ notions, in terms of mere signs and the syntactical rules for their construction. But the key notion of form in Wittgenstein's account of the tautological symbol and therefore of the notion of a presentational symbol is the notion of *form*$_2$.

In Black's view Wittgenstein is very close to the standard logical positivist view on this matter.[18] Black is not alone in such a position. Nakhnikian says:

> Following Wittgenstein, the positivists accounted for the necessity of tautologies in terms of formal structure devoid of content. For example, letting "p" and "q" stand for any statements and defining "p or q" to mean it is not the case that p and q are false simultaneously, the formula "p v~p" is a formal truth. This fact can be proved by mechanical calculation. It is in this sense only that formal truths are known a priori.[19]

It is a common view that both the Wittgenstein of the *Tractatus* and the positivists understand the notion of the 'a priori' only in terms of a mechanical calculation. This is a well entrenched dogma about the *Tractatus,* and yet the text of the *Tractatus* makes clear that this is not Wittgenstein's intended view.

Black is correct that the nature of a calculation does appear in the *Tractatus*. But it is noteworthy that Black refers the reader to 6.233 and 6.2331 for textual support:

> 6.233 The question whether intuition is needed for the solution of mathematical problems must be given the answer that in this case language itself provides the necessary intuition.
>
> 6.2331 The process of calculating serves to bring about that intuition.
>
> Calculation is not an experiment.

Two points are striking here. In order to explain the autonomy of logical propositions, Black refers the reader to a discussion not of logical propositions, but of mathematical ones! Second, Wittgenstein's remarks at 6.2331 make clear that if there is any autonomy to mathematical (and presumably logical) propositions, it is because of the "intuition" provided by "language itself." Calculation is only a *means* to achieving that "intuition."

Wittgenstein does discuss calculation in connection with the logical propositions (6.126–6.1265):

> 6.126 One can calculate whether a proposition belongs to logic, by calculating the logical properties of the *symbol*.
>
> And this is what we do when we "prove" a logical proposition. For, without bothering about sense or meaning, we construct the logical proposition out of others using only *rules that deal with signs*.
>
> The proof of logical propositions consists in the following process: we produce them out of other logical propositions by successively applying certain operations that always generate further tautologies out of the initial ones (and in fact only tautologies *follow* from a tautology).
>
> Of course, this way of showing that the propositions of logic are tautologies is not at all essential to logic, if only because the propositions from which the proof starts must show without any proof that they are tautologies.

Here, Wittgenstein makes clear that the process of calculation is not the key idea involved in his account of the autonomy of logic. For this process of calculation itself depends on the fact that the tautologies on which the "proof" (the calculation) is based must, independent of any calculation, "show that they are tautologies."

Obviously the "intuition provided by language itself," or the idea that every tautology shows "without any proof . . . that it is a tautology," is what is basic in Wittgenstein's account of the autonomy of logic. Admittedly this portion of Wittgenstein's thought is obscure. This helps explain why some commentators have felt compelled to defend interpretations which are so clearly unwarranted by the text.

Fortunately, an account of these notions is readily available on the present interpretation. A tautology is true by virtue of that which is presented with its symbol. The meaning component of the symbol is the thought, and thus the tautology is true by virtue of the general internal structure of thought. The truth conditions of the tautological symbol are provided by the language itself in the sense that they are internal to the thought component of the linguistic symbol. The tautological symbol is self-guaranteeing (autonomous) in the sense that what it is about is presented with its meaning component—the thought. In concrete terms, this means that thoughts themselves have a general structure, and that structure is what is internal to the symbol and is relevant to the truth value of the tautology.

Wittgenstein's notion of the 'a priori' is explicable in these terms. He writes:

> 3.05 A priori knowledge that a thought was true would be possible only if its truth were recognizable from the thought itself (without anything to compare it with).

A thought is a priori only if its truth is "recognizable from the thought itself," that is, only if that which is relevant to the truth value of the thought is presented with the thought itself. (Recall the similar remark at 6.113, where Wittgenstein tells us that it is "the peculiar mark of the logical propositions that one can recognize that they are true from the symbol alone, . .")

Wittgenstein's account is not conventionalistic. There is something which logical propositions are about—the general internal structure of thoughts—and that is not settled by convention. Neither does Wittgenstein wish to appeal to a notion of self-evidence. But the idea that a tautology shows itself that it is a tautology, or that "language itself provides the necessary intuition . . . for the solution of mathematical problems" looks very much like a notion of self-evidence. Clearly a distinction is needed here, and not any mere parroting of Wittgenstein's rejection of self-evidence.

The notion of self-evidence to which Wittgenstein refuses to appeal is that of obviousness, or subjective certainty. He writes:

> 5.1363 If the truth of a proposition does not follow from the fact that it is self-evident to us, then its self-evidence in no way justifies one's belief in its truth.

That is, that it is self-evident *to us* or to a cognizing subject does not justify one's belief in its truth. Any account which involves such a notion of self-evidence can explain, at most, only how a subjective certainty is attainable.

In Wittgenstein's view, the self need not go beyond that which is presented with the symbol itself by any subjective act of intuition or understanding. The knowing self is, to speak, passive before the symbol. The fact of the passive relation of the knowing subject to the symbols is an important part of Wittgenstein's view, and especially of his alternative to the notion of self-evidence.

> 6.124 We have said that some things are arbitrary in the symbols that we use and that some things are not. In logic it is only the latter that express: but that means that logic is not a field in which *we* express what we wish with the help of the signs, but rather one in which the nature of the absolutely necessary signs speaks for itself.

This picture is not the traditional one of a mind reaching out with a special act of intuition and grasping something, but is instead that of the self becoming passively aware of something given to it.

The burden of the a priori is transferred from the self, traditionally overworked in philosophy and with relatively little to show for it, to the symbol itself. Though the *Tractatus* has been likened to Kantian views in many respects, its significance lies in the fact that Wittenstein has developed an entirely different account of the a priori. Wittgenstein's view puts the symbols themselves to work. His account of the "a priority" of the logical propositions in terms of his notion of a presentational symbol is an extreme example of a purely objective certainty.[20]

II.7 A Comparison of Wittgenstein and Russell

Russell's four suggestions are:

S1 Logical propositions contain only variables.

S2 Logical propositions do not mention any particular thing.

S3 Logical propositions are about the forms of propositions in the sense that their constituents are the forms of propositions.

S4 Logical propositions are true by virtue of their own form.

I will compare Wittgenstein's final view with these four suggestions in order.

(1) According to Wittgenstein, the components of logical propositions are not variables. Expressions like 'p v$\sim$$p$', where '$p$' is a variable, are merely useful schemas for referring to the actual tautologies in an indeterminate way. They are also useful in that they make explicit the fact that the particular subject matter and truth value of the component propositions are irrelevant to the truth value of the tautology. It is very important for Wittgenstein that the actual tautologies contain genuine propositions. Since the tautologies are presentational symbols, what they are about must be presented with their symbol. But if they were composed of variables, the tautologies would be *representations* of that which the variables range over (stand for). By contrast, in Wittgenstein's view a tautology is a logical combination of propositions which is true by virtue of the most general features of that which is presented with the symbol, that is, by the general form of a proposition. Only that which possesses the general form of a proposition can be presented with the symbol in a tautology, such that the tautology is true. But only genuine propositions possess the general form of a proposition.

(2) Wittgenstein accepts *S2*, but not, like Russell, because he accepts *S1*. Russell seems to accept *S2* because he holds that the logical proposition is composed "wholly and solely of variables." For Wittgenstein the re-

markable fact about the logical propositions is that they contain propositions which do mention some thing external to their symbol, but the logical proposition itself does not mention those things. '$P \vee {\sim} P$' is not just another disjunction. It is qualitatively different from disjunctions like '$P \vee Q$' since in a tautology, propositions which do mention particular things in the world are logically combined in such a way that the compound expression does not mention these things.[21]

(3) Wittgenstein rejects *S3*, for the logical propositions have no constituents at all. They are not about anything external to the symbol, whether "particular things" or "forms" of propositions. The logical propositions *present* with their symbol that which is relevant to their truth value; they do not represent it from a position outside it. In the sense in which ordinary propositions are about something, that is, represent it, logical propositions are about nothing. That is their unique status. Of course a logical proposition can be about something in a different sense. It is "about" the forms of propositions in the sense that it presents propositions in such a logical combination that only that which is presented with the symbol and is common to all propositions determines its truth value.

The import of Wittgenstein's view is that there are at least two classes of symbols (though up to the present point the existence of propositions which are about something independent of the symbol has only been assumed). One class has truth conditions, the specification of which essentially involves reference to something external to the symbol. The specificaion of the "truth conditions" of the second class, the logical propositions, does not essentially involve such a reference.

(4) Wittgenstein does not accept *S4* in the form suggested by Russell, but rather he accepts *S4'*, namely, the view that the logical propositions are true by virtue of the general form of the component propositions. His notion of an analytic proposition is not of a proposition which is true by virtue of the meanings involved, nor of a proposition which is true by definition. An analytic proposition is a *formal₂* truth, a proposition which is true by virtue of the most general features of that which is presented with its symbol.[22] But that is the general propositional form. Thus, the tautologies show the general propositional form. The foundation of the argument of the *Tractatus* is complete. The next question is: How can one read off the various features of the general propositional form from the tautologies?

CHAPTER III

The Sole Logical Constant or General Propositional Form

In the preceding chapter Wittgenstein's fundamental idea is employed in an interpretation of the tautologies with the result that the tautologies are found to be presentational symbols. But this interpretation of the logical propositions can be employed in a demonstration of the nature of the non-logical, or "genuine," propositions. In the present chapter, the first step in this demonstration is taken. Specifically, genuine propositions are, according to the *Tractatus,* contingent. Every genuine proposition is possibly true and possibly not true. But if genuine propositions are contingent, then that they are contingent must be implicit in the general propositional form. Since the general propositional form is shown by the tautologies, the tautologies must also show that "genuine" propositions are contingent. And so there must be a demonstration, which is in some sense based upon the tautologies, that genuine propositions are contingent. The particular tautology employed in this demonstration is the *law of the excluded middle.*[1]

III.1 Wittgenstein's 'Fundamental Principle'

To construe the tautologies as presentational symbols means that (1) the tautologies are made true by virtue of that which is presented with their symbol, and (2) that which is presented with their symbol which is relevant to their truth value are genuine propositions combined in such a way that all particular features of genuine propositions drop out as irrelevant to the truth value of the tautology. In short, tautologies present with their symbol, and are made true by virtue of, the general propositional form.

One could say that *if* a tautology made an assertion, what it asserted would be the general propositional form.

This interpretation has a consequence which is expressed at 5.47 and again at 5.551 in his 'fundamental principle'.

> 5.47 It is clear that whatever we can say in advance about the forms of all propositions we must be able to say all at once.

> 5.551 Our fundamental principle is that whenever a question can be decided by logic it must be possible to decide it without more ado.

> (And if we get into a position where we have to look at the world for an answer to such a problem, that shows that we are on a completely wrong track.)

What one can "say in advance" about the forms of all propositions, or decide "without more ado," is the list of the components of the general form of a proposition. The reason why, in principle, a complete account of the general form of a proposition can be given *all at once,* is because that which "contains" the answer to all of one's logical questions about genuine propositions in general is implicit in a tautology. One need not await any future developments in logic, psychology or ontology. Of course, the fact that the answers to one's logical questions are implicit in a tautology does not imply that one knows how to read off those answers from the tautology.

These consequences are also connected with his interrelated views that logic (including a large part of philosophy) is "a self-contained system" (5.4541). The fact that one can recognize the truth of the tautologies from the symbol alone "contains the whole philosophy of logic" (6.113). One can recognize the truth of the tautologies from the symbol alone, since the tautologies present with their symbol that which is relevant to their own truth value. This fact contains the whole philosophy of logic, and determines the entirety of the philosophical system. This is true in the sense that when one provides the proper interpretation of the tautologies, it becomes clear that what is presented with the symbol of the tautologies which is relevant to their own truth value is the general form of *all* genuine propositions. The "whole philosophy of logic," the entirety of the philosophical system, consists in the statement of the nature of all propositions. So, if a way is found of reading off the general features of all propositions from the tautological symbol, then the whole philosophy of logic is implicit in the tautological symbol itself. The fact that Wittgenstein's fundamental idea, his fundamental principle, his remark about the nature of the self-contained philosophical system, and so forth, are comprehensible on the present interpretation is strong evidence that the interpretation is on the right track.

There is, therefore, reason to hope that an exhaustive accounting of the features of the general propositional form can be given. But there are limits to what we can expect to be derived from the tautologies. Wittgenstein writes:

> 5.55 We now have to answer *a priori* the questions about all the possible forms of elementary propositions.
>
> Elementary propositions consist of names. Since, however, we are unable to give the number of names with different meanings, we are also unable to give the composition of elementary propositions.
>
> 5.554 It would be completely arbitrary to give any specific form.

The interpretation of the tautologies justifies us in expecting an account of the *general form* of a proposition, but it does not justify us in deciding upon any "specific" form.

To use Wittgenstein's own example from 5.5541 and 5.5542, it is impossible to decide a priori whether one of the specific forms of propositions which is possible involves a 27-termed relation. My interpretation of the tautologies is neutral with respect to all such questions. Those questions are answered by "the application of logic"—a notion which cannot be developed here. The interpretation of the tautologies bears on questions about genuine propositions *in general,* that is, whether they are one and all contingent, whether they one and all involve some relations or other, and so on. Those features which are presented with the symbol and are *common to all* genuine propositions can be determined a priori. We can not expect to derive any specific form from the tautologies.

III.2 The Sole Logical Constant

Given that a tautology "shows the general form of a proposition," how does one derive any consequences from that fact? Following Wittgenstein's lead, one must attend to the structure of some particular tautology, not merely to a schema or to tautologies in general.

In the particular instantiation of, say, the law of the excluded middle *('P* v∼*P')* that which is presented with the symbol of the tautology is a particular proposition upon which certain logical operations are performed, specifically: affirmation, negation and disjunction.[2] According to a standard view, the tautologies express something about the logical connectives. That is, *'P* v∼*P'* tells us something about negation and disjunction, and what it tells us is embodied in the truth-table of the tautology.

But how is it that in the logical proposition all this logical apparatus can be applied to propositions? Is it simply a given fact that propositions can be affirmed, negated, disjoined and conjoined? Wittgenstein's answer is that it is not an accident. If a logical operation *"O"* is performable on a proposition, then it must be by virtue of the general form of the proposition that *"O"* can be performed on it. To put the point most directly and simply, the fact that one can perform those logical operations on propositions must be inherent in the general propositional form. This is the key idea which enables one to exploit the tautological structure in order to demonstrate the features of the general propositional form. That is, the fact that it must be implicit in the general propositional form that genuine propositions can be affirmed and negated, turns out to pave the way to the proof of their contingency.

If the possibility of performing logical operations on propositions were not inherent in the general propositional form, then that which is relevant to the truth value of the tautology would not be determined by that which is presented with its symbol. (In addition, there would be an "accident" in logic.) A tautology is true by virtue of the most general features of that which is presented with its symbol. Since *'P* v∼*P'* is a tautology, it is by virtue of the general form of a proposition that every genuine proposition or its negation is true. But then it must be inherent in the general form of a proposition that genuine propositions are both affirmable and negatable.

This interpretation is supported by key remarks in the text. At 5.47 Wittgenstein writes (numbering added for convenience of reference):

5.47 (1) It is clear that whatever we can say in advance about the forms of propositions we can say all at once.

(2) An elementary proposition really contains all logical operations in itself. For 'Fa' says the same thing as '(∃x) Fx.x=a'.

(3) . . . .

(4) One could say that the sole logical constant was what all propositions, by their very nature, had in common with one another.

But that is the general propositional form.

Line (1) is a consequence of Wittgenstein's view that there is a general form common to all propositions and that this is shown by the tautologies.

Lines (2) and (4) are of special significance in the present connection. In line (2) Wittgenstein makes the point that all the logical operations are "already contained" in an elementary proposition. What does he mean by this?

The general propositional form is identified as the "sole logical constant." This must mean that there is a sense in which the multiplicity of logical constants are in some sense reducible to the general propositional form. That propositions can be affirmed, negated, and so on, is inherent in the general propositional form. (Ultimately it becomes clear that this means that genuine propositions have a *very concrete structure* which determines the possibility of negating them, conjoining them with one another, and performing other operations on them.)

The same idea is involved at 3.42 where the connection with Wittgenstein's fundamental idea is also explicit. Wittgenstein writes:

3.42 A proposition can determine only one place in logical space: nevertheless the whole of logical space must already be given by it.

(Otherwise negation, logical sum, logical product, etc., would introduce more and more new elements in coordination.)

Part of what it means to say that the whole of logical space is already given by a proposition, is equivalent to the view of 5.47 that any proposition contains all logical operations in itself. Thus, it is implicit in the affirmative proposition 'P' that 'P' can be negated, conjoined with others and so on. It is implicit in the affirmative proposition, in the sense that the affirmative proposition possesses the general form of a proposition, and it is inherent in the general form of a proposition that a proposition can be negated, among other operations.

The remark at 3.42 makes clear that the significance of the fundamental idea is that the logical propositions, rather than introducing "new elements," are merely expressions of possibilities which are implicit in the general form of a proposition (in the general structure of the elements which make up the propositional symbol). That the logical operations are performable on propositions is not an accident; it is explicable in terms of the fact that the possibility of these operations is implicit in the general propositional form, or—as Wittgenstein calls it—*the sole logical constant.*

III.3   The Contingency of Genuine Propositions

All genuine propositions are contingent. In order to prove the general thesis of contingency, one must show that there are at least two possible truth values for every genuine proposition. But in order to demonstrate fully the specific form in which Wittgenstein holds that genuine propositions are contingent, one must also show that there are at most two possible truth values for every genuine proposition. That is, Wittgenstein holds that there are exactly two possible truth values for every genuine proposition. In any instance of excluded middle, one is presented with a propositional symbol which is both affirmed and negated. This means that it must by virtue of its own general form be affirmable and negatable. If to affirm a proposition is to say that it is true, and to negate it is to say that it is false, then that it is possible to say that the given proposition is true, and that it is possible to say that it is false, are implicit in the general form of that proposition. In other words, that there are two possible truth values for that proposition is implicit in the general form of that proposition. Since the same argument applies to any proposition to which excluded middle applies, to the class of "genuine" propositions, the conclusion can be generalized to include all genuine propositions.

The same conclusion can be reached in a somewhat less direct but related argument. This second argument illuminates the connection between the contingency thesis, the view of 5.47 that the general propositional form is the sole logical constant, and other remarks in the *Tractatus*, specifically, with the views that there are no "accidents" in logic and that there can be no superfluous devices in logic. The view that the general propositional form is the "sole logical constant" is the view that the possibility of performing logical operations on these propositions must be implicit in the general form of a proposition. If this is true, then (1) that it is possible to perform logical operations on propositions is not an accident; these must be allowed by the general propositional form. (2) There can be no superfluous or avoidable applications of logical operations on propositions. If these operations are really avoidable, then that they are possible operations on propositions is not implicit in the general propositional form and so they have nothing to do with propositions. Wittgenstein writes:

> 5.452 But if the introduction of a new device has proved necessary at a certain point, we must immediately ask ourselves, 'At what point is the employment of this device now unavoidable?' and its place in logic must be made clear.

The strong requirement of 5.452 is a consequence of Wittgenstein's view that the applicability of the logical constants to propositions must be by virtue of the fact that their possibility is implicit in the general propositional form. This establishes the ground of the second argument that genuine propositions in general are contingent.

If it is possible to affirm or negate a proposition, then this possibility must be unavoidable; that it is possible must be already implicit in the general propositional form. Thus, it cannot be superfluous, redundant or avoidable that one can affirm and negate propositions. This means that it must accomplish something to affirm or negate a proposition. That is, it could not be implicit in the general form of a proposition that one can affirm or negate it, if the symbol of a genuine proposition has already accomplished that which would be accomplished in affirming or negating it. But if to affirm a proposition is to say that it is true, and to negate it is to say that it is false, then the symbol of the general proposition cannot determine its own truth value. That affirmation and negation are possible operations on genuine propositions by virtue of their own general form means that, unlike the presentational symbols of the tautology and contradiction, the genuine propositional symbol does not determine its own truth value.

(It is important to recognize that that type of presentational symbol, the type possessed by tautologies and contradictions, does not satisfy the conditions of being a genuine proposition.) Tautologies are presentational symbols that present with their symbol that which determines their own truth value. The tautological symbol itself accomplishes what would be accomplished by affirming it—it determines its own truth. (This means that it does not make sense to affirm, or negate, a tautology, and appearances to the contrary, this is clearly the view in the text of the *Tractatus*.) Those propositional symbols which can be meaningfully affirmed and/or negated are those which are not presentational symbols in the sense in which tautologies are. That is, they are those which do not determine their own truth value. Tautologies and the propositions whose general form they show have contrasting natures.

Wittgenstein's specific view about the truth possibilities of genuine propositions is that there are exactly two truth possibilities for genuine propositions. It must, therefore, also be demonstrated that the law of the excluded middle shows that there are at most two possible truth values for genuine propositions. In this argument the result of the first chapter, that '*P*' and '~*P*' have the same sense which is affirmed or negated, "whole and undivided," plays a key role. Suppose that '*P*' takes some truth value other than true. It must be shown that there is only one truth value other than true which is possible for '*P*'. If '*P*' is other than true, then since '~*P*' only says that that which '*P*' says is not true, '~*P*' is true. But in '~*P*' the "whole and undivided sense" of '*P*' is negated. So the assertion made by the proposition '*P*' must be considered "whole and undivided" to be not true. That is, there is only one way in which '*P*' can fail to be true. But then there is no third possibility.

For this reason it is probably less misleading to represent the two truth possibilities of propositions as '*true*' and '*not true*' instead of as '*true*' and '*false*'. The latter designation conceals the relationship between the truth possibilities and makes them appear as distinct properties. Just as '*red*' and '*yellow*' need not, and in fact are not, the only color possibilities of objects, one may be led to suspect that '*true*' and '*false*' are not the only truth possibilities of propositions. Perhaps it is even better for some purposes to think in terms of one truth value which a proposition *either has or not*. In fact, this might be regarded as one of the very important corollaries of the fact that '*P*' and '~*P*' have the same sense.

This constitutes the demonstration of the contingency of genuine propositions.[3]

III.4   The Structure of the Genuine Propositional Symbol

Not only are genuine propositions contingent, but also the fact of their contingency must be embodied in a structural feature of the genuine propositional symbol. That this additional conclusion is warranted can be seen by paying careful attention to the manner in which the contingency thesis is demonstrated.

The tautologies are formal truths in the sense that they are true by virtue of that which is presented with their symbol. The argument that genuine propositions are contingent is based upon that which is presented with the tautological symbol (specifically the symbol of the law of the excluded middle) which is relevant to its truth value. Therefore, that genuine propositions are contingent must be determined by that which is presented with the tautological symbol. And that which is presented with the tautological symbol and is relevant to its truth value is nothing but genuine propositional symbols combined in such a way that all their individuating features drop out as irrelevant to the truth value of the tautology. But then the fact that genuine propositions in general are contingent is determined by that which is presented with the symbols of these genuine propositions.

In concrete terms, this means that the fact that genuine propositions are contingent is embodied in the structure of their own symbols, a structure which all genuine propositions share (the *general* propositional form). To say that the tautologies are formal truths (*formal₂* truths, see II.6), is to say that the genuine propositions which, when combined in a certain way, are taut∩logies, have a certain structure which they share in general, and it is that structure which is relevant to the truth value of the tautologies. Wittgenstein writes:

> 6.12 . . . if propositions are to yield a tautology when they are connected in a certain way they must have certain structural properties. So their yielding a tautology when combined in this way shows that they possess these structural properties.

What is provided in the preceding section is the argument that genuine propositions, when combined in accordance with the schema '$p \vee \sim p$', have a certain structural property. When Wittgenstein tells us that there is a connection between tautologies and the structural properties of propositions, or between tautologies and the "logical form of language and the world," he is not making an eccentric or exaggerated statement. The cash value of this statement is that the concrete and specific structural properties of propositions in general can be clearly and rigorously demonstrated by exploiting that which is presented with the tautological symbol.

The idea that the contingency of genuine propositions is embodied in a structural feature of the propositional symbol is very abstract. The process of rendering the idea more concrete will occupy several more chapters. But it may not be unhelpful to point out that what the idea boils down to in concrete terms is that the genuine propositional symbol *is itself a fact which may or may not obtain*. Its symbolic properties are embodied in its factual character. In other words, the idea that the genuine propositional symbol presents with itself the fact that it is contingent really only means that the genuine propositional symbol itself has the structure of a fact which itself may or may not exist.

In addition, this conclusion can be generalized. *Anything* which is demonstrated on the basis of that which is presented with the symbol of a tautology (as in the preceding argument) can be inferred to be embodied in a structural feature of the genuine propositional symbol. For example, if in the subsequent chapter we demonstrate that genuine propositions are about something which is external to their symbol, then we can infer at the same time that this fact must be embodied in a formal (structural) feature of the genuine propositional symbol. In that case one could infer that the genuine propositional symbol contains names, or proxies, for that subject matter.

This is quite important. In demonstrating the logical properties of genuine propositions in general, one at the same time demonstrates that genuine propositions have concrete structures which embody those logical properties. (What has emerged here is the most fundamental reason why the genuine propositional symbol must be a picture of a fact.)[4]

III.5   Tautology and Contradiction as Cases of the "Disintegration" of the Combination of Signs

It might appear that the argument of the present chapter commits Wittgenstein to an obvious absurdity. He is committed to the view that if a proposition is affirmable and negatable, then it is contingent. But tautologies and contradictions are affirmable and negatable, yet they are not contingent.

Appearances to the contrary, a contradiction is not the negation of a tautology. Thus, strictly speaking, it is not correct to say that either a tautology or its negation is true. In an important sense, neither tautologies nor contradictions are either affirmable or negatable. Rather, they are cases of "the disintegration of the combination of signs" (4.466). In '∼(P v∼P)' the combination of signs has disintegrated and so, in a sense, '∼' cannot be conceived as playing the normal role of negation.

Although Wittgenstein's view on this matter appears very implausible, it turns out to be reasonable and to fit very well into his system. First, to say that a tautology is not negatable does not mean that signs like '∼(P v∼P)' do not exist. Obviously they do exist. As Wittgenstein states at 4.4611:

> Tautologies and contradictions are not, however, nonsensical. They are part of the symbolism, just as '0' is part of the symbolism in arithmetic.

Tautologies and contradictions do have *a role*. The question is: Is the role of symbols like '∼(P v∼P)' like the role of genuine negative propositions? *What role* do tautologies and contradictions have and what roles do they— notwithstanding the appearances—not have?

In saying that '∼(P v∼P)' is not the negation of a tautology, one is making a point about the *nature* of the symbol; one is not challenging its existence. In symbols like 'P v∼P' and '∼(P v∼P)' *none* of the symbols involved are performing their usual function. This claim has already been foreshadowed in Chapter II with the recognition that in tautologies and contradictions, propositions with a particular subject matter are logically combined in such a way that their subject matter is not relevant to the truth value of the symbol. Tautologies and contradictions are not about the subject matters of the component propositions. That is not a trivial fact. The genuine propositions involved are not performing their usual function. But neither are the logical constants. That this is so can be illustrated in a striking way.

It has already been argued that contingent propositions are affirmable or negatable, because with them it accomplishes something to affirm or negate them. Since the symbol of a contingent proposition does not determine its own truth value, it is not superfluous to affirm or negate it. Tautologies and contradictions, however, do determine their own truth value "from the symbol alone." According to the interpretation in Chapter II, these symbols present with themselves, or "show," that which is relevant to their own truth value. The tautological symbol shows its own truth and the contradictory symbol shows its own falsity. This must be taken into account when considering the question of whether tautology and contradiction can be affirmed or negated.

For example, a tautology and its apparent negation are, respectively, 'P v$\sim P$' and '$\sim(P$ v$\sim P)$'. If one makes explicit in writing that which these respective symbols show, one is only explicitly representing that which is actually presented with the symbol. The first symbol (tautology) becomes " '$(P$ v$\sim P)$' *is true*" while the second becomes " '$\sim(P$ v$\sim P)$' *is false*" (where the italicized portion corresponds to that which is *shown* by the symbol). Note that when one writes in that which a contradiction shows, the contradiction '$\sim(P$ v$\sim P)$' becomes '$\sim(P$ v$\sim P)$' *is false*. Assuming that saying of something that it is false is equivalent to negating it, that which the contradiction shows in a certain sense *negates* that which it appears to say. But also, note that when one writes in that which the tautology shows, the tautological symbol does not suffer from this being-at-odds with itself.

Though it is of course too crude to put the point so directly, if saying that a proposition is true is equivalent to affirming it, and saying that it is false is to negate it, then the symbol of the tautology remains the same, but the symbol of the contradiction reduces to '$\sim$ $\sim(P$ v$\sim P)$'. Cancelling the double negation signs, one is left with the symbol of the tautology! This is a striking result. We began with what seems to be a tautology and its negation. But when one reckons in the unusual feature of the tautology and contradiction, the contradiction appears, so to speak, to negate itself, and therefore reduces to the tautology. In the *Notebooks* Wittgenstein asks: "Is there really such a thing as the duality: tautology-contradiction?" (p. 47). The present interpretation explains why he doubts that this apparent duality is genuine.

That which is presented with the symbol in a tautology, which is relevant to the truth value of the tautology, is the general propositional form. But, of course, exactly the same sorts of considerations apply to contradictions as to tautologies. That which is presented with the symbol in a tautology, and which determines that it is true, is the same thing presented with the symbol in a contradiction, determining that it is false.

This is the general propositional form. The only difference is that the truth value of the tautology is true and that of the contradiction is false. One might put it this way: By showing its own falsity a contradiction expresses *the same thing* that a tautology expresses by showing its own truth. Both express the general form of a proposition.

These results are a symptom that the normal function of the negation sign is not being performed by the first negation sign in '$\sim$ $(P \vee \sim P)$'; the symbol has at least partially "disintegrated." The normal function of the negation sign '$\sim$' is that '$\sim$' is employed in the construction of a proposition '$\sim P$', which expresses the *alternative possibility* to that which is expressed by 'P'. The negation sign can only perform its normal function if the original proposition can take either of two possible truth values, that is, if it is contingent. Though '$\sim (P \vee \sim P)$' appears to be the negation of '$P \vee \sim P$', it is not and cannot be. For '$P \vee \sim P$' and '$\sim (P \vee \sim P)$' *do not express alternatives,* and they do not express possibilities (in the sense of mere possibilities—or contingencies).

'$P \vee \sim P$' and '$\sim (P \vee \sim P)$' express exactly the same thing, the general propositional form, because of the fact that the contradiction, by showing its own falsity, reduces to the tautology. Both express one and the same thing, the general propositional form. It is as if, in trying to construct a symbol which expresses an alternative to that which the tautologies express, the essence of the "materials" always keeps the symbols one step ahead of you. So that which one finally constructs, the contradiction, shows its own falsity and thus aborts the whole attempt.

Wittgenstein writes:

> 6.1202   It is clear that one could achieve the same purpose by using contradictions instead of tautologies.

The purpose involved is that described at 6.12, where Wittgenstein says that tautologies "show the logical form of language and the world." That which tautologies express (or show) is the general form of the proposition. At 6.1202 Wittgenstein tells us that *both* tautologies and contradictions show the logical form of language and the world! Both show the *same* thing, that is, the general form of a proposition. Despite the appearances, the contradiction does not express the negation of the tautology.

That which can be affirmed or negated is that which, by virtue of its own form, it makes sense to affirm or negate, namely, a contingent proposition. In such a case, the negation sign is employed in the construction of a proposition (which expresses a contingent possibility) out of another proposition which expresses the *alternative* contingent possibility. Tautologies and contradictions determine their truth value from the symbol alone, so such symbols cannot be affirmed or negated. For the result of the argument in the preceding section is that negation is an operation which constructs one logical place out of another, that is, the alternative possibility out of a given possibility. And this can occur only in the case of a genuine contingent proposition.

But if we attempt to negate a tautology in order to form a contradiction, we have not constructed one logical possibility out of the alternative possibility. Rather, both tautology and contradiction express the same thing—the general form of a proposition. The essence of the symbols intervenes to frustrate the attempt to construct a symbol which expresses an alternative to that which a tautology expresses.

It is just as impossible to construct an "illogical symbol" as it is to construct an illogical situation. The first negation sign in '$\sim(P \ v\sim P)$' does not function as a genuine negation. This is only one symptom of the fact that the tautology and contradiction are cases of the "disintegration of the combination of signs."

It is only possible to negate a proposition if it is contingent. The function of negation is to produce out of one proposition another which expresses the *alternative* possibility. Only propositions whose general form includes contingency can be affirmed and negated. Neither tautologies nor contradictions are contingent. Therefore, neither possesses the general form of a proposition. Both tautology and contradiction show the general form of a proposition, but neither has that form. And so *none* of the logical operations, which are performable on genuine propositions by virtue of their form, are performable on the logical propositions.

It is, therefore, strictly speaking, incorrect to say that either a tautology or its negation is true. Despite the appearances to the contrary, a tautology has no negation. Thus there is no danger in saying that any proposition whose general form is such that either it or its negation is true, is contingent. The purported counterexamples, tautology and contradiction, are not counterexamples when properly interpreted.

The first negation sign in '$\sim(P \ v\sim P)$' does not function normally. And it is not the only sign in '$\sim(P \ v\sim P)$' and '$P \ v\sim P$' which is functioning abnormally. *None* of the signs, the logical signs or the signs of the genuine propositions involved, are functioning normally. The complete remark at 4.466 is as follows (numbering added for convenience of reference):

> 4.466 (1) What corresponds to a determinate logical combination of signs is a determinate logical combination of their meanings. It is only to uncombined signs that absolutely any combination corresponds.
>
> (2) In other words, propositions that are true for every situation cannot be combinations of signs at all, since, if they were, only determinate combinations of objects would correspond to them.
>
> (And what is not a logical combination has *no* combination of objects corresponding to it.)
>
> (3) Tautology and contradiction are limiting cases—indeed the disintegration of the combination of signs.

In line (1) Wittgenstein notes that if a proposition is a determinate logical combination of its components, then its meaning is simply a combination of the meanings of its components. This is exactly the significance of the 'fundamental idea,' that the logical contants do not enter into the representational content of the proposition. If they did enter into the representational content of the proposition, then a determinate logical combination of propositions (a conjunction, disjunction, and so forth) would not be merely a combination of the meanings of its components. But in Wittgenstein's view, the meaning of 'P v Q' is simply a particular combination of the meanings of 'P' and 'Q'. That is, if 'P' is about the object a, and 'Q' is about the object b, then 'P v Q' is about those same objects a and b.

But 'P v$\sim$$P$' is not about the object a, even if 'P' and '$\sim$$P$' separately are about a. That which is relevant to the truth value of 'P v$\sim$$P$' is that which is presented with the symbol of the tautology which is common to all propositions. For it is the same thing which determines that 'P v$\sim$$P$' is true that determines that 'Q v$\sim$$Q$' is true, and that does not involve *any* particular objects at all. The meaning of 'P v$\sim$$P$' is *not* a logical combination of the meanings of its component propositions. This is what Wittgenstein says at 4.466. And it has quite surprising consequences.

If 'P v Q' is a disjunction in the sense that its meaning is a particular logical combination of the meanings of its component propositions, then

'P v~P' is not a disjunction! This point is parallel to the claim that symbols such as '~$(P$ v~$P)$' are not the negations of tautologies. It is an expression of the fact that in a tautology *none* of the symbols are functioning normally.

That 'P v~P' is not a disjunction can be seen in the following way: 'P v Q' is a disjunction since the specification of its truth conditions involves the specification of two possible situations, each of which is relevant to the truth value of 'P v Q'. But the specification of that which is relevant to the truth value of 'P v~P' does not involve any possible situation at all. In specifying that which is relevant to the truth value of 'P v~P', one does not specify the possible situation represented by the proposition 'P'. What is relevant to the truth value of 'P v~P' is the general propositional form, that is, it is that which is presented with the symbol of the proposition 'P' which is common to all propositions. The truth conditions of 'P v~P' have nothing to do with any particular situation. The particular proposition 'P' only occurs accidentally in the symbol.

Wittgenstein makes this clear in the second sentence in line (1). Since "any combination [of meanings] corresponds" to a tautology, the tautology is an "uncombined sign." By saying that any combination of meanings corresponds to a tautology, Wittgenstein is merely pointing out that it does not matter which proposition is substituted for 'P' in 'P v~P'. Any proposition may be substituted for 'P' without altering that which is relevant to the truth value of the logical proposition. 'P v~P' appears to be a logical combination (disjunction) of propositions, but it is not. For the particular propositions which seem to be disjoined in the tautology *are not essential to the symbol at all.* Just as '~$(P$ v~$P)$' is not a negation of a proposition, 'P v~P' is not the disjunction of two propositions.

It is the role of negation to produce out of one genuine proposition another genuine proposition which is merely a logical "combination" of the meaning of the original proposition. '~P' is a logical combination of the meaning of 'P', in the sense that '~P' has the same sense as 'P', *not a distinct sense.* So too it is the role of disjunction to produce out of a pair of propositions another proposition whose meaning is a mere combination of the meanings of its components. It must be remembered that to say that 'P v Q' is a mere combination of the meanings of its components is to say that 'P v Q' is not about "a single objective fact which is disjunctive." It is only a compound expression which is about two possible facts—those expressed by 'P' and 'Q' when they are taken separately.

Disjunction has the role of combining two contingent propositions into *another contingent proposition*, whose meaning is merely a combination of the meanings of its component propositions. Therefore, 'P v~P' is not a disjunction. For in 'P v~P', two propositions with a meaning appear to be combined, but their meanings are not disjoined. Or in the language of 4.466, the tautologies "cannot be combinations of signs at all."

At 4.4661 Wittgenstein admits that in some sense the signs are combined in tautologies and contradictions:

> 4.4661 Admittedly the signs are still combined with one another, even in tautologies and contradictions—i.e. they stand in certain relations with one another—but the relations have no meaning, they are not essential to the symbol.

Here Wittgenstein makes the distinction between sign and symbol. The signs are combined in a tautology, but the symbol is not that which it appears to be. To deny that the symbol is that which it appears to be is to deny that 'P v~P', for instance, is a disjunction. It is to deny that in 'P v~P' the particular proposition 'P' is involved at all.

So despite the physical combination of signs which usually expresses a disjunction, 'P v~P' does not express that which a genuine disjunction would express. But even if the symbol in 'P v~P' is not the symbol of a disjunction, it does not follow that there is no symbol of any kind involved. If there is a positive account of the tautological symbol (and we have already seen in Chapter II that tautologies can at the very least be said to present the general form of a proposition) then there is a symbol of some kind involved. (See VII.7 "Throwing Away the Ladder")

It is interesting that, according to the fundamental idea, the logical constants do not affect the representational content of the proposition in which they occur. But the logical constants do not seem to conform to this requirement in the logical propositions. For the result of disjoining 'P' and '~P' is an expression in which not only is the meaning not a mere combination of the meanings of the component propositions, but the representational content is cancelled out altogether. In tautologies and contradictions the logical signs (like '~' and 'v') do not behave according to the fundamental idea. They are not performing their normal logical role. This is the more fundamental reason why tautologies and contradictions, while not being contingent, are not propositions which are negatable, affirmable, and so forth.

III.6   The Application of the Tautologies in Inference

Wittgenstein's account of the logical propositions can be used to resolve traditional paradoxes in the philosophy of logic. One of these, a logical version of the paradox of Achilles and the Tortoise, is discussed here. In addition, Wittgenstein's view anticipates the modern development of Relevant and Paraconsistent Logics. However, the results of the present section are tangential to the developing argument of the *Tractatus,* and nothing in the remainder of the book depends on the views sketched here.

Since tautologies and contradictions show the general propositional form, a tautology could be said to *apply* to genuine propositions. For example, it is by virtue of the general form of genuine propositions that either a proposition 'P' or its negation is true, that is, that the law of the excluded middle *applies* to 'P'. But since a tautology does not itself possess the general form of a proposition, it cannot be applied to itself. This is why Wittgenstein holds that "There is not, as Russell thought, a special law of contradiction for each 'type'; one law is enough since it does not apply to itself " (6.123). It must be emphasized that the fact that tautologies do not apply to themselves is not decided arbitrarily, or even in order to resolve such problems as "types", but it arises naturally out of the preceding interpretation of the logical propositions.

But there are prima facie difficulties with this view. For tautologies appear to apply to themselves. If 'P v~P' is a tautology, then so too is '(P v~P) v~(P v~P)'—where 'P v~P' has been substituted for 'P' in 'P v~P'. But the appearance that tautologies (or contradictions) apply to themselves is an illusion, suggested by the fact that it is possible to substitute tautologies and contradictions for genuine propositions in a tautology, and still have a tautology. One must make a distinction between the kind of symbols to which tautologies and contradictions apply, and those which can be substituted *into* a tautology such that the resulting expression is still a tautology.

In denying that tautologies apply to themselves, Wittgenstein is not denying that one can substitute a tautology or contradiction for a genuine proposition in a tautology such that the resulting expression is also a tautology. But the fact that a symbol like '$(P \lor \sim P) \lor \sim (P \lor \sim P)$' exists is not an expression of the fact that either '$P \lor \sim P$' or its negation is true. '$P \lor \sim P$' has no negation. Rather, that which is expressed by that complex tautology is something about *genuine propositions,* namely that *any genuine proposition,* when combined in accordance with the schema '$(P \lor \sim P) \lor \sim (P \lor \sim P)$' yields a tautology. The resulting expression also shows the form of the component genuine proposition, and is itself true by virtue of the general form of the component genuine proposition. The complex tautology '$(P \lor \sim P) \lor \sim (P \lor \sim P)$' applies to the component genuine proposition 'P', not to its middle-sized component '$P \lor \sim P$'.

Since tautologies express the general logical features of genuine propositions, it is possible to apply tautologies to genuine propositions in order to make valid inferences from one genuine proposition to another. But since tautologies do not apply to themselves, one must distinguish a proof of a contingent proposition by means of logic from a "proof" of a logical proposition.

> 6.1263 Indeed, it would be altogether too remarkable if a proposition that had a sense could be proved *logically* from others, and *so too* could a logical proposition. It is clear from the start that a logical proof of a proposition that has sense and a proof *in* logic must be two entirely different things.

Wittgenstein's distinction between these two sorts of "proofs" is simply an extension of the distinction between the application of tautologies to genuine propositions, and the substitution of tautologies (and contradictions) into tautologies.

The following is a "logical proof of a proposition," that is, a proof in which a genuine proposition is "proved logically" from other genuine propositions:

1. P

2. $P \supset Q$

$\therefore$ 3. Q

The logical law applied to genuine propositions in this proof is *modus ponens,* '$\{[P \cdot (P \supset Q)] \supset Q\}$'. But the premises and the conclusion of this proof are contingent propositions. The logical law is applied to the premises in this argument in order that the conclusion may be derived. It *can* be applied to the premises since, as a tautology, it is nothing other than an expression of the general form of the genuine propositions involved in the proof. The strongest statement of this is 6.122, where Wittgenstein states that one can actually "do without logical propositions," since "in a suitable notation we can in fact recognize the formal properties of propositions by mere inspection of the propositions themselves." The reason we can apply the logical proposition to the genuine ones is the same as the reason why it is possible to do without the logical propositions.

The characteristics of a "logical proof of a proposition" are: (1) *all* premises and the conclusion are genuine (contingent) propositions; (2) the inference is made by means of a logical proposition which is itself simply an expression of the general form of those contingent propositions.

The role of the logical proposition is such a proof is similar to that of a mathematical proposition in "real life."

> 6.211   Indeed, in real life a mathematical proposition is never what we want. Rather we make use of mathematical propositions *only* in inferences from propositions which do not belong to mathematics to others that likewise do not belong to mathematics.

Similarly, in a logical proof of a proposition, both premises and conclusion are genuine (non-logical) propositions.

Thus a logical law is not, and cannot itself be, a line in the proof. In this way Wittgenstein avoids the logical version of the Paradox of Achilles and the Tortoise, namely, that 'Q' follows from 'P' and '$P \supset Q$' only if an infinite number of logical propositions are premises in the proof. The paradox may be stated as follows. Suppose the two premises in an argument are 'P' and '$P \supset Q$'. In order to draw the conclusion 'Q', one must employ modus ponens. But then modus ponens is just another premise in the proof. Now, one must argue that if 'P' and '$P \supset Q$' and '$(P \cdot (P \supset Q)) \supset Q)$', then '$Q$'. But then one needs a more complex rule of inference yet . . . and so on ad infinitum. Thus the proof must be infinitely long:

1. P

2. $P \supset Q$

3. $[P \cdot (P \supset Q) \supset Q]$

4. $[(([P \cdot (P \supset Q)] \cdot \{[P \cdot (P \supset Q)] \supset Q\} \supset)Q]$

.

.

.

ad infinitum

∴ Therefore Q

But that which one seeks to add in lines 3, 4, and beyond, is already implicit in the general form of the genuine propositions in lines 1 and 2 of the proof. Logical propositions do not function at all like premises in a logical proof of a genuine proposition. The paradox results from treating a tautology too much like a genuine proposition, that is, by regarding the tautology itself as a proposition with logical properties over and above those possessed by the genuine propositions. The infinite regress never even gets a chance to begin.

A logical proof of a proposition must be distinguished from a proof "within" logic. The proof of 'Q' from 'P' and '$P \supset Q$' is of an entirely different character from, for instance, the "proof" of Q' from '$P \cdot \sim P$'. This "proof" goes as follows:

1. $P \cdot \sim P$ hypothesis

∴ 2. P 1. simplification

∴ 3. $P \vee Q$ 2. addition

∴ 4. $\sim P$ 1. simplification

∴ 5. Q 3,4 disjunctive syllogism

In this "proof" the sole premise is a contradiction. The inference from line 1 to line 2 is justified as an instance of the rule of simplification, that is, '$(P \cdot Q) \supset P$'. But according to Wittgenstein it is, strictly speaking, inaccurate to think of this as an inference from one proposition to another by means of an application of the rule of simplification. For the rule of simplification is expressed in a tautology, and one cannot apply a tautology to a contradiction. One can only apply a tautology to a proposition whose general form is shown by the tautologies, that is, a genuine contingent proposition.

It does seem odd to speak of a "proof" that anything follows from a contradiction (the learned intuitions of logicians aside). That such a proof cannot be conceived as an application of logical laws to propositions, in order that inferences can be made, follows from Wittgenstein's account of the logical propositions. An earlier version of his objection to the view that one can *infer* anything from a contradiction is stated in the *Notebooks*, p. 54:

> But then! Won't a contradiction be a proposition that says the most? From 'P. ~P' there follows not merely 'P' but also '~P'. All propositions follow from none!? But I can't infer anything from a contradiction just because it is a contradiction.

In comprehending this view it is important to remember that Wittgenstein is making a point about the nature, not challenging the existence, of the "proof." When Wittgenstein denies that '~(P v~P)' is the negation of a tautology, he is not denying the existence or importance of the sign. So too he is not denying the interest or utility of the "proof that anything follows from a contradiction." Rather, he is only saying that this "proof" must be conceived differently from the proof of a genuine proposition by means of logic.[5]

Wittgenstein has a positive account of a "proof within logic:"

> 6.1262 Proof in logic is merely a mechanical expedient to facilitate the recognition of tautologies in complicated cases.

Strictly speaking, nothing is proved in the "proof" that anything follows from a contradiction. In this "proof" one has merely, in a mechanical manipulation of signs, shown that something is a tautology. One has only, in a mechanical manipulation of signs, shown that '(P. ~P)⊃Q' is a tautology.

Rather than considering the sequence of steps in the "proof that anything follows from a contradiction" as a proof that a genuine proposition follows from a contradiction, it is only proper to think of it as a mechanical procedure which enables one to sort out tautologies from other expressions.

6.126 One can calculate whether a proposition belongs to logic by calculating the logical properties of the *symbol*.

And this is what we do when we 'prove' a logical proposition. For without bothering about sense or meaning we construct the logical propositions out of others using only *rules that deal with signs*. . . .

Note that Wittgenstein puts the word "prove" into quotation marks when it is used in connection with the "proof" of a logical proposition. For in this case one is not inferring one proposition from another by means of logic. One is only "calculating" with mere signs ("without bothering about sense or meaning").

Though it does not make sense to say that 'P' is inferred from '$P \cdot \sim P$', it is obviously not impossible to set up rules, as in a game. If one encounters and expression of the form '$P \cdot \sim P$', on the "game board," one is allowed to write down 'P' in a subsequent line on the board. And this is all that one does in a proof within logic. Naturally, these rules are set up to insure that the results of the mechanical manipulations are *useful* for logicians. That is, if one plays the game properly it is possible to write down '$(P \cdot \sim P) \supset Q$' in a later line on the board. Logicians aim to set up the rules of the game in such a way that corresponding to the mere *signs* reached at the conclusion of the game, is a symbol which is syntactically indistinguishable from the sign, and is a tautology. By using mere syntactical rules for dealing with *signs,* logicians may achieve results which can be *interpreted* in such a way that they are useful in determining the logical properties of *symbols.*

Wittgenstein's account of how the tautologies apply to genuine propositions explains why the tautologies can be employed in inferences from one genuine proposition to another. In such an inference one does not appeal to some rule which is given independently of the genuine propositions themselves. A tautology may appear to be distinct from the genuine propositions to which it is applied, but it is not, since it is only an expression of the general form of those propositions. So to appeal to a tautology is not to appeal to anything which is not already given with the genuine propositions involved anyway. Furthermore, Wittgenstein's account enables one to understand why—appearances to the contrary— tautologies do not apply to themselves or to contradictions. That is important insofar as a great gain in conceptual clarity is thereby realized. In concrete terms this gain in conceptual clarity is manifested in the solutions to paradoxes like the Paradox of Achilles and the Tortoise, and in the manner in which Wittgenstein avoids the infinite regress of "types" of propositions.

CHAPTER IV

Logical Form and the Form of Reality

In addition to showing that genuine propositions are contingent, the tautologies also show (1) that every genuine proposition is about something external to its symbol, and (2) that this subject matter is or is not in some contingent state. Corresponding to each of these ontological theses there is a corresponding "linguistic" thesis about the structure of the propositional symbol. These and other ontological and linguistic theses are demonstrated in the present chapter. Some of these demonstrations may appear to be too simple. Such simplicity is not found in other reconstructions of the *Tractatus*. Yet it is a requirement of the *Tractatus* itself. "The solutions to the problems of logic must be simple since they set the standard of simplicity" (5.4541).

IV.1 The Subject Matter of Propositions

It has already been demonstrated that the law of the excluded middle shows that genuine propositions are contingent. That which is presented with the symbol of the genuine proposition does not determine which of the two truth values the proposition has. But excluded middle also shows that the truth value of the genuine proposition is determined. So either 'P' or '~P' is true (which is simply an expression of excluded middle itself), and the other is not true. But since the truth value of the genuine proposition is not determined by that which is presented with its symbol, then unless its truth value can be determined by nothing at all, its truth value must be determined by reference to something external to the symbol.

But the truth value of the genuine proposition cannot be determined by nothing at all. In Chapter II we assumed that propositions are in some sense about *something*.[1] There is something in accordance with which their truth value is determined. It follows that the truth value of the genuine proposition is determined by something external to its symbol.

This is an argument that the law of the excluded middle shows that any genuine proposition "represents" its subject matter from a position outside it (2.173). The point at 2.173 is stated with respect to "pictures," not explicitly with respect to propositions. But since it is Wittgenstein's final view that every genuine proposition contains a picture, it is obviously not inadmissible to employ the remark in the preceding fashion. Rather than being inadmissible, that which is demonstrated in the preceding argument is nothing but an important first step in the demonstration that a genuine proposition contains a picture (in Wittgenstein's sense).

The next question is: Is this external subject matter the same for 'P' and '$\sim P$'? Could 'P' be about some subject matter S, and '$\sim P$' be about some S' where $S \neq S'$? Wittgenstein holds that if 'P' is about S, then so too is '$\sim P$' about S. In the completed view of the *Tractatus*, the subject matter of genuine propositions is the object(s) it is about. And if, for example, 'P' is about the objects a and b, then so too is '$\sim P$' about those same objects and no other. How does the law of the excluded middle show that this is so?

First, it is obvious that any view in which 'P' and '$\sim P$' have different subject matters must be a dualistic view of the sort discussed in Chapter I. And Wittgenstein rejects all such dualistic views for the reasons presented there. But despite the fact that we have long recognized Wittgenstein's view to be anti-dualistic, it is still illuminating to develop his view in a continuation of the current argument.

We know that '$P \vee \sim P$' is a tautology, and also that the fundamental idea can be employed in an argument that the genuine propositions, which are the components of the tautological symbol, 'P' and '$\sim P$', have the same sense₁ (*see* Chapter I). But since the specification of the sense of the genuine proposition is the specification of that which is relevant to its truth value, and since 'P' and '$\sim P$' have the same sense, it follows that they have the same subject matter.

IV.2   The Proxy

The fact that genuine propositions are about something external to their symbol must be embodied in a formal feature of the propositional symbol.[2] Since the fact that genuine propositions are about something external to their symbol is demonstrated on the basis of that which is presented with the symbol in the law of the excluded middle, it follows that the fact must be embodied in a feature of that which is presented with the symbol of a tautology. But the tautological symbol is composed of the symbols of genuine propositions, which are combined in such a way that everything which distinguishes one genuine proposition from another drops out as irrelevant to the truth value of the tautology. Therefore, it is a feature of genuine propositions in general that they contain a structural feature which embodies the fact that they are about something external to their symbol.

This argument and its language are very abstract. What it means in concrete terms is that the propositional symbol must contain a *proxy* for its subject matter. Since the propositional symbol "represents its subject matter from a position outside it," it cannot actually contain its subject matter. But since the fact that it is about an external subject matter is presented with the symbol of the proposition, the genuine propositional symbol must contain a proxy for that subject matter.

In addition, the fact that 'P' and '$\sim P$' are about the same subject matter must be reflected in that which is presented with their respective symbols. In concrete terms, this means that 'P' and '$\sim P$' must contain *the same* proxy. Sameness of subject matter must be reflected in a sameness in the structure of the respective symbols. That 'P' and '$\sim P$' are about the same subject matter is determined by formal considerations in that sense.

At this point the line of thought which connects this view with the view that the tautologies are presentational symbols should have become clear. That '$P \vee \sim P$' is a tautology is determined by that which is presented with its symbol. But then, that 'P' and '$\sim P$' are contradictories must be determined by that which is presented with their symbols. But they are contradictory only if they have the same sense, and therefore the same subject matter. Thus, that they have the same subject matter must be determined by that which is presented with their symbols, that is, they must contain the same proxy.

If 'P' and '~P' did contain distinct proxies to stand for a common subject matter, then that they are about the same subject matter *would not be determined by the formal features of the two propositional symbols*. In that case, that 'P' and '~P' are about the same subject matter would not be embodied in that which is presented with the propositional symbol alone.[3]

This line of argument can be pushed further. It is a well known position of the *Tractatus,* and a position commonly brought up in discussions of logically perfect languages during the *Tractatus* period, that there would be no ambiguity or redundancy in the names of such a language. Russell writes, "In a logically perfect language there will be one word and no more for every single object, . . ."[4] This view can also be demonstrated in an extension of the foregoing argument.

The fact the 'P' and '~P' are about the same subject matter must be reflected in the structure of their respective symbols. But, since the propositional symbol must present with itself whatever subject matter it concerns, then if 'P' and 'Q' are about the same subject matter, where 'Q' is not logically related to 'P' (by for example, not being its contradictory), then 'P' and 'Q' must contain the same proxy. Similarly, if 'P' and 'Q' are about different subject matters, they must contain different proxies. This is so because the question of whether any logical combination of propositions is a tautology is a formal matter; it must be determined by that which is presented with its symbol. If proxies were employed ambiguously or redundantly, then there would be facts about the sense of expressions which would not be determined by that presented with, or shown by, the symbols involved.

The meaning of the parenthetical remark at 3.203, which has so perplexed commentators, can be explained based on this interpretation.

3.203 A name means an object. The object is its meaning. ('A' is the same sign as 'A').

Taken by itself, the parenthetical remark seems trivial. But taken within the context of the rest of 3.203, the point that 'A' is the same sign as 'A' is intended to have something to do with the meaning of the sign. Sameness of symbol reflects sameness of subject matter. Thus, within the context of the rest of 3.203 the parenthetical remark means that the sign 'A' in one of its occurrences, for instance in the proposition 'P', means the same object as that same sign in another of its occurrences, for instance in '$\sim P$'.[5]

The interesting thing about this view is that it means that the multiplicity of subject matters (objects) in the world must be matched in a one-to-one correspondence by proxies within the symbolic medium. Since this requirement placed on logically perfect languages is a familiar one, the really interesting development here is the unexpected method of derivation of the view. It is demonstrated on the basis of the view that tautologies are true by virtue of that which is presented with their symbols.

The notion of 'showing', as it pertains to symbols, is defined in terms of the presentational powers of symbols. Insofar as the tautologies present with their symbol that which is relevant to their value, they show that which is relevant to their truth value. That is, they "show that they are tautologies" (6.127). But genuine propositions cannot present their subject matter with their symbol. They cannot, so to speak, show their subject matter. But they do present something with their symbol which stands in for their external subject matter. Because of this, one might be tempted to say that they show their subject matter in an indirect sense. But to avoid confusion, it is better to say only that they show *that* they are about some particular subject matter. And one of the requirements for achieving this is that there be no ambiguity or redundancy in the proxies which constitute the symbolic language. That is, the multiplicity of subject matters in the world is matched, one to one, by the multiplicity of proxies in the symbolic medium.

It would not be incorrect, but neither would it be quite sufficient, to call this proxy a "name." It is not that proxies are not names, but that merely calling them "names" does not reveal that they must perform a quite remarkable function: they must not merely stand for their subject matter, but *the proxy must present with itself the fact that it stands for a subject matter which cannot itself be presented with the propositional symbol.* This function is not associated with the notion of a name as a matter of course.

In summary, (1) the propositional symbol must contain proxies for its external subject matter, (2) sameness or difference of subject matter must be reflected in sameness or difference of proxies in the propositional symbols, (3) the proxies must perform the remarkable function of showing that they are about some specific external subject matter, and (4) these conclusions are all derivable by virtue of the fact that if 'P v$\sim P$' is a tautology, then it must be true by virtue of that which is *presented with its symbol.*

IV.3   Pictorial Form

The genuine proposition is about something external to its symbol. But we also know that such a proposition is contingent. The genuine proposition must, therefore, say that its subject matter is or is not in some contingent state. The main result which is demonstrated in the present section is that, unlike the subject matter of the genuine proposition, the contingent state expressed by the proposition is not external to the propositional symbol. That this is so must, of course, be demonstrated on the basis of that which is presented with the symbol of the tautologies.

Suppose that '*S* is *F*' is such a genuine proposition, and it says of *S* that it is in the contingent state *F*. Then '*S* is *F* or it is not the case that *S* is *F* ' is a tautology. As such it is true by virtue of that which is presented with its symbol. But then that which is presented with its symbol must determine that it is possible for *S* to be *F*, and also possible that *S* not be *F*. If this were not so, then there would be a condition of that tautology's truth value which is not determined by that which is presented with the tautological symbol. And that, as we know, cannot be. Thus, that which is presented with the symbol of the genuine proposition involved must determine both that it is possible that *S* be *F*, and that it is possible that *S* not be *F*.

In short, that which is presented with the symbol of the genuine proposition involved must determine: (1) that it makes sense to say that *S* is *F*, and (2) that it makes sense to say that *S* is not *F*. The first condition would not be satisfied if *S* were simply of the wrong category to be *F*. The second condition would not be satisfied if *S* were necessarily *F*, for *F* is only a *contingently* possible state of its subject matter. Thus, that which is presented with the symbol of the proposition must determine both that *S* may be *F*, but also that it may not be *F*.[6]

But how can the propositional symbol, which is external to its subject matter, present with itself the possibility that its external subject matter may or may not be in some contingent state? This would seem to be a difficult requirement to satisfy. A concrete structural feature of the propositional symbol must determine something about the possible contingent states of that subject matter which is *external* to its symbol.

The answer is that the propositional symbol is *itself* a contingent fact. It presents with itself the contingent state in which the subject matter is represented by the proposition. It does this by presenting the proxies in the very same contingent state in which the objects are represented. Since the proxies are themselves actually presented in the relevant contingent state, it follows that the propositional symbol itself presents the possibility that objects may be in that state. But also, that which is presented with the propositional symbol determines that the objects may not be in the contingent state *F*, since the propositional symbol is itself a *contingent* fact which may or may not obtain. That is, the proxies are only contingently in the state *F*.

Thus, that the propositional symbol is itself a contingent fact, composed of proxies presented in the same contingent state as that in which objects are represented, enables it to embody in a concrete way (present with its symbol) the possibility that its external subject matter may be in that contingent state. It also embodies the possibility that it may not be in that contingent state. This is the claim Wittgenstein is making in his discussion of pictorial form.

> 2.15 The fact that the elements of a picture are related to one another in a determinate way represents *[stellt vor]* that things are related to one another in the same way.
>
> Let us call this connexion of its elements the structure of the picture, and let us call the possibility of this structure the pictorial form of the picture.
>
> 2.151 Pictorial form is the possibility that things are related to one another in the same way as the elements of the picture.

That is, the propositional symbol presents with its symbol the contingent state in which its external subject matter may or may not be, by virtue of the fact that the propositional symbol has pictorial form. The proxies are themselves in the same contingent state in which the subject matter of those proxies is represented to be or not be. ("Our problems are not abstract but perhaps the most concrete that there are" 5.5563.)

The fact that the propositional symbol has pictorial form means that, unlike the subject matter of the genuine proposition, *the contingent state involved is not external to the propositional symbol.* It is literally presented with the propositional symbol. Wittgenstein's explanation of the way in which the contingent state is presented with the propositional symbol consists in his view that the contingent state has no proxy standing in for it. It is literally presented with the propositional symbol.

The proxies which are components of the propositional symbol are themselves in the contingent state in which their subject matter is represented. That is, the correct description of a genuine propositional symbol (for example, the proposition which says of its subject matter, the objects *a* and *b,* that they are in the contingent state *R*) would not be that the propositional symbol is composed of proxies for *a* and *b* and a proxy for *R.* Rather, a correct description of the symbol would be that it is composed only of two proxies, those for *a* and *b,* where those proxies are actually in the relation *R.*

That the genuine propositional symbol does not contain a proxy for the contingent state involved, but is composed of proxies for its subject matter, which are themselves actually in that contingent state, means that the propositional symbol is itself a fact. It also means that, as regards the contingent state involved, the symbol-fact is identical with the possible fact, that is, the state of affairs, which is represented by the proposition.

> 2.161 There must be something identical in a picture and what it depicts to enable the one to be a picture of the other at all.

Such remarks are often interpreted to mean that the proposition-fact and the possible fact in the world must be identical in structure only in some very abstract sense. That is, it is often thought that if they are both facts with the same "logical multiplicity"—for instance, if both are composed of two objects in a binary relation which is not necessarily the same binary relation—then the one fact is capable of being a picture of the other.

Urmson, for example, in his comment on 3.1432, writes: "Thus, one fact states another by means of its internal structure. The relation of the picturing, depends. . .on the identity of structures of the two facts."[7] The example employed by Urmson is the following: the fact, or "complex sign," 'glass on dish' says 'Wisdom has killed Al Capone.' That is: the glass is a proxy for Wisdom, the dish is a proxy for Al Capone, and the relation *"on"* (top of) goes proxy for the distinct relation "has killed!" In general commentators have failed to take account of the notion of pictorial form, and have regarded a proposition as a picture only in the sense that the propositional sign and the pictured fact are isomorphic in structure (see section V.3).

Wittgenstein's view is that the propositional symbol is a picture of the possible fact involved in the sense that the contingent state involved is the same in the propositional fact and in the possible fact it pictures. The notion of isomorphic structures is not the only notion of a picture in the *Tractatus*.

The genuine proposition says that the subject matter external to its symbol is or is not in some contingent state, and that contingent state is literally presented with the propositional symbol. Wittgenstein writes:

> 4.022 A proposition *shows* its sense.
>
> A proposition *shows* how things stand *if* it is true and it *says* that they do so stand.

A proposition shows how things stand if it is true, in the sense that the contingent state in which things are represented to be or not be is literally presented with or contained in its symbol. And it is presented with its symbol in the sense that the proxies which are the components of the symbol are themselves in that contingent state. Wittgenstein's view that the genuine proposition shows how things stand if it is true *is* the view that the genuine propositional symbol has pictorial form.

It is important to recognize that in the argument that the propositional symbol has pictorial form (the argument that it shows how things stand if it is true) there are two intimately related but distinguishable arguments being made. First, if the propositional symbol were not itself a fact, then nothing presented with its symbol would determine the possibilities of the being and non-being of facts. For of course, what is affirmed or negated in logical affirmation and negation is the being and non-being of facts. The second argument is that we have demonstrated considerably more than that the propositional symbol is just any type of fact. We have argued that it must have pictorial form. And how does it come about that this can be demonstrated? Since 'P v~P' is a tautology, it is true by virtue of that which is presented with its symbol. Thus, that it makes sense to affirm or negate the existence of the state of affairs involved must be determined by that which is presented with the propositional symbol involved. What this means is that the fact that the genuine propositions involved *have sense* must be determined by that which is presented with their symbols. Thus, the genuine propositional symbol cannot be just any fact, for it must *present with itself the conditions of its own meaningfulness:* "A thought contains the possibility of the situation of which it is the thought" (3.02).

Tautologies are presentational symbols in the sense that they present that which is relevant to their truth value with their symbols. Genuine propositions cannot be presentational symbols in that sense, since they are about a subject matter which is external to their symbol. But the fact that the genuine propositional symbol has pictorial form means that it presents with its symbol the conditions of its own meaningfulness, that is, presents entities (the proxies) which are actually in the very contingent state which is involved in its own sense.

Wittgenstein's view that the genuine propositional symbol has pictorial form is one of the most important and most underemphasized views of the *Tractatus*. It means that (1) unlike the subject matter of the proposition, the contingent state involved in the sense of the proposition is not external to the propositional symbol, and (2) the conditions of the meaningfulness of the genuine proposition are presented with its symbol.[8]

IV.4   The Propositional Bond

Any account of the genuine proposition must explain the fact that the genuine proposition is not merely a list of symbols. The proposition says that something *is* such and such. In the *Notebooks* Wittgenstein asks: How does "the *propositional bond* come into existence?" (*NB*, p. 5). In everyday language the propositional bond is expressed by the copula '*is*'. Wittgenstein's account of the propositional bond is implicit in his view that the propositional symbol has pictorial form. According to the *Tractatus*, the contingent state expressed by a proposition is not stood in for by a proxy, but it is not only the contingent state involved which is not stood in for by a proxy. The propositional bond is not expressed by a symbol either. The only components of the genuine propositional symbol are the proxies which stand for the subject matter of the proposition. The genuine propositional symbol does not contain the copula 'is'.

Wittgenstein might appear to be uniquely open to the charge that according to his view the proposition is understood as a mere list of names. For in his view the proposition contains no symbol for the copula. Here a propositional symbol looks like *a b,* where *a* and *b* are each symbols which stand for objects. But the fact that the propositional bond is not present in the person of an additional symbol does not imply that it is not present. Quite the contrary, Wittgenstein's holds that the only way the proposition can contain a propositional bond is if it is *not* present in the form of a symbol.

The fact that the propositional symbol has pictorial form means that the contingent state expressed by the proposition is not expressed by a proxy which stands for that contingent state, but by the fact that the proxies for the subject matter are themselves in that same contingent state. One does not say that *a* is *F* by somehow combining a proxy for *a* and a proxy for *F.* Nor does the propositional symbol say that something *is* such and such by virtue of the fact that it contains a symbol which stands for its subject matter, and *another symbol* which stands for "is-ness." The propositional symbol does not *indirectly allude* to what it is to *be the case* by representing being with a proxy, that is, 'is.' Quite the contrary, the propositional symbol says that something is the case by virtue of the circumstance that *it is itself something which is the case.* The propositional symbol is an *immediate presentation* of what it means for something to be the case.

What it means for something to *be* is not in some obscure fashion *represented* by a symbol 'is', but is itself literally presented with the symbol. Just as the contingent state involved is not represented by means of a proxy, but is actually present in the symbol of the proposition, so too, being is *itself* presented by the propositional symbol. Wittgenstein's account of the propositional bond is not abstract. The propositional symbol is bonded together in *exactly the same fashion* as the possible fact represented by that proposition. ("Our problems are not abstract, but perhaps. . . .")

That which is affirmed or negated by genuine propositions is the being of states of affairs, that is, that a subject matter *is* in some contingent state. The notion of being which is expressed by genuine propositions, and what it means for something to be in a contingent state, is literally presented with the genuine propositional symbol by virtue of the fact that the propositional symbol is itself composed of objects in a contingent state.

Sections III.2 and III.3 contained the argument, based upon the interpretation of the tautologies as presentational symbols, that the possibility of affirming and/or negating geunine propositions must be inherent in the general form of genuine propositions ("the sole logical constant"). This is one of the key insights in the argument of the *Tractatus*. We now see that the possibility of affirming and negating genuine propositions is inherent in the general propositional form in the sense that the genuine propositional symbol is itself composed of objects in the same contingent state in which the proposition's subject matter is represented. What this means is that affirmation is nothing but the affirmation of the sort of being which is presented in the propositional symbol, the *being in a contingent state of objects*. The same is true of negation, and this is well worth a careful examination.

Suppose that 'P' is a genuine proposition which says that its subject matter is in the contingent state F. Then the symbol 'P' is itself composed of entities in the *same* contingent state F. Since 'P' is itself composed of entities (the proxies) which are only contingently F, then that which is presented with its symbol determines that its subject matter may not be F. The propositional symbol is itself a fact which *might not exist*, and it is a fact involving just that contingent state in which its subject matter is represented. Despite the fact that the propositional symbol presents something being F, it is still true that that which is presented with the propositional symbol also determines that its subject matter may not be F. And this is how what is presented with the propositional symbol determines the possibility that the proposition is negatable.

The important points are: (1) The proposition is bonded together in the same sense in which facts are. (2) The sort of being which is bound up with affirmation and negation is actually presented with the propositional symbol. (3) This sort of being is the being of contingent facts. (That this is so is a consequence of the fact that the possibility of affirming and negating propositions must be determined by that which is presented with their symbols.) (4) The view that the sort of being which is bound up with the sense of the genuine proposition is *itself* presented with the symbol of the proposition is an important part of the view that the genuine propositional symbol presents with its symbol the conditions of its own meaningfulness.

IV.5   Substance

In the *Tractatus* the subject matter of propositions is substance; it is "unalterable" and "subsistent" (2.027). But the mere fact that genuine propositions say that their subject matter is or is not in some contingent state does not by itself entail that that subject matter itself exists non-contingently, that is, that it is the *constant* or unalterable element in the world. As usual, this conclusion must be demonstrated on the basis of that which is presented with the symbol in the tautology 'P v~P', and not on the basis of any extraneous assumptions.

Affirmation and negation are bound up with the sort of being which is literally presented with the genuine propositional symbol, the "being in a contingent state of entities." Of course, affirmation and negation are only a special case: The whole machinery of the logical constants is bound up with that sort of being which can be presented with the genuine propositional symbol.

The importance of these facts in the present deduction is this: The fact that the subject matter of the genuine proposition is external to the propositional symbol means that its existence cannot be either affirmed or negated. The point at which one comes up against that which is external to the propositional symbol, that which cannot be presented with the propositional symbol, is the point at which the whole of the logical machinery breaks down. And that point is the point at which the proxies stand in for their external subject matter.

Furthermore, we know that 'P' and '~P' each present with their symbols the fact that they are about the same external subject matter. Thus, it is only the contingent state of the subject matter which is presented by the symbol as contingent. The proxies which stand in for the subject matter are constant between 'P' and '~P'. Thus, the subject matter of propositions is the *constant* or *abiding* element in the world, and only its "configuration" or contingent state is presented as "unstable" (see 2.027).

But is the matter this simple? The answer to this question is "yes" if one is clear about exactly what has been demonstrated in the argument. The answer is "no" if one wants to make a very natural, but unwarranted, assumption about the meaning of the conclusion. The most glaring indication that one must qualify the nature of the conclusion is that we have demonstrated not only that the existence of the subject matter cannot be negated, but also that it cannot be affirmed. It would be a mistake to conclude from the argument that we can affirm the existence of substance. But if the argument commits us to the view that the existence of substance is not affirmable, then what is demonstrated in the argument?

As far as that which is presented with the symbols is concerned, the existence of the subject matter of propositions is constant while only its contingent state is "unstable." But in order to determine more precisely what this means, let us test this conclusion. Is it not consistent to hold that the proxies are constant between 'P' and '$\sim P$', and also to hold that the subject matter stood in for by those proxies is not *in actuality* constant and abiding? Why is the external world bound by the way in which it is presented by the propositional symbol? What justifies one in inferring from the fact that the symbolic representation of something is constant, that it *really is* constant?

Nothing justifies making such an inference, for one is here at the point at which something can no more be inferred than affirmed or negated. All that one can conclude on the basis of the argument is *that there is a constancy in the meaning (Bedeutung)* of the proxies in the propositional symbol. To put it in another way, all that one can justifiably mean by saying that the subject matter of propositions exists, or constantly exists, is that as far as that which is presented with the symbols goes, everything behaves as if there is a subject matter—a constantly existing subject matter—in the world. And even this explanation can be made more concrete. In the positive and negative propositions, the proxies remain constant while their arrangement or contingent state is what can be or fail to be.

If one wants to go on and ask: But does this constancy in the meaning of the proxies correspond to the actual constant existence of something "in the world?," then one has introduced a notion of existence, into the discussion without warrant. The question whether the subject matter of propositions *really exists,* or is the abiding existent in the world, is illicit. It is not that there is a question here which cannot be answered, but that there is no question. For the notion of existence involved in the question is without any meaning. And it is without meaning because the fundamental notion of meaning in the *Tractatus* is that of a presentational symbol, and therefore *all* meaningful notions must be defined in terms of that which can be presented with the propositional symbol. And since the subject matter of the genuine proposition is precisely that which cannot be presented with its symbol, that it exists or not cannot be presented with the propositional symbol.

This contrasts with the notion of existence involved in the existence of facts. The existence of facts can be presented with the propositional symbol for the simple reason that the symbol is itself a fact, a being-in-a-contingent-state of things. But no notion of the "real existence" of the subject matter of genuine propositions can be presented with the symbol of the genuine proposition. So we have no means of defining such a "transcendent" notion of existence in terms of that which can be presented with the propositional symbol. That means that there is no such notion.

Thus, the qualification of the meaning of the conclusion of the argument that the subject matter of propositions is the constant element in the world, has to do with the notion of existence which is involved in any such view. That is, since the subject matter cannot be presented with the propositional symbol, *all* meaningful notions which pertain to that subject matter, including the notions of its existence and its substantiality, must be defined in terms of that which can be presented with the genuine propositional symbol. So *all that it can mean* to say that a genuine proposition is about a constantly existing subject matter in the world is that, as far as that which is presented with the symbols goes, the meaning of the proxies is constant, while only their configuration is "changing and unstable" (from 2.027).

It is important to realize that it is quite natural that some such indeterminacy appears at just this point in the argument of the *Tractatus*. The key insight which powers the argument of the *Tractatus* from start to finish is that the truth value of the tautologies is determined by that which is presented with their symbols. That means that the key to the account of the logical constants, and to the account of the sense of the genuine proposition, is the notion of that which is presented with the propositional symbol. *But in dealing with the subject matter of the genuine proposition, one is dealing precisely with that which cannot be presented with the propositional symbol.* It is precisely in connection with considerations which pertain to the external subject matter of the genuine proposition that one wants to say that one has run up against the limits of language. For nothing about that external subject matter itself can be captured in definitions which are based upon that which can be presented with the propositional symbol. And Wittgenstein would hold that the fact that there is this indeterminacy at this point is not *his* problem. Anybody who holds that propositions are about something external to their symbol must acknowledge this same indeterminacy, these same limits.

The whole doctrine that there are limits to language must be understood in light of the fact that the fundamental notion of meaning in the *Tractatus* is that of a presentational symbol. These limits must be encountered at any point at which one attempts to deal with that which cannot be presented with the propositional symbol, that is, its subject matter. What the proposition says about its subject matter, that it is or is not in some contingent state, is within the limits of that which can be expressed by language only because the being-in-a-contingent-state of an entity can be presented with the propositional symbol. But the existence or nature of the subject matter itself, apart from its contingent states, is beyond the limits of language. This is because it has to do, by hypothesis, with that which cannot be presented with the propositional symbol.

Did Wittgenstein himself recognize the difficulty posed here, or did he simply make the inference to the existence of the substance of the world (in the notion of an existence transcending symbols)? After all, he does make some very strong statements concerning the existence of the substance of the world in the 2.02's, and especially at 2.0211. Also at 5.5521 he writes, "We might put it this way: If there could be a logic even if there were no world, how then could there be a logic given that there is a world?" This rhetorical question clearly suggests that he held that the "existence of logic" (presumably to be spelled out in terms of the truth of the tautologies, and so forth) is not independent of the existence of the world. And there is no hint of any qualification.

Wittgenstein did recognize the problem posed above, and he did not make the inference to the "symbol-transcendent existence" of substance. First, as regards the very strong statements at 2.0211 and 5.5521, it is not Wittgenstein's style in the *Tractatus* to state a position each time with all of the qualifications and explanations which might be given. It would be tedious to do so. And since there is a notion of the existence and constancy of the subject matter of propositions (that as far as that which is presented with the symbols is concerned, the meaning of the proxies remains constant), the statements at 2.0211, 5.5521 and elsewhere can be interpreted in accordance with those definitions.

There is also direct evidence in the text that Wittgenstein conceived the problem as it is described above. 6.124 is the fourth comment on 6.12, which is the governing statement about the connection between the tautologies and the logical form of language and the world. At this key place in the text Wittgenstein writes:

6.124 The propositions of logic describe the scaffolding of the world, or rather they represent *[darstellen]* it. They have no 'subject matter'. They presuppose *[voraussetzen]* that names have meaning *[Redeutung]* and elementary propositions sense; and that is their connection with the world. . . .

The connection between the propositions of logic and the "world" is that the propositions of logic "presuppose" that names have meaning and elementary propositions, sense. This is a way of stating the "connection" which is oriented toward the symbols, and that which can be presented with a symbol, rather than toward the unqualified statement of the existence of the subject matter external to those symbols. Thus, when Wittgenstein writes, "and that is their connection with the world," one may well hear him saying—"and that is all that one can mean by saying that the propositions of logic are connected with the world."

One cannot object to this interpretation of 6.124 on the grounds that Wittgenstein says that the propositions of logic presuppose that names have meaning *[Bedeutung]*, and a proposition cannot have *"Bedeutung"* unless it refers to something *existent*. For *even if* one interprets *Bedeutung* to mean reference (which, as Fogelin points out,[9] is not warranted by the text), one cannot *presuppose* that a name can only refer to something if that something exists. First, such a principle is not obvious. But more importantly, according to Wittgenstein's view, any such principle must be demonstrated on the basis of that which is presented with the symbol of the tautologies. And we have already seen that not only is such a view not demonstrable, but also that it is just such views which transgress the limits of language. The notion of existence intended in such a principle cannot be defined in terms of that which can be presented with the symbol of the genuine proposition.

It is not, however, a main concern to decide here whether Wittgenstein recognizes that the inference to the unqualified existence of the substance is unwarranted. The main point is that there is a demonstration, based on that which is presented with the symbol of the tautologies, of the substantiality of the subject matter of propositions (given that the notion of existence involved has been appropriately qualified). That demonstration is the cash value of the view of 5.5521 that the existence of logic is not independent of the existence of the world. And understanding the qualifications which must be made in connection with this demonstration illuminates the view that there are limits to what can be expressed by language. Given that the fundamental notion of meaning is that of a presentational symbol, plus the fact that it is precisely the subject matter which cannot be presented with the propositional symbol, it is clear exactly where and why those limits must be encountered.

Admittedly, this view that there are limits to language, and that they are encountered at just this point and in just this way, is one of the most problematic views of the *Tractatus.* The connection between the proxies and the subject matter "in the world" is clearly one of the most mysterious parts of Wittgenstein's theory. The view must not be allowed to escape criticism, but it is more fruitful to take up the criticism after the whole theory has been stated. For the present we shall simply develop Wittgenstein's view and assume that the propositional symbol contains proxies which present with themselves the fact that they are about an external subject matter. The criticism of this view, and other views in the *Tractatus,* must be developed in a sequel.

IV.6 The Symbolic Representation of the Substantiality of the World

As usual, any demonstration of an ontological thesis is accompanied by a parallel thesis about the structure of the propositional symbol. Thus, that genuine propositions are about a constantly existing subject matter in the world must be embodied in a structural feature of the genuine propositional symbol. But in this case the alleged ontological thesis concerns that which cannot be presented with the propositional symbol. Therefore, the allegedly ontological thesis must really be a disguised thesis about the structure of the propositional symbol. The point at which one runs up against the limits of language is the point at which all apparently ontological theses are reducible to theses about the structure of the propositional symbol.

In other words, that genuine propositions are about a constantly existing subject matter in the world only means that, *as far as that which is presented with the symbol is concerned,* the meaning (*Bedeutung*) of the proxies remains constant. But what, in concrete terms, does this mean about the structure of the propositional symbol? It means that though the proxies which stand in for the subject matter of the world must be entities which can have contingent states, they must not themselves be contingent complexes. That is, the proxies for the subject matter of the proposition must constitute a constant, or unalterable, component of the genuine propositional symbol. The proxies cannot themselves belong to the category of contingent facts.

But why could it not turn out that the proxies for the subject matter are themselves structures, composed of components in contingent states, and that those components are themselves contingent structures, and so on ad infinitum? If by this is meant that there are really no proxies, but only deeper and deeper levels of contingent structure to the world, then there would really be no qualitative difference between a subject matter and its contingent state. There would not really be any proxies for an external subject matter. True, in this view there would appear to be a qualitative difference between the subject matter of propositions and its contingent state, since at any given level of analysis of a proposition there would be: prima facie unstructured entities, the *apparent* proxies, and also the contingent state which they are in. But in this view the appearance of a qualitative difference between the two elements of the propositional symbol would be illusory. For it would always be possible to analyze away any apparent proxy into a further level of contingent sub-structure. There would be no point at which one would come to the proxy for a subject matter which cannot itself be presented with the propositional symbol.

But that is impossible. We have demonstrated that (1) there is subject matter external to the propositional symbol, (2) it may or may not be in some contingent state, and (3) there is a disanology both between the subject matter and its contingent state, and between the way in which they are expressed by the propositional symbol. This is not the mere appearance of a disanalogy. The subject matter is external to the propositional symbol, while the contingent state is literally presented with the symbol.

The preceding line of thought is an attempt to give lip service to the thesis of the externality of substance, while holding that the subject matter of propositions is not really incapable of being presented with the propositional symbol. There must be objects, an external subject matter for propositions, and they must be capable of being represented as being in some contingent state, where the contingent state is presentable with the propositional symbol. The world cannot be a bottomless well of contingency.

The fact that the world is not a bottomless well of contingent sub-structures, the fact that genuine propositions are about a constantly existing subject matter in the world, must be embodied in structural features of the propositional symbol. And, in concrete terms, that means only that the propositional symbol contains proxies which are not themselves contingent structures, while it is only their configuration, or "relation," which is changeable and unstable.

IV.7   Interim Review

There is a danger tht the real simplicity of the argument of the *Tractatus* will be lost amidst the complexity of explanatory comments, discussions of side issues, and commentaries. For these reasons it is worthwhile to state in summary form the argument from Chapter II to the present point.

In Chapter II, the 'fundamental idea' is used in an argument that '$P \vee \sim P$', like all tautologies, is true by virtue of that which is presented with its symbol. But tautologies are composed of genuine propositions combined in such a way that their individuating features drop out as irrelevant to the truth value of the tautology. Thus, that which is presented with the symbol of the tautology and is relevant to its truth value is a genuine proposition which, in that context, functions as an exemplar of genuine propositions in general. That is, the tautologies present with their symbol, and are true by virtue of, the general propositional form. The key idea which is needed in order that one can demonstrate the features which constitute the general propositional form is that the general propositional form is "the sole logical constant." This means that the multiplicity of the logical constants is "reducible" to features of the general propositional form. And ultimately, this means that the possibility of performing logical operations on propositions must be determined by concrete structural features of the propositional symbol.

Thus, in the tautological symbol '$P \vee \sim P$', genuine propositions are affirmed, negated and disjoined. It is argued in Chapter III that a genuine proposition is only affirmable and/or negatable by virtue of its own general form, if that which is presented with its symbol does not determine its own truth value, and indeed, even determines that the genuine proposition may be either true or not true. Thus, genuine propositions in general must be contingent. This demonstration of the contingency of genuine propositions, and of the intimately associated fact that that which is presented with the symbol of the genuine proposition does not determine its truth value, is the foundation for all of the inferences made in the present chapter.

In the present chapter it is argued that, since that which is presented with the symbol of the genuine proposition in general does not determine which of the two truth values it has, its truth value must be determined either by reference to nothing at all or by reference to something external to its symbol. But we have assumed from the beginning that there *are* symbols, that propositions are about something in some sense. Thus, the genuine proposition must be about something external to its symbol. This conclusion is extended to include the fact that genuine propositions and their negations are about the same external subject matter, since we know that 'P' and '$\sim P$' have the same sense.

Continuing the argument, we infer that since the genuine proposition is contingent, 'P' and '$\sim P$' must say of their common subject matter that it is or is not in some contingent state. If 'S is F' is such a genuine proposition, then 'S is F or not-S is F' is a tautology, and is true by virtue of that which is presented with its symbol. Thus that S may but may not be F must be determined by that which is presented with its symbol. Otherwise there would be conditions of the truth of the tautology which are not presented with its symbol. That S may but may not be F is presented with the symbol of the genuine proposition only if (1) the genuine propositional symbol is itself a fact which may be or may not be, and (2) it has pictorial form. That is, the contingent state in which the subject matter is represented must be the same contingent state in which the proxies for that subject matter themselves are found in the propositional symbol.

That the genuine propositional symbol has pictorial form explains how it is that the possibility of affirming and negating a proposition is inherent in the general propositional form: (1) The propositional symbol itself has the structure of a contingent fact which may be or not be the case. (The propositional symbol is itself bonded together in the same sense as a contingent fact is bonded.) (2) That it makes sense to affirm or negate the existence of a state of affairs involving the particular contingent state is determined by the fact that the propositional symbol is itself a presentation of entities in that same contingent state. It is, therefore, "not an accident" that one can affirm and negate genuine propositions, for the possibility of affirming and negating them is determined by the fact that the genuine propositional symbol has concrete structural features which embody its logical properties.

An important consequence of this interpretation is that the genuine proposition cannot affirm or negate the existence of its subject matter. Since the subject matter of genuine propositions is external to its symbol, and since the whole machinery of logic has to do with the structural features presented with the symbols of propositions, the subject matter of propositions is outside the reach of language and logic. The existence of this subject matter is presupposed by logic in the sense that that which is presented with the symbols of 'P' and '$\sim P$', respectively, embodies the fact that each of these propositions is about the same external subject matter. But that is the most that can be said. In fact, the most that can be said about the existence of this subject matter of propositions is that, as far as that which is presented with the symbols goes, the proxies remain constant while contingent states are presented as variable.

Corresponding to these "ontological" theses is a series of parallel theses concerning the structure of the propositional symbol. These "linguistic" theses follow, since the aforementioned ontological theses are demonstrated on the basis of that which is presented with the symbol of the tautologies, that is, the general form of genuine propositions.

The genuine proposition must contain a proxy or proxies for the subject matter which cannot be presented with the propositional symbol. But the contingent state expressed by the proposition is not stood in for by a proxy. It is expressed by virtue of the fact that the proxies are themselves actually in that contingent state, and that explains how the propositional symbol "shows how things stand if it is true."

Finally, the fact that 'P' and '$\sim P$' have the same sense must be embodied in that which is presented with their symbols. Thus 'P' and '$\sim P$' are, in general, composed of the same proxies, and these proxies are, in each of the respective propositions, in the same contingent state. If 'P' is composed of the proxy 'a' in the contingent state F, then '$\sim P$' is composed of the same proxy 'a' in the same contingent state F. Otherwise they would have different senses, and we would be faced with a dualism of propositions and a dualism of facts as described in Chapter I. (That 'P' and '$\sim P$' can have opposite truth values is not paradoxical on this interpretation, since 'P' affirms the actuality of the possibility represented and '$\sim P$' negates the actuality of the same possibility.)

It is important to recognize that in this argument we did not even assume that propositions are about facts (as did Russell). That genuine propositions are about facts, and that the structure of their symbols must also have the structure of facts—that genuine propositions involve pictures— is *demonstrated,* not assumed. And it is demonstrated not on the basis of any imported metaphysical, linguistic or even commonsensical assumptions, but on the basis of that which is presented with the symbols of the tautologies. There are, of course, assumptions which must be made (for instance, the fundamental idea), but these are much fewer and thinner than is generally the case in philosophical adventures.

The reader is reminded here that it is not being assumed that Wittgenstein's views are wholly true, or that his strategy is wholly satisfactory. The present aim is to state his views and strategy accurately. But neither is it assumed that his views and strategy are totally wrong. In fact, Wittgenstein's views and strategy are closer to the truth than they might appear to be. But how near or far they are from the truth cannot be settled here, and is the theme of the sequel to the present book.

CHAPTER V

The Perceptible Propositional Signs and Sign-Systems

It is obvious that the sorts of things which one ordinarily thinks of as propositional symbols, that is, the perceptible sentences of everyday language, do not themselves have the special logical properties or structure which has emerged in the argument of the *Tractatus*. Wittgenstein's view is that the propositions of everyday language already have the required structure even though it is not exhibited directly in their perceptible component. Thus, he is not an advocate of constructing an artificial or ideal language that conforms to the features of language laid out in the *Tractatus*. Wittgenstein distinguishes between the perceptible propositional sign and the imperceptible thought. The propositional symbol is composed of the perceptible propositional sign, together with its accompanying thought. The thought or meaning component of the proposition conforms to the a priori requirements of the argument of the *Tractatus*. The perceptible part of the symbol is designed for practical, and other, purposes; its structure and nature cannot be determined a priori (though it is sometimes constructed so as to approximate to the a priori structure of the thought). The general structure of meaning, of the thought, is a priori. The structure of the perceptible propositional sign is not. The present chapter focuses on the perceptible part of the propositional symbol. It is, therefore, a departure from the strictly a priori portion of the argument of the *Tractatus*. The a priori account of the thought is picked up in the subsequent chapter.

V.1   The Surface and the Underlying Structure of Language

a. Logic and the Underlying Structure of Language

The sentences of everyday language do not, apparently, have the logical structure attributed to the propositional symbol in the argument of the *Tractatus*. They are not composed of proxies which are in the same contingent state in which their subject matter is represented, that is, they do not have pictorial form. Even if an occasional sentence approximates to the structure, this seems to be an accidental feature of the sentence and does not have anything essential to do with the fact that the sentence expresses the sense that it does. Suppose, for example, that in the sentence "Stephen is larger than Mary," the sign "Stephen" is in fact larger than the sign "Mary." That these signs stand in that relationship is purely accidental, and it would be ludicrous to suggest that the signifying capacity of the sentence has anything to do with this fact about the size of the signs involved.

In general, the sense or meaning of the everyday sentence does not stand in any simple relationship to its structure. In everyday language sentences with different structures can have the same meaning, and sentences with the same structure can have different meanings. These are nothing other than, respectively, sentence synonymy and ambiguity. Since, in the view of the *Tractatus,* the sense of the proposition is determined purely by its structure, the contrast between the sentences of everyday language and Wittgenstein's requirements for the genuine propositional symbol is great. Not only do the sentences of everyday language not have pictorial form, but they would seem, from the point of view of logic, to be in a state of structural disorder.

Russell, in his Introduction to the *Tractatus,* interprets this discrepancy to mean that Wittgenstein's description of the general propositional form is merely the blueprint for the construction of the sentences of an ideal language:

> Mr. Wittgenstein is concerned with the conditions of a logically perfect language—not that any language is logically perfect, or that we believe ourselves capable, here and now, of constructing a logically perfect language, but that the whole function of language is to have meaning, and it only fulfills this function in proportion as it approaches to the ideal language which we postulate.[1]

But at 5.5563 Wittgenstein writes: "The propositions of our everyday language, just as they stand, are in perfect logical order." The sentences of everyday language do have the refined logical structure, pictorial form, and so on which have been attributed to the propositional symbol in the argument of the *Tractatus*. Obviously Wittgenstein must distinguish between the real and the merely apparent structure of sentences.

One cannot identify the observable structure of sentences with their logical structure. One must distinguish the sentence as a symbol from the sentence as its observable manifestation. A symbol is a combination of a sign and a thought; the sign is perceptible and the thought is imperceptible (see *Tractatus* 3.32). Thus, one can distinguish between the sentential symbol and the sentential sign, the latter being the perceptible component of the former. The fact that the perceptible part of the symbol does not possess the required logical structure does not mean that the imperceptible part, the thought which accompanies it, does not have it. The sentences of everyday language are in "perfect logical order" in the sense that, though the sentential sign does not have the necessary logical structure, the sign is merely the perceptible "clothing" (4.002) of the imperceptible thought, and the thought does have it.

Wittgenstein can, thus, consistently hold that the sentential signs of everyday language do not have pictorial form, but that the everyday sentential symbol does have it. What is his argument? There are many sorts of arguments which can be given for the claim that the propositional symbol has such an underlying imperceptible structure. However, only those sorts of arguments which are derivative from the philosophy of logic of the *Tractatus* are presented here.[2]

The argument of the *Tractatus* is the demonstration of the general form of genuine propositions. This general form is demonstrated on the basis of that which is presented with the symbol of the tautologies which is relevant to their truth values. The particular tautology employed in this demonstration is the law of the excluded middle. Thus, if one admits that the law of the excluded middle applies to the propositions expressed in everyday language, that is, that either they or their negations are true, then one must admit that these propositions *already* have the general form of a proposition (pictorial form, for instance).

This argument is not without force, but it may not be totally convincing, since it is not out of the question to deny that the tautologies apply to the propositions of everyday language just as they stand. There are, after all, considerations of vagueness, indeterminacy, and so forth, and some would argue that these considerations mean that the tautologies do not apply to the sentences of everyday language, or at least that they apply to them only to a certain degree. Obviously the views that (1) logic does not apply to everyday propositions, and (2) that it only approximates to them, are not unproblematic, but they are not without some intuitive appeal. Furthermore, both Russell and Wittgenstein do consider such views. Russell actually endorses such a view in his Introduction to the *Tractatus* by his suggestion that a language only "has meaning" in the "proportion" to which it approximates to the "ideal language which we postulate."[3] Wittgenstein himself considers such a view in the *Notebooks* (see pp. 66–70). So since it can be denied that the tautologies apply "straightaway" (*NB*, p. 66) to everyday propositions, then it is reasonable to ask for a more direct and compelling argument on the matter.

Wittgenstein's most basic argument on this matter derives from his account of the logical constants. The possibility of performing logical operations on propositions is determined by the general structural features of the genuine propositional symbol. For example, that it is possible to affirm or negate a genuine proposition is determined by the fact that the propositional symbol is *itself* a structure which may or may not be the case. Thus, if it is possible to affirm or negate the propositions of everyday language, then they do have the structural features attributed to the propositional symbol in the argument of the *Tractatus*. Though it may seem plausible to deny that the law of the excluded middle applies to the propositions of everyday language, it is much less plausible to hold that they cannot be affirmed or negated, or that they can only be affirmed or negated in a certain "proportion." The sentences of everyday language are, therefore, in perfect logical order in that they are the perceptible manifestation of the underlying structure. This (1) determines the sense of the proposition, (2) has the refined logical structure which has emerged in the argument of the *Tractatus,* and (3) is the component of the propositional symbol to which the logical apparatus applies.

The conclusion of these arguments is that the logical structure of everyday propositions is, in fact, embodied in an underlying structure. It is, however, the stronger view of the *Tractatus* that it *must* be embodied in an underlying structure, that the meaning component of the proposition has a nature which no mere perceptible entity can have. The explanation of Wittgenstein's complete view on this matter involves considerations concerning the unique nature of the thought which are taken up in the subsequent chapter.

It is also important to recognize that the present argument does not have the same logical status as the argument of the *Tractatus* itself. The argument of the *Tractatus* itself, the demonstration of that which is presented with the symbols of the tautology which is relevant to their truth value, includes among its conclusions certain views about the structure of meaning. The argument of the *Tractatus* is rigorous and a priori in a way in which the present argument is not. The present argument rests upon certain *facts* and certain *intuitions* about everyday language. The structure of meaning is a priori; the view that everyday language has that structure is not.

b. *Wittgenstein's Alternative Account of Vagueness*

Wittgenstein does have an interpretation of those phenomena of everyday language, such as vagueness, which have led some to deny that logic applies "straightaway" to them. Wittgenstein's discussion of these issues in the *Notebooks* also lends support to the interpretation put forward in the present discussion.[4]

Not only Russell, but even Wittgenstein, considered for a time the view that logic does not fully apply to ordinary propositions. Wittgenstein writes:

> Yes, this is the point: Can we apply logic just as it stands, say in *Principia Mathematica* straight away to ordinary propositions? (*NB*, p. 66)

In the same series of remarks Wittgenstein goes on to ask:

> But could it be possible that the sentences in ordinary use have, as it were, only an incomplete sense . . . and that the propositions in physics, as it were, approach the stage where a proposition really has complete sense? (*NB*, p. 67)

Here Wittgenstein considers a view akin to Russell's view in the introduction to the *Tractatus*—that a certain artifically constructed sign system, that of physics in this case, is better suited to have sense (or "complete sense") than the signs of everyday language. Since Wittgenstein's view in the

Tractatus is that the meaning component of the proposition is not its perceptible component, but an accompanying imperceptible one, one should expect this discussion in the *Notebooks* to move away from the idea that the artificially constructed sign language of physics is better suited than the everyday sign language to have meaning. It should move toward the view that the meaning component of the proposition is not its perceptible component.

Wittgenstein goes on:

> When I say, "The book is lying on the table," does this really have a completely clear sense?" (AN EXTREMELY important question.) But the sense must be clear, for after all we mean *something* by the proposition, and as much as we certainly mean must surely be clear. (*NB*, p. 67)

Contrary to expectations, the everyday proposition does have a clear sense *insofar as we "mean something"* by it. Wittgenstein does not here explicitly mention an imperceptible component which has determinate sense, but the reference to the fact that, insofar as the proposition is *meant* it is determinate, does suggest such a view. And this is not the end of Wittgenstein's discussion.

> Then are the propositions of physics and the propositions of ordinary life at bottom equally sharp, and does the difference consist only in the more consistent application of signs in the language of science? (*NB*, p. 68)

The view that both kinds of propositions are "at bottom equally sharp" is a first formulation of the distinction between the surface and underlying structure of the proposition. When Wittgenstein says that the two kinds of propositions are at bottom equally sharp, he is driving at three related points: (1) that both sorts have an underlying structure, (2) that the sense or meaning of the propositions is determined by that underlying structure, and (3) that the underlying structure is in both cases equally determinate.

The difference between ordinary propositions and the propositions of physics does not concern their underlying meaning components, but their surface components. The "surface" or perceptible component is *applied*, and it is in the *"consistency" of the "application"* of these perceptible signs that the two languages differ. But how do they differ in the application of their respective perceptible parts?

> But it may also be that the proposition "The book is lying on the table" represents my sense completely, but that I am using the words, e.g., "lying on," with a *special* reference here, and that elsewhere they have another reference. What I mean by the verb is perhaps a quite special relation which the book now actually has to the table. (*NB*, p. 68)

Here Wittgenstein suggests one way to take the remark that in the language of physics signs are applied "more consistently" than are the propositional signs of everyday language. The signs in the language of physics are used with a "special reference." In ordinary life one counts many sorts of situations as cases in which the book is lying on the table. For example, the book may be entirely within the area of the table top, or it may extend outside the area to a considerable degree, and still count as lying on the table. But in physics, when one is interested in setting up and describing experiments, one may not wish to count cases of the latter sort as cases in which the book is said to be "on the table." This is so in order to minimize or eliminate entirely certain kinds of physical effects which occur when the book teeters on the edge of the table.

The artificial language of physics is not better suited to have sense or meaning in some basic philosophical sense; it is simply designed to enable one to express certain *particular senses* which one does not normally have the need to express in daily life. In ordinary life one uses the expression—"The book is lying on the table"—to cover a wide range of cases. This does not mean that the sentence is used with indeterminate sense, for it can be quite determinate that this particular wide range of cases will include cases of the book lying on the table, while others will be left out. One might imagine the sense of this everyday sentence quite determinately expressed by a very lengthy disjunction. The difference is that in the language of physics the disjunctions are simply much shorter. In the two languages, different senses are expressed, different discriminations made. For this reason it is probably better to think of the language of physics as a *specialized* language than as an ideal language. This point is very important, for it means that the language of physics is not ideal in the sense of conforming to certain *philosophical* ideals (Russell's notion of an ideal language), but in that it is specially designed for certain scientific endeavors.

The view which is in the process of development in the *Notebooks* exploits the fact that there are two components to the propositional symbol, one perceptible and one imperceptible. The meaning component is the imperceptible part, and thus the two kinds of propositions, so different in their perceptible components, can each have determinate sense. Vagueness and precision have to do with the perceptible part of the proposition and the manner, or "consistency," of its application (for example, to how many different kinds of situations are the words "is lying on" applied?). The notion of determinate sense and the notion of precision (in the sense in which the language of physics is more precise than the everyday language) are, therefore, fundamentally different notions, and they even pertain to fundamentally different components of the propositional symbol. Determinate sense is properly located in the account of the *meaning* or imperceptible component of the propositional symbol, whereas precision has its place in the account of the *application* of the perceptible propositional sign.

The phenomenon of the vagueness of everyday propositions and signs only appears to imply that logic, the tautologies, and so forth, apply only approximately to these propositions. The question of whether logic applies to a proposition has to do with the sense or meaning of the proposition, and that involves the imperceptible underlying structure of the proposition. Vagueness and precision have to do with an entirely different dimension of the language, that is, the application of the perceptible propositional sign. The perceptible part of language may be characterized by vagueness, for instance, as well as by what has been called "structural disorder," and the language still be "in perfect logical order just as it is."

These passages from the *Notebooks* do not contain the fully worked out distinction between the surface and underlying structure of the propositional symbol, nor the key notion of the "application" of the perceptible propositional signs. It is also not clear that Wittgenstein's account of vagueness is adequate to all of the types of linguistic vagueness. It is, for example, designed to deal with the sense in which "The thing is in Asia" is vague (vague because Asia is so big), but not with the kind of vagueness involved in borderline cases, cases where it is not determined whether a description applies to a subject or not. If there are genuine cases of such borderline vagueness, then Wittgenstein's account of vagueness may be incomplete in a fundamental way. However, it is even possible that this sort of vagueness could be handled in Wittgenstein's account. That is, he could perhaps hold that even these sorts of cases do not have to do with the logic or sense of the proposition, but with the application of the propositional signs to situations. In short, he could hold that there is no vagueness of this sort in our thought, or in the world, but only in our *use* of the mere perceptible signs. This is a fascinating possibility, but it goes beyond the limits of our present purpose, which is simply to outline the role of this issue in Wittgenstein's reasoning that one must distinguish between the surface and underlying structure of language.

V.2 The Propositional Sign of Everyday Language

If the contrast between the structure of the everyday propositional sign and its real logical structure is so great, and if the perceptible part of the symbol is not its meaning component, then what is the purpose of the everyday propositional sign? Wittgenstein does not provide a very detailed account of the purposes of the everyday propositional sign. The general outlines of his view can be gleaned from his remarks in the *Tractatus,* and fleshed out by reference to the somewhat more detailed remarks of the *Notebooks.*

Wittgenstein writes:

4.002 Man possesses the ability to construct languages capable of expressing every sense without having any idea how each word has meaning or what its meaning is—just as people speak without knowing how the individual sounds are produced.

Everyday language is a part of the human organism and is no less complicated than it.

It is not humanly possible to gather immediately from it what the logic of language is.

Language disguises thought. So much so, that from the outward form of the clothing it is impossible to infer the form of thought beneath it, because the outward form of the clothing is not designed to reveal the form of the body but for entirely different purposes.

The tacit conventions on which the understanding of everyday language depends are enormously complicated.

Wittgenstein distinguishes the "outward form of the clothing" from the form of thought beneath it. By the "outward form of the clothing" he means the perceptible signs of everyday language. These perceptible signs are said to have a different purpose from "the form of thought beneath it," that is, from the underlying imperceptible structure. Wittgenstein does not explain the purpose of the everyday sign, but he does state that it is connected to the form of thought beneath it by "enormously complicated conventions." The facts that there are such connections and that they are enormously complicated are a result of the purposes to which the everyday sign is put.

Wittgenstein explains the importance of these complex conventions in the *Notebooks:*

> To anyone that sees clearly, it is obvious that a proposition like "This watch is lying on the table" contains a lot of indefiniteness, in spite of its form being completely clear and simple in outward appearance. So we see that this simplicity is only constructed.
>
> It is then also clear to the *uncaptive* mind that the sense of the proposition "The watch is lying on the table" is more complicated than the proposition itself.
>
> The conventions of our language are extraordinarily complicated. There is enormously much added in thought to each proposition and not said. (*NB*, pp. 69–70)

The thought, which embodies the sense of the proposition, is much more complicated than its "outward appearance." Much is "added in thought" which is not reflected in the perceptible sentence. The simplicity of the perceptible sentence is "merely constructed." In short, the simplicity of the perceptible sign is achieved by allowing very complicated conventions which connect it with the underlying thought.

This simplicity is of value since the peceptible sign must serve the purposes of daily life. Russell expresses such a view in the *Lectures* and there is no doubt that the same sort of view is shared by Wittgenstein.

In a logically perfect language the words in a proposition would correspond one by one with the components of the corresponding fact, . . . In a logically perfect language there will be one word and no more for every simple object and everything that is not simple will be expressed by a combination of words, by a combination derived, of course, from the words for the simple things that enter in, one word for each simple component. . . . Actual languages are not logically perfect in this sense, and they cannot possibly be if they are to serve the purposes of daily life. A logically perfect language, if it could be constructed, would . . . be intolerably prolix, . . .[4]

The purposes to which the outward sign must conform are, in a broad sense, the practical purposes of daily life. Specifically, the perceptible propositional sign must serve the purposes of communication. For this reason the "outward form of the clothing" must be simpler than the structurally much richer thought "beneath" it.

How is it possible to get by in daily life with a simplified perceptible sign? After all, if the perceptible sign does *not* reflect the rich structure of the thought involved, will not its use occasion constant misunderstanding? Wittgenstein addresses this question in the *Notebooks:*

It is clear that I know what I mean by the vague proposition. But now someone else doesn't understand and says: "yes, but if you mean that then you should have added such and such"; and now someone else again will not understand and will demand that the proposition should be given in more detail still. I shall then reply: Now *that* can be taken for granted. (*NB,* p. 70)

In order to serve the purposes of daily life, the perceptible sign must be simpler than the thought involved. It can be simpler because normally a great deal can be "taken for granted." Nevertheless, the sign must be connected to the underlying thought, and this connection is expressed in the conventions which connect the thought with the perceptible sign. To the degree that the sign is very simple and the underlying thought very complex, the connecting conventions must themselves be very complex.

The connection of the everyday perceptible propositional sign with both the thought and the relevant state of affairs is, therefore, constituted by the complex tacit conventions involved. The sense in which the everyday propositional sign is a picture is definable in these terms:

4.011 At first sight a proposition—one set out on a printed page, for example—does not seem to be a picture of the reality with which it is concerned. But no more does musical notation at first sight seem to be a picture of music, nor our phonetic notation (the alphabet) to be a picture of our speech.

And yet these sign-languages prove to be pictures, even in the ordinary sense, of what they represent.

4.0141 There is a general rule by means of which the musician can obtain the symphony from the score, and which makes it possible to derive the symphony from the groove on the gramophone record, and, using the first rule, to derive the score again. That is what constitutes the inner similarity between these things which seem to be constructed in such entirely different ways. And that rule is the law of projection which projects the symphony into the language of musical notation. It is the rule for translating this language into the language of gramophone records.

The propositional sign, structurally so dissimilar to the relevant state of affairs, is a picture of that state of affairs only if it is taken together with a complex rule for systematically deriving the former from the latter. In the case of everyday language, the rules involved are the tacit conventions which connect the perceptible sign with the imperceptible thought. Insofar as the projection rule connects the propositional sign with the thought, it also connects it with the relevant state of affairs. This is because the thought, with pictorial form, is *structurally identical* with the relevant state of affairs.

Wittgenstein even tells us that the everyday perceptible propositional sign is a picture "in the ordinary sense" of the word. It is not ordinarily required that there be much similarity between a picture and that which is pictured. A photograph may be two dimensional and small, and the pictured object three dimensional and large. The photograph may be black and white, and the object colored. What makes the photograph a picture of the object, despite these great differences, is the fact that there are projection rules which systematically connect the former with the latter. (For example: "when the human face is photographed in normal light, the existence of elevation in the face (such as prominent cheekbones) is embodied, not in elevations on the picture, but in the appearance of shadows of such and such a kind" is the schema of such a projection rule.)

One might infer from the remark at 4.011 that the fundamental notion of picturing involved in the *Tractatus* is the ordinary notion of a picture. But this inference would be hasty. There are two very different notions of a picture, and each has a place in Wittgenstein's account. An ordinary picture and that which it pictures need not have much in common since the lack of commonality is made up for in the supplementary projection rules. But the thought, the underlying structure, is a picture in a much stronger sense. The thought has pictorial form: how the proxies are in the thought *literally coincides* with how the pictured objects in the world may be. Ordinary pictures need not have pictorial form, and it turns out that nothing which we ordinarily think of as a picture is a picture in the strong sense in which a thought is a picture.

A common mistake of the commentator on the *Tractatus* has been to emphasize the notion of a picture which is appropriate to the perceptible propositional sign, at the expense of that which is appropriate to the imperceptible thought. (It is as if the investigator of an economic system on the gold standard were to emphasize the paper currency, with its properties and use, but ignore the gold in the vault which backs it up and is the thing of real value.) The fundamental notion of a picture in Wittgenstein's account of meaning is the notion of a picture which pertains to the imperceptible thought, the notion which is characterized by pictorial form. It is by reference to the thought which has these very extraordinary pictorial properties that the fundamental philosophical questions concerning meaning must be answered. The everyday propositional sign is a picture in the ordinary sense, but it is only the perceptible part of the symbol. It is designed for the practical purposes of daily life, especially for the purpose of communication—not in order to "touch" reality or "show how things stand if it is true."

Wittgenstein's view is that (1) there are two components to the everyday propositional symbol, an imperceptible and a perceptible component. (2) Each of these is suited to serve different purposes, that is, the imperceptible component is suited to be the meaning component of the propositional symbol, and the perceptible component is suited to be adequate for the purposes of communication. (3) In order for the imperceptible component to be suitable to be the meaning component, it must be a *perfect picture* of the relevant state of affairs, that is, it must be *structurally identical* with the relevant state of affairs. (4) In order for the perceptible component to be suitable to be the perceptible indicator of the underlying meaning, it must be a picture of the relevant state of affairs. But it *cannot* be a perfect picture of that state of affairs, and (5) the perceptible indicator of the meaning must instead be a picture in a derivative sense: it is a structure which is *systematically* related to the underlying thought by means of connecting "projection" rules.

V.3   The Ideal Propositional Sign and Sign-System

In his introduction to the *Tractatus* Russell writes that Wittgenstein is interested in the conditions for a logically perfect language. But, ideal for what purposes? We have already seen that the everyday propositional sign is well suited for the practical purposes which it must serve, while the "logically perfect" sign is far too unwieldy for those practical purposes. The program of constructing an ideal language is not motivated by such practical considerations.

It is Russell's view in the Introduction to the *Tractatus* that the ideal sign and ideal language serve a particular purpose which we can call "theoretical," in order to contrast it with the practical purposes which the propositional sign must serve in daily life. Russell writes: "The whole function of language is to have meaning and it only fulfills this function as it approaches to the ideal language which we postulate."[5] Russell's notion of an ideal language is the notion of a language whose propositional signs are better suited to "have meaning" than the everyday propositional signs. But Wittgenstein rejects this view, since he holds that it does not fall to the perceptible part of the symbol to determine meaning in the first place. Thus, the existence of an idealized propositional sign is irrelevant to the capacity of language to "have meaning." The very idea of Russell's ideal language is regarded by Wittgenstein as conceptually confused.

Wittgenstein holds that each part of the everyday propositional symbol, both the perceptible and the imperceptible parts, is ideally suited for the *different* purposes which they must fulfill. If, therefore, there is a notion of an ideal language in the *Tractatus,* it is the notion of the everyday language "just as it is." But this notion of the ideal is not the same as Russell's, insofar as Wittgenstein's notion does not involve the idea of a perceptible sign which is designed to have meaning. There are passages in the *Tractatus* which suggest that Wittgenstein is interested in the construction of an ideal language (a language different from the everyday language), but these remarks have a different point. In them Wittgenstein is concerned with the construction of an ideal *sign-system*. This is not to be equated with the construction of an ideal language.

If a language is a *symbolic* system, that is, a system in which signs are *meaningfully* employed, then Wittgenstein is not interested in the construction of an ideal language. Since the everyday propositional symbol is, in both its components, ideally suited for the purpose for which that component is designed, no philosophical purpose is served by altering everyday language.[6] Wittgenstein's purpose in constructing an ideal sign system is not, therefore, to construct a propositional sign which is better suited for either practical purposes or for the purpose of "having meaning." The ideal sign system is of no use to the language user. It is, however, of utility to the philosopher of language, that is, it is useful for those whose task it is to understand the nature of language. It is the view of the *Tractatus* that the ideal propositional sign is an aid in philosophical *reflection* on language.

If the meaning of a sentence is determined by the imperceptible thought, and if the everyday sign is not designed to reveal the structure of thought, but is used for practical purposes, it follows that one cannot base a correct account of the nature of the propositional *symbol* on an examination of the everyday propositional sign. In Wittgenstein's view, therefore, philosophers can benefit from having before them a *perspicuous perceptible image of the imperceptible thought*. Furthermore, the philosopher is not interested in any particular thought, but in the general nature of thought and in the general sorts of similarities and differences between thoughts. For these reasons the philosopher will not construct just one ideal propositional sign, but enough to illustrate the general sorts of similarities and differences between thoughts. The philosopher may even wish to formulate rules for the generation of ideal propositional signs, and among other things, rules for the transformation of one into another. For this illuminates the nature of thoughts in general. Thus, it is useful to construct not merely one, or a few ideal propositional signs, but an ideal sign system which mirrors the general structure of the imperceptible thought and the general sorts of similarities and differences between thoughts.

In other words, the role of the ideal propositional sign in philosophy is analogous to that of the plastic copy of the human body in medical science. What one really wants to understand and study in medical science is the living human body. For various reasons one cannot always directly study the real object of interest. Nevertheless the structure of the living body can be duplicated to a considerable degree, and the artificial approximation can be quite useful for some, if not for all, of the purposes of the medical scientist. This is true despite the fact that it lacks life (which is of basic importance to the medical scientist). Similarly, though what the philosopher is primarily interested in is the imperceptible thought, it can be quite useful to construct a perspicuous perceptible image of it, despite the fact that the ideal propositional sign does not itself have the "life," the *meaning,* which is possessed by the imperceptible meaning component or thought.

It is important to realize that in order to fulfill this philosophical purpose, it is not necessary that the ideal propositional sign actually have a meaning, that is, it is not necessary that it be actually correlated with any particular thought. The same holds true of the copy of the human body, which need not be actually correlated with any particular human being in order to fulfill its purpose. The philosopher is interested not in particular thoughts, but in thoughts in general. The philosopher's use of a particular propositional sign, and the employment of it as if it were the perspicuous perceptible expression of a particular thought, does not indicate an interest in the meaningful expression of any particular thought, any more than the mathematician's use of a particular triangle to illustrate a point about triangles in general indicates an interest in some particular triangle. The reason why it is easy to forget that the ideal propositional sign need not have any meaning in order to fulfill its purpose, is that its propositional sign is employed *as if* it were the perceptible image of a particular thought.

These points about the use of the ideal propositional sign are really quite trivial, but it is just such trivial misunderstandings which can, and *have,* misled commentators into believing that the ideal propositional sign is intended to be ideal for some actual linguistic duty. It is just such trivial misunderstandings which have led to the suggestion that Wittgenstein is interested in the construction of an ideal language in Russell's sense.

Any interpretation of the *Tractatus* which makes the ideal propositional sign itself the object of primary interest is mistaken. One cannot imagine the analogous mistake in medical science, that is, one cannot imagine anyone inferring that all the attention and care exercised in constructing, assemblying and disassembling plastic cadavers betrays a real interest in these lifeless objects for themselves. The reasons for this are obvious. Whereas scientists often concern themselves with the properties of artificial copies of the human body, they also often directly study the real object of interest, the living human body. Philosophers however, are not so fortunate. Though what is of real interest to the philosopher is the thought, it is only approached through some means involving a perceptual representation. This is one manifestation of the *abstract* character of philosophical logic as compared to that of medical science. Russell himself emphasizes that the "fearfully difficult" and "elusive" character of "abstract" studies such as philosophical logic makes it easy to attribute to the thing the properties which belong only to its "tangible" symbol.[7]

From Wittgenstein's point of view, Russell has himself made the converse error, that is, he has attributed to the perceptible image of the thought some of the characteristics of the thought itself. Russell has mistaken the image for the reality. Russell has observed that the everyday perceptible sign is unsuited to have meaning and has wrongly inferred that a more carefully constructed perceptible sign might have meaning. But, for one who shares Wittgenstein's point of view that the imperceptible component of the propositional symbol is its meaning component, this is a philosophical fantasy.[8] The ideal propositional sign could no more itself have meaning than a carefully constructed plastic cadaver could come to life.

Interpretations of the role of the ideal propositional sign in the scheme of the *Tractatus* have not always emphasized that its role is to be a means for philosophical reflection on the imperceptible thought. Textual support for the present interpretation is, therefore, required. The major textual support occurs in two important discussions of the ideal sign and sign system. The first of these is numbers 3–3.2.

3   A logical picture of facts is a thought.

3.1   In a proposition a thought finds an expression that can be perceived by the senses.

3.143 Although a propositional sign is a fact this is obscured by the usual form of expression in writing or print.

3.2   In a proposition a thought can be expressed in such a way
         that the elements of the propositional sign correspond to
         the objects of the thought.

At 3.2 Wittgenstein describes a propositional sign which "can" be constructed and which reflects the structure of the thought. The need for this
construction is generated by the fact that the everyday propositional sign
"obscures" (3.143) this structure. In general, this series of remarks displays
the intimate link between the construction of the ideal propositional sign
and the purpose of perspicuously exhibiting the structure of the thought.

Another important series of remarks occurs in the early 4's. At 4.0031
Wittgenstein says that "all philosophy is a critique of language." This is
explained in terms of the view, attributed to Russell, that "the apparent
logical form of a proposition need not be its real one." Thus, all philosophy
is, in one way or another, concerned to ferret out and understand the
"real" logical form of language. The context of this remark includes 4.002,
where Wittgenstein states that the "form of thought" is "disguised" in
everyday language. If one can identify the "real logical form" of language
with "the form of thought beneath it," one can infer that "all philosophy"
is concerned to elucidate and understand the form of thought. Though
this is probably too narrow a description of Wittgenstein's own philosophical
efforts in the *Tractatus,* it does describe a central and underemphasized
dimension of the *Tractatus.* Wittgenstein accepted Russell's distinction
between the apparent and the real logical form of a proposition, and
interpreted it as a distinction between the perceptible and the underlying
structure of the propositional symbol. Thus, when in this context Wittgenstein enters into a discussion of the ideal propositional signs and sign
system, the presumption is that these ideal propositional signs are intended
as perspicuous perceptible images and reminders of the "form of thought."[9]

Assuming that this interpretation is fundamentally correct, the question
arises whether, or to what degree, the perceptible medium is suitable for
its intended purpose. That is, constructing a perceptible image of the
imperceptible thought is none too easy a thing to do. It is not obvious
that one can be wholly successful in this enterprise. One very important
remark on the construction of the ideal propositional sign is 3.1432.
Wittgenstein writes:

3.1432 Instead of, 'the complex sign "aRb" says that a stands to b in the relation of R'; we ought to put 'That "a" stands to "b" in a certain relation says that aRb.'

This remark has been the subject of considerable philosophical discussion. But its connection with the view that the ideal propositional sign is intended to be the perspicuous perceptible image of the imperceptible thought has not been brought out. In addition, part of the point of 3.1432 is that the perceptible image of the thought is by its very nature an imperfect image of the thought.

Urmson offers an interpretation of 3.1432 which is not entirely correct but whch makes several important points.

> Now the meaning of the statement in 3.1432 which at first sight is so very perplexing becomes clear. We have: 'we must not say "The complex sign 'aRb' says 'a stands in relation R to b' "'; but we must say, "that 'a' stands in a certain relation to 'b' says that aRb." ' Let that aRb be the fact that Wisdom has killed Al Capone; then Wittgenstein is saying: 'we must not say "The complex sign 'glass-on-dish' says 'Wisdom has killed Al Capone' "'; but we must say "That the glass is on the dish says that Wisdom has killed Al Capone." ' That the glass is on the dish is a fact; that Wisdom has killed Al Capone is another. Thus, one fact states another, by means of its internal structure. The relation of the picturing fact, the sentence, to the pictured fact, the relation of picturing, depends, according to all our authorities, on the identity of structure of the two facts.[10]

According to Urmson's view, the fact that the glass is actually on the dish is, in effect, an ideally constructed sign which pictures the fact that Wisdom has killed Al Capone. The notion of a picture which is developed here involves, first, the idea that that which pictures a fact is *itself* a fact. Second, the ideal propositional sign is not just any fact. The one fact pictures the other by means of its "internal structure." Each fact is composed of two individuals, glass and dish, and Wisdom and Capone, and each are in a binary relation, on (or on-top-of) and has-killed, respectively. That is, the ideal propositional sign is a picture in the sense that it is *isomorphic* with the pictured fact. If the ideal propositional sign is intended to be the perspicuous perceptible image of the imperceptible thought, then it should, unlike the everyday propositional sign, faithfully reflect the structure of the underlying thought.[11]

The ideal propositional sign is constructed so as to have a high degree of structural analogy with the underlying thought. But why is it not constructed so as to be completely structurally accurate to the thought? Why does Wittgenstein relax the requirement of pictorial form and require only that the ideal propositional sign be isomorphic with the pictured state of affairs? It is clear that he does not require pictorial form of the ideal propositional sign, and this is reflected in Urmson's view. The relation in which the signs are put is not the *same* relation in which the objects are represented. And in the text of the *Tractatus* itself, at 3.1432, instead of saying that in order to represent a's being R to b, we should put a and b in the same relation R, Wittgenstein only says that the proxies should be put "in a certain relation."[12] The question is: "why?" If the ideal propositional sign is supposed to be our perspicuous perceptible image of the imperceptible thought, where the thought has pictorial form, then why not require that the ideal propositional sign measure up fully to the thought? After all, the ideal propositional sign is something which *we construct,* and it would seem that we can require it to measure up to any standard which we choose.

Wittgenstein holds that the mere surface form of everyday language is not its "real" or logical form. His version of this view is quite radical; he is committed to a radical type of *new level* analysis of everyday propositions. In a "same level" analysis of propositions, the original proposition is rewritten into a new proposition(s), but the gain is only in clarity, for instance, not in ontological commitment or in the type of entity involved. In a new level, or "reductive" analysis, the original proposition is recast into a new proposition, where the ontological commitment of the two propositions is different.[13]

It is a point commonly made about the *Tractatus* that the real subject matter of the proposition is nothing so complex as entities like Wisdom and Capone, glasses and dishes. The real subject matter of propositions consists of simple objects. There has been much debate about how this notion of a logically simple object is to be understood. Wittgenstein himself worries about this a great deal. He asks, for example, whether a watch could be a simple object (see *Notebooks,* p. 60). The view which I believe Wittgenstein finally adopted, and which is a commitment of his views, is that a watch cannot be a simple object, that a "simple object" is an entirely new category of object. Wittgenstein writes:

> *And it keeps on* forcing itself upon us that there is some simple indivisible, an element of being, in brief a thing. (*Notebooks,* p. 62).

Whereas Wittgenstein may have considered the possibility that the apparent necessity of postulating simple objects is simply the need that something be *treated* as simple in any given representational system (something which is, in itself, an ordinary complex object like a watch), his final view is that the notion of a simple object is to be taken logically and ontologically more seriously. An accurate representation of the sense of the proposition would require that an everyday proposition be rewritten in a radical new level analysis where the real subject matter of the proposition is disclosed to be an ontologically new type of object.[14]

Just as the real subject matter of the proposition is much simpler than the subject matter which is suggested by the surface form of everyday propositions, so too the real contingent states or universals involved are much simpler than those contingent states or universals which are suggested by the surface forms of propositions. This is related to Wittgenstein's remark that all relations are *logical* relations (see *Notebooks,* p. 8). Wittgenstein is committed to a quite radical type of new level analysis of everyday propositions where the shift in ontological commitment extends to both the category of objects and the category of contingent states or universals involved. Commentators have in general tried to develop a *plausible* interpretation of Wittgenstein's account of the analysis of everyday propositions, but at the expense of making it out to be more akin to a same level analysis.[15]

The relevance of Wittgenstein's conceptions of analysis to this problem can be illustrated by analogy with a standard philosophical view. It is common in philosophical discussions of perception to distinguish between the "object" as it is perceived, and the object as it really is. For example, one perceives an object as pink and homogeneous, but it is "really" atoms in a great void. If one holds such a view, and if one finds it useful to construct a perspicuous perceptible image of the "real" imperceptible elements of perceptible things, then one must explain that though our perspicuous perceptible image of the imperceptible hydrogen atom is blue and white, the real hydrogen atom itself is not composed of blue protons and white electrons. It would be a mistake to think that any of the perceptible qualities of our perceptible model of the atom are actually exhibited by the real atom. The use of such a perceptible model of imperceptible atoms requires, therefore, that it be accompanied by a commentary in which both the benefits and the limitations of the perceptible model are detailed. It must be explained that our perceptible model of the imperceptible atom is itself a "middle-sized" object which has the perceptible qualities of the "commonsense framework," and that the atom itself has none of these qualities but has much simpler and more basic attributes.

The account of the construction and utility of the ideal propositional sign is analogous to the account of the classroom model of the atom. If Wittgenstein is committed to a very radical type of new level analysis of everyday propositions, then there is an analogy between the conceptual limitations on the adequacy of our perceptible image of the thought, and those on our perceptible image of the atom. The ideal propositional sign is our perspicuous perceptible image of the structure of thoughts in general, but it makes no more sense to suppose that the ideal propositional sign has pictorial form, than to suppose that the gross perceptible properties of the classroom model of the atom coincide with the qualities of the real atom. To require pictorial form of the ideal propositional sign is not only spurious, but it is as nonsensical as the view that the classroom model of the atom, as perceived, has 'spin' and 'charm.'

The similarity between the ideal propositional sign and the thought is, therefore, limited. First, one can guarantee that the ideally constructed sign is a fact, and even that it strikes us as a fact. Second, there is no reason to suppose that an ideal sign could not be made which is *isomorphic* with the relevant thought and state of affairs. This is not to say that it would be practical to construct a perceptible sign which is isomorphic with even the simplest of thoughts involved in everyday languages, but only that there is no theoretical objection to the possibility of an isomorphism between the ideal propositional sign and both the relevant thought and state of affairs. But the real contingent states involved in the thought cannot always be duplicated in the gross perceptible medium. In the final analysis, that is the reason why it does not make sense to say that the ideal propositional sign is characterized by pictorial form. It does not make sense to say that the ideal propositional sign is composed of proxies which are put in *the same* contingent state as those in which the objects in the world may be.

The ideal propositional sign has, in principle, a greater degree of structural analogy with the relevant state of affairs than does the everyday propositional sign, but a lesser degree than does the thought. The ideal propositional sign is, unlike the everyday propositional sign, *isomorphic* with the relevant state of affairs. But it is not, like the thought, composed of proxies which are in the very same contingent state that is involved in the relevant state of affairs.

There are several different sorts of "symbolic" entities which are countenanced on Wittgenstein's view and which have a refined logical structure, and it is of the greatest importance that claims about one sort are distinguished from claims about the other. Specifically, it is important that claims about the "ideal" propositional sign are distinguished from claims about the thought. The ideal propositional sign is not intended for actual linguistic duty, but to be a perspicuous perceptible image of the imperceptible thought. It is not a perfect image of the thought. The ideal propositional sign must, therefore, like the classroom model of the imperceptible atom, be accompanied by a commentary in which the nature and limitations of the perceptible image, or model, of the imperceptible entities are explained. Wittgenstein's failure to provide such a clear and explicit commentary has led to the view that there is only one type of "symbolic" entity with a refined logical structure, the one described at 3.1432. But that is only the idealized propositional sign *(Zeichen)*, the mere perceptible and imperfect image of the thought. This error is one special type of a more general sort of misinterpretation of the *Tractatus*.

V.4   The Perceptible "Image of the Truth"

There are, altogether, three different notions of a picture in the overall account of the *Tractatus*. The everyday propositional sign is a picture in the ordinary sense of the word, that is, it is a *picture₁* of a state of affairs in the sense that it is a fact which is projected upon that state of affairs, by means of what are normally very complex projection rules. In the case of the everyday propositional sign, these projection rules are in fact the "tacit conventions" which are presupposed in the use of everyday language. Because these supplementary projection rules are very complex, the everyday propositional sign need not have much in common with the pictured state of affairs, and it need not even be isomorphic with the relevant state of affairs.

The ideal propositional sign is, in principle, a *picture*$_2$ of a state of affairs in the sense that it is a fact which is isomorphic with the relevant state of affairs. The ideal propositional sign also needs to be supplemented by a projection rule. For example, the relation is-on-top-of has in itself nothing to do with the relation has-killed, and so Urmson's ideal propositional sign, which pictures the state of affairs of Wisdom's having killed Al Capone, would have to be supplemented by a projection rule which projects the fact that the glass is on the dish onto the relevant state of affairs. Since in this case the picture and the state of affairs which is pictured are isomorphic, the projection rules can be much simpler than those underlying the use of the everyday propositional sign.

The thought, by contrast, is a picture in the strongest sense of the word. The thought is a *picture*$_3$ of a state of affairs insofar as it has pictorial form. The thought has pictorial form, and so it is not merely isomorphic with the pictured state of affairs. But it satisfies an additional condition which the ideal propositional sign does not. The thought is composed of proxies which are in *the same* contingent state as that in which the subject matter is represented. The thought is not merely similar on an *abstract* structural level with the pictured state of affairs. Rather, how the proxies are combined in the propositional symbol literally coincides with how the objects are in the relevant state of affairs.

The first two notions of a picture pertain to the sense in which a *perceptible* propositional sign, either the everyday or the ideal propositional sign, can be a picture. The third notion pertains to the thought. The tendency in the commentaries has been to emphasize one or both of the notions which pertain to the perceptible signs. But the fundamental notion of a picture is the notion which pertains to the thought. All the important logical properties of the propositional symbol are explained by reference to the fact that the propositional symbol, specifically the imperceptible thought component of the propositional symbol, has pictorial form.

Neither the everyday nor even the ideal propositional sign is characterized by pictorial form. Neither of these can "show how things stand if it is true" or "touch reality." That is obvious in the case of the everyday propositional sign, which has very little in common with the relevant state of affairs. This is why the connection of the everyday propositional sign with the relevant state of affairs must be mediated by a structurally richer thought which underlies it. That is, the everyday perceptible sign is connected with the thought by means of extremely complex "conventions," and the thought is perfectly structurally congruent with the relevant state of affairs.

The ideal propositional sign is not much better off. Urmson's example illustrates this point very well. Not only does the glass stand in for Wisdom and the dish for Capone, but the relation is-on-top-of *stands for* the relation has-killed. The contingent state in which the proxies are put is itself *just another proxy for something distinct from it* (in this case a distinct contingent state). A crucial dichotomy in the *Tractatus* lies between that which can only be stood in for by a proxy (represented from a position outside it), and that which is literally presented with the symbol (is actually internal to the symbol). The ideally constructed propositional sign is composed of proxies throughout. It does not touch reality or show how things stand it if is true. One cannot give an account of the notion of meaning, of the connection between symbols and the world, solely by reference to perceptible propositional signs, ideal or otherwise.

Urmson's account of the notion of a picture in the *Tractatus* is correct if it is taken as the account of the sense in which the ideal propositional sign can be a picture of a state of affairs. The error is the view that the notion of a *picture*$_2$ is the fundamental notion of a picture in the *Tractatus*, that it is sufficient for an account of how the propositional symbol "touches reality," and so forth. This error is, however, one example of a quite pervasive kind of misinterpretation of the *Tractatus*, a type of misinterpretation which Wittgenstein anticipated.

> 5.5563 In fact, all of the propositions of our everyday language, just as they stand, are in perfect logical order.—That utterly simple thing, which we have to formulate here, is not an image of the truth, but the truth itself in its entirety.
>
> (Our problems are not abstract, but perhaps the most concrete that there are.)

By "the truth" here, I take it that Wittgenstein means the *essential* factor in an account of the meaning of propositions. Any account of the propositional symbol which makes reference only to the perceptible part of the symbol (and here it does not matter whether that reference is to the everyday propositional sign or to an "ideal" propositional sign) is an account only of the mere perceptible image of the thought. It is only by reference to the unique characteristics of the thought that the account of the connection between symbols and the world can be given.

There are many forms which this misemphasis on the perceptible "image of the truth" can take. The emphasis on the everyday propositional sign, or on the construction of an ideal language, are two most common misinterpretations. Other forms include those which give an account of the meaning of the proposition by reference merely to the perceptible behavior which is involved in linguistic contexts, or which concentrate on questions concerning how the meaning of a proposition is stated, specified or conveyed. Each of these programs may capture one dimension of the total phenomenon of meaning, but they can capture at best only a dimension of the perceptible *image* of the thought or meaning component of the proposition. Such phenomena as the perceptible propositional sign and perceptible behavior are, from Wittgenstein's point of view, the mere *epiphenomena* of meaning. The real connection between symbols and the world is not even approached by reference to such phenomena alone.

Commentators on the *Tractatus* have in general overemphasized one or more of the various perceptible phenomena which are mentioned by Wittgenstein, and underemphasized both the role of the imperceptible thought in Wittgenstein's account, and the fundamental differences between the nature of the thought and the nature of the perceptible parts of language. The notions of the $picture_1$ and/or the $picture_2$ (the "images of the truth") have been overemphasized at the expense of the notion of $picture_3$ (the "truth itself") which pertains to the thought and its unique possession of pictorial form. Wittgenstein's account of the thought is given in the subsequent chapter.

CHAPTER VI

The Imperceptible Part of the Propositional Symbol: The Thought

The present chapter is a return to the strictly a priori portion of the argument of the *Tractatus*. The refined logical structure of a picture with pictorial form characterizes the imperceptible part of the propositional symbol, the thought. But there is considerably more to Wittgenstein's notion of the thought than this. The thought, the meaning component of the proposition, has an essential mental dimension. Wittgenstein's account of the thought ties in with certain classical accounts of the mental, such as Brentano's, and with contemporary developments in the theory of meaning.

VI.1 Russell's 1919 Account of the Proposition

In order to get at Wittgenstein's notion of the thought, it is useful to employ Russell's 1919 essay, "On Propositions: What they are and how they mean."[1] There are certain notions present in Russell's 1919 account of the proposition which are not present in his account of the proposition in the *Lectures,* but which are key notions in the *Tractaus.* Specifically, Russell adopts the view that a proposition involves a perceptible propositional sign and an imperceptible thought, and that the thought is characterized by pictorial form. Furthermore, Russell adopts a version of Brentano's notion of a "mental entity" in his 1919 essay and its form has definite points of similarity to the view of the *Tractatus.* This is useful preparation, both conceptually and historically, for the treatment of Wittgenstein's version of these views and notions in the subsequent section.

a. Russell's 'Mental' Propositions and Brentano's Notion of the Mental

Russell asks "whether the word *proposition* can stand for anything except a form of words."[2] The proposition as a "form of words" is "the most tangible thing" and its existence is not questioned.[3] Given this, Russell writes:

> The first question to be asked is: Can the relation called 'meaning' be a direct relation between the word as a physical occurrence and the object itself, or must the relation pass through a 'mental' intermediary which could be called the idea of the object?[4]

Russell's answer to this question is that "the behaviouristic theory of language is inadequate, in spite of the fact that it suggests much that is true and important."[5] Thus Russell distinguishes between the proposition as a form of words, his "word-proposition," and the proposition as a mental intermediary between word-propositions and the facts, his "image-proposition."[6] Russell does not hold that a significant use of words always involves such a mental accompaniment. He acknowledges the case in which one acquires a "word-habit." But even in such cases it is "the possibility" of having the mental accompaniment which "makes the essence of the 'meaning' of the words."[7]

Russell explains the connection between word-propositions, image-propositions, and the fact in the world as follows:

> A word-proposition apart from niceties, 'means' the corresponding image-proposition, and an image-proposition has an objective reference depending on the meanings of its constituent images.[8]

What one initially wants to know is how word-propositions, ordinary perceptible (or physical) sentences, "mean" objects or states of affairs. In order to answer this question, Russell finds it convenient to analyze this "relation" of meaning into various subcomponents. Since he posits a mental intermediary between word-propositions and facts, he posits a relation between word-propositions and these mental image-propositions (which he unfortunately calls the "meaning relationship", and another relation of a *different kind* between the image-proposition and the fact, which he calls "objective reference." Both Russell and Wittgenstein do distinguish these two components of the "relationship" between the perceptible word-proposition and the relevant state of affairs, and both hold that the relationship of objective reference which holds between the image-proposition and the relevant state of affairs has a quite remarkable character (a character which is definitive of an important notion of the mental).

Russell holds that, in general, the connection between propositions and facts involve their *structural similarity*.

> The most important thing about a proposition is that, whether it consists of image or words, it is . . . an actual fact, having a certain analogy of structure—to be further investigated—with the fact which makes it true or false.[9]

But though *both* the word-proposition and the mental image-proposition have an analogy of structure with the relevant fact, there are important differences in the degree of analogy achieved in each case.

Russell finds the case of propositions involved in memory most illuminating in this regard. He writes: "the simplest possible schema of correspondence between the proposition and the objective [the fact] is afforded by such cases as visual memory images."[10] The case considered by Russell in order to illustrate his point is the case in which one remembers the window being to the left of the fire:

> In this case I have a complex image, which we say analyse, for our purposes, into (a) the image of the window, (b) the image of the fire, (c) the relation that (a) is to the left of (b). The objective consists of the window and the fire with the very same relation between them. In such a case the objective of the proposition consists of the meaning of its constituent images related (or not related as the case may be) by the same relation as that which holds between the constituent images in the proposition.[11]

The image-proposition is composed of images (which are really a special kind of proxy for objects) and these images are in *the same* relation in which the represnted objects in the world may be. Wittgenstein's notion of pictorial form involves the notion of a picture in which the proxies are in the same relation in which the objects in the world are represented. The appearance of the notion of pictorial form in Russell's 1919 essay is of great historical interest, especially since (1) Russell places great weight on this notion, calling it "the simplest possible schema of correspondence" and (2) it is the *mental* component of the propositional symbol to which Russell attributes pictorial form.

Of course, the word-proposition does not have pictorial form:

> But such idyllic simplicity of correspondence is rare. It is already absent in the word-propositions which mean such simple visual image-propositions. In the phrase 'A is to the left of B,' even if we treat 'is-to-the-left-of' as one word, we have three terms with a triadic relation, not two terms, with a dyadic relation. The linguistic symbol for a relation is not itself a relation, but a term as solid as the other words of the sentence. Language might have been so constructed that this should not have been always the case: a few specially important relations might have been symbolized by relations between words. For instance, 'AB' might have meant 'A is to the left of B.' It might have been the practice that pronouncing A on a high note and B on a low note meant that A was B's social superior. But the practical possibilities of this method of symbolizing relations are obviously very limited, and in actual language relations are symbolized by words.[12]

Russell distinguishes between the way the propositional sign is constructed in everyday language, and the way it could have been constructed. The propositional sign could have constructed, in special cases, so as to be isomorphic with the relevant state of affairs. However, though one of Russell's two examples involves a mere isomorphism between the artificially constructed propositional sign and the relevant state of affairs, the other is an example of a propositional sign which is composed of words which are put in *the same relation* as that relation which is involved in the relevant state of affairs. Russell gives no indication that he is conscious of this difference between his two examples. For the present, the notion of isomorphic structures is emphasized as the paradigm case of the way propositional signs could have been constructed. But in the ensuing discussions I return to a discussion of the fact that one of Russell's examples is not a case of merely isomorphic structures.

Russell distinguishes the same three notions of a picture which are present in the *Tractatus*. Russell gives an account of the propositional symbol according to which it is composed of a perceptible sign (his "word-proposition") and an imperceptible thought (his image-proposition). The imperceptible thought is the meaning component of the proposition, and it is a picture in the strongest possible sense, that is, it is characterized by pictorial form.[13] The perceptible propositional sign admits of two degrees of structural analogy with the relevant state of affairs. The "ideal" propositional sign is isomorphic with the relevant state of affairs, and the everyday propositional sign in a structure, but is not even isomorphic with the relevant state of affairs. The most important of these for the theory of meaning is the thought or image-proposition. It is "essentially" the meaning component of the proposition, and the account of how the thought "means" the relevant state of affairs involves the fact that it is a *perfect* picture of that state of affairs. But a complete account of the thought also involves the view that this perfect picture is mental in a sense which it is our primary purpose to define.

One symptom of the fact that Russell's 1919 notion of the meaning component is, essentially, the notion of a *mental* entity is this: though Russell admits that in very special cases the word-proposition could have been set up so that the relation between the proxies is the *same* as that involved in the relevant state of affairs—he does not emphasize this case at all. Even if word-propositions might be made which involve the very same relation which is involved in the relevant state of affairs, it is for some reason important that the entity which is perfectly structurally congruent with the relevant state of affairs is the *mental* component!

The relevant notion of the mental is even implicit in Russell's original question. The question is whether the relation called 'meaning' is a direct relation between the word proposition and the objective, or whether a mental intermediary is involved. His answer is that a mental intermediary is involved. The obvious question is: If the relation of the word-proposition to "the objective" requires a mediating entity, then *why does that mediating entity itself not also need something to mediate its relation to the objective?* That is, what is the unique nature of the mental entity with pictorial form which distinguishes it in this respect from a perceptible word-proposition, which happens to be perfectly structurally congruent with the relevant state of affairs?

Russell wants to explain the connection between the symbolic entity and the world. His view is that the meaning connection is not forged by the mere perceptible sign itself, so the perceptible sign must be accompanied by something else which makes the meaning connection with the world. Furthermore, if this accompanying entity were not fundamentally different in nature from the mere "word-proposition," then it too must be accompanied by another entity . . . and so on. Obviously this meaning chain must come to an end. There must be a terminal point in the symbolic medium at which the connection between the symbol and the world is made. There must be a component of the propositional symbol which is the locus of meaning. Russell holds that his image-proposition is this *meaning locus*. The meaning of the perceptible propositional sign is determined by something extrinsic to it (by the thought which accompanies it), but the meaning of the thought is determined by the thought itself, not by something extrinsic to it. The thought, unlike the perceptible propositional sign, is meaningful *in itself*. But how can something be meaningful in itself? Russell's answer to this question lies in his understanding of Brentano's view.

In his 1919 essay Russell makes clear that he is concerned to work out an account of the proposition which incorporates Brentano's notion of the mental. In his *Psychology From an Empirical Standpoint,* Brentano gives two formulations of his notion of a mental entity, one in the text and one in an appendix. In the first, an entity is said to be mental if it is characterized by the intentional "in-existence" of an object. In the second, an entity is mental if it has a very special kind of relation to an object.[14] Both of Brentano's formulations are vague and conceptually problematic, but Brentano is groping toward an important insight. What is important here, though, is only Russell's understanding of Brentano's insight.

A few years after his 1919 essay, in his *Analysis of Mind* (1921), Russell writes that he is "concerned to combat" Brentano's view since he had once held it himself:

> Until very lately I believed, as he [Brentano] did that mental phenomena [sic] have essential reference to objects, . . . Now I now longer believe this, even in the case of knowledge.[15]

In a second formulation, he writes:

> Even those [entities] which are purely mental will not have that intrinsic reference to objects which Brentano assigns to them and which constitutes "the essence of consciousness" as ordinarily understood.[16]

Russell's key idea is that Brentano's notion of a mental entity is the notion of an entity which is *essentially* or *intrinsically* related to an object. Russell understands Brentano's notion of an entity which contains an object, or state of affairs, *within itself* as but a colorful way of saying that the mental phenomenon is *intrinsicially* related to that object or state of affairs.

The same notion of intrinsic meaningfulness is present in his 1919 essay, but in different words. There Russell refers to Brentano's reformulated notion. He characterizes Brentano's second notion of the mental entity as the notion of an entity which is "relational in its own nature."[17] To say that a mental entity is relational *in its own nature* is to say that in itself, or intrinsically, it bears the meaning relationship to an object or state of affairs. But how does Russell explain how the meaning locus is intrinsically meaningful?

Part of the account of the intrinsic connection between the symbol and the relevant state of affairs is that the structure of the symbol is perfectly congruent with the structure of the relevant state of affairs. This is Russell's picture theory. The notion of a picture involved, that is, the notion of congruent structures, is, prima facie, a straightforward notion.[18]

The notion of the meaning locus is, howeer, not fully explained in terms of structure or congruent structures. A non-mental entity which has a structure perfectly congruent with that of some state of affairs does not intrinsically mean anything at all. It is just another meaningless fact in the world. The structure of an entity is semantically relevant only if it is *the structure of a meaning.* The notion of the meaning locus is *the notion of an "entity" whose intrinsic nature it is to "project" its structure.* The essence of the mental is constituted by this second component of the notion of the meaning locus. We say that an entity is mental, not because it has a structure which is perfectly congruent with that of some state of affairs, but because it is intrinsic to that entity that its structure is "meant" (or "projected") onto an external subject matter. This is the basis of Russell's intuition that it is essential that it is something which is *mental* in some sense which satisfies the conditions of perfect structural congruence with the relevant state of affairs. Russell's account of Brentano's notion is a conceptual advance over Brentano's, not only in that Russell explicitly introduces the notion of intrinsic meaningfulness, but also that Russell's account facilitates the analysis of Brentano's notion into two components. This enables one to isolate the real essence of the mental. The full fledged notion of the meaning locus is the notion of an entity which is such that (1) what it means in particular is intrinsic to it, that is, it is determined by its structure, and (2) it is intrinsic to it that its structure is "meant" or projected, that is, it is a mental entity.

Russell's original question is whether the meaning relation is a direct relation between word-propositions and facts, or whether it must "go through a mental intermediary." He answers that it must pass through a mental intermediary, but he relies on merely suggestive and inexplicit formulations of his notion of the mental intermediary. Nor does Russell even make the motivation behind his original question completely explicit. These formulations and motivations have now been clarified.

Russell's original question is founded on the insight that the word-proposition is only arbitrarily connected with some particular state of affairs, and it is only arbitrarily connected with a meaning at all. The "word-proposition" could, in itself, mean anything or nothing. The word-proposition has nothing essential to do with the particular state of affairs which it means, and it is even a contingent fact that it means anything at all. Furthermore, the meaning of the word-proposition cannot be constituted by its connections with other word-propositions, or even with gestures such as pointing. Like the original word-proposition, each of these gestures and word-propositions could, in themselves, mean anything or nothing. To take the most extreme case, it is conceivable that all these words and gestures are just a meaningless pattern of physical behavior, just "sound and fury, signifying nothing." Something so remarkable as a *meaning* cannot be fashioned with such crude perceptible tools. The propositional symbol must, therefore, involve an entity which has a nature fundamentally different from that of such perceptible signs: a *meaning locus*. The apparent need to postulate the existence of such an entity is behind an intuition that one must countenance a place for the mental in the world.

The implicit pattern or argument in his 1919 essay parallels that of cosmological arguments for the existence of God. In such arguments it is pointed out that something exists which has a radically *dependent* kind of being. It is then argued that the existence of such a dependent thing cannot be explained solely by reference to other things with the same type of being. For example, the existence of the thunder is not completely explained by reference to the existence of lightning since the latter's existence is itself in need of explanation. Therefore, one must either accept an infinite regress, which is then argued to be absurd on various grounds, or one must postulate that the regress terminates in something whose nature contrasts with that of the entity whose existence needs explaining. This postulated entity must have such a nature that it does not depend for its being on something extrinsic to it. It must be intrinsic to it in some sense (such as necessary or self-caused existence) that it exists. The concept of the "unmoved mover" is the concept of a *'being locus'*. In Russell's essay this same pattern of argument is duplicated, but in connection with the problems of linguistic meaning. Russell points out that sentences have meaning, but that they have such a nature that they are radically dependent for their meaning on something extrinsic to them. Therefore one must either accept an infinite regress, which seems unacceptable, or one must admit that that which determines the meaning of word-propositions must be something with a fundamentally different nature, the nature of a meaning locus.

Russell's "image-proposition" is an entity which contrasts with perceptible signs in that it means a certain state of affairs intrinsically. His account of how, what the image-proposition means in particular is intrinsic to it, consists in his view that the image proposition is a perfect picture; it is perfectly structurally congruent with the relevant state of affairs. But it must also be intrinsic to it that its structure is "meant." The structural dimension of the notion seems relatively straightforward, but the mental dimension of the notion is more mysterious. In the following subsection Russell's attempt to deal with the mental dimension of the notion of the meaning locus is sketched.

b. Russell's Account of the Mental Dimension of the Meaning Locus

The mental dimension of the notion of the meaning locus cannot be explained solely by reference to the notions of structure and structural congruence. For this reason Russell does not, in his 1919 essay, embrace Brentano's notion of the mental without qualification. He writes:

> Brentano's view . . . that mental phenomena are characterized by
> 'objective reference' cannot be accepted in its obvious sense.[19]

He goes on to state that he wishes to formulate a view which is "less relational" than Brentano's.[20] What are these qualifications?

Perhaps the most basic mystery which is involved in the notion of the meaning locus consists in the idea that it is intrinsically directed toward, or means, something distinct from itself. According to such a view the notion of meaning is analogous to the notion of a necessary connection between distinct existences. The thought is one entity, the relevant state of affairs is another, and there is an intimate connection between the two. The notion of a necessary connection between distinct existences has traditionally proved troublesome, and analogous difficulties can be raised in connection with the notion of the intrinsic meaning connection. How can one explain how a thought intrinsically means something external to it?

The first component of the view that what the thought means in particular is intrinsic to it is not so mysterious. The view that the propositional symbol and the relevant state of affairs are perfectly structurally congruent constitutes an account of how what the symbol means in particular is intrinsic to it. The mysterious part of the meaning connection is the notion of something which is intrinsically "directional" or "projected."

Russell attempts to give an account of how the intrinsic directionality of the meaning locus must be understood. In his discussion of the phenomenon of memory Russell writes:

> Images, in accordance with what has just been said, are not to be regarded as relational in their own nature; nevertheless, at least in the case of memory images, they are felt to point beyond themselves to something which they 'mean.'[21]

Here Russell denies that images are to be regarded as intentional or mental in Brentano's sense. He states that they are only "felt to point beyond themselves to something which they mean." Russell's view is that the image-proposition is not, taken solely by itself, the complete meaning component of the proposition. The mental charcter of the proposition, that is, that which determines that it is intrinsic to it that its structure is "meant", is constituted by a feeling which accompanies the image-proposition.

Russell's complete account of the proposition is that there are two components to the thought which accompanies the word-proposition. The image-proposition is a structure which is perfectly congruent with the relevant state of affairs. Given that it is meaningful, what it means is determined by its structure. But the fact that it is meaningful in the first place, that is, the fact that its structure is projected or "meant," is determined by the feeling which accompanies it. It is these feelings, and not the image-propositions, which are the real intrinsically meaningful or directional entities in Russell's view.

According to Russell's 1919 view, the two components of the *notion* of the meaning locus correspond to two distinct *entities* in the thought. It is only the compound entity—composed of both a structure and a feeling—which is a thought, a meaning locus in the full fledged sense. Russell's 1919 view is itself a version of the view that what the image-proposition means in particular is intrinsic to it, while the fact that it is meaningful in the first place is determined by something extrinsic to it, that is, by the feeling which accompanies it. Russell's suggestion concerning the most fundamental mystery which pertains to the notion of meaning—the question of how there can be meaning at all, how there can be something "directional" in the world—is that there are feelings with these special powers.

Russell's reason for stating a view which is less relational than Brentano's is that "the theory which analyzes a presentation into an act and object no longer satisfies me . . . [because the] act, or subject, is schematically convenient, but not empirically discoverable."[22] In this remark Russell refers to Brentano's second formulation and, on the grounds of a more attentive empiricism, rejects Brentano's act-object model because he denies that the act is empirically discoverable. The function which Brentano had assigned to the act must be taken over by something. Russell, under the influence of James, finds feelings with unique powers, but no mental acts, to be empirically discoverable. The function of transforming a mere meaningless structure into a projected structure is assigned to a feeling.

Perhaps this interpretation makes too much of a causal remark that images are sometimes felt to point beyond themselves. It is possible that his mention of a *feeling* of relationality is not advanced with the intention that it be invested with such philosophical weight. However, in the 1919 essay itself, Russell quotes James' view that "In its inner nature, belief, or the sense of reality, is a sort of feeling more allied to the emotions than anything else." Also, "In the main this view seems inevitable."[23] Similarly, in his subsequent *Analysis of Mind,* his account of various mental phenomena explicitly involves feelings which constitute or accompany them. For example, he postulates that "there may be a specific feeling which could be called the feeling of pastness, especially where immediate memory is concerned," and he also postulates "feelings of reality" and of "familiarity."[24] Russell's writings in this period reveal a definite tendency to postulate feelings with special powers in order to resolve philosophical problems.

It is illuminating to take Russell's talk about these feelings seriously, since one must explain in what sense Russell qualifies his acceptance of Brentano's notion. The suggestion is that Russell admits that there is a role for the mental in his account, and this role is assigned to a feeling. But because the mental component of the meaning locus is constituted by a *mere feeling,* the notion of the mental cannot be accorded the objective status in the conceptual edifice of science which Brentano assigns to it.[25]

There are two components to the notion of the meaning locus, and one of these components can apparently be explained in objective scientifically acceptable terms. The view that what a proposition means is intrinsic to it is explained in terms of the structural congruence of the image-proposition and the relevant state of affairs. The concept of the structure of an entity, and the concept of congruent structures, certainly seem to be objective scientifically acceptable concepts. It is important that there is *an* objective component to the notion of meaning, and it is part of Russell's task to explain this objective component.

It is the second component of the notion of the meaning locus to which Russell refuses to accord the status of an objective scientific concept. The significance of the fact that Russell places such weight on these feelings in his account of meaning is that feelings are subjective entities in a special sense, and this means that Russell's concept of the mental cannot be accorded the status of an objective or scientific concept. There is a long and diverse tradition which holds that concepts of private entities are not acceptable scientific concepts, since science is an intersubjective enterprise. Science cannot, therefore, employ concepts of entities which are not open to intersubjective examination.

There is also another, though related, point which may be involved. The analogy between the notion of meaning and the notion of a necessary connection between distinct existences has already been suggested, and it is illuminating to press it again here. Hume asks whether we can understand the notion of a necessary connection between distinct existences, and he answers that we cannot. But this does not mean that such a notion is a complete fabrication. Though there is no valid notion of a necessary connection between distinct existences, he does not deny that one event may occasion the *feeling* that another event must happen. Put in another way, though Hume denies that there is an "objective" notion of a necessary connection, he does not deny that we have some sort of notion of a subjective feeling of such a connection.[26]

Both Russell and Hume insist that there is an objective component to the particular notions each wishes to analyze. Hume's account of the objective component of the notion of causality is given in terms of spatial and temporal contiguity and constant conjunction. In Russell's analysis of the meaning connection, the "objective" component consists in the structural congruence of the image-proposition and the relevant state of affairs (as well as certain causal connections which it has not been necessary to discuss here). But both of these philosophers also insist that a certain very important dimension of their respective phenomena of interest reduces to a subjective feeling of connection between the distinct "entities."

Hume's point in denying that we have an objective notion of a necessary connection between distinct existences is that there is no *real* relation or connection between these distinct existences which answers to the notion of a necessary connection. Similarly, insofar as the meaning connection involves a private or inner feeling, then there are good grounds for saying that the meaning connection (in that respect, though not necessarily in others) does not involve a *real* connection between the image proposition and the relevant state of affairs. To put it most directly, the relation of meaning in the sense of the "intentional" connection extends no further than the inner limits of the private consciousness. It is not merely that since the relation of meaning involves a private feeling that it is not open to intersubjective examination, and is not, therefore, an acceptable scientific concept. The additional point is that insofar as the relation of meaning involves a private feeling, then it does not, in that respect, constitute a real relation to an objective state of affairs.[27] Russell's view is that the image-proposition is merely felt to be, as opposed to really being, intentional in Brentano's sense.

There are two senses in which the view here attributed to Russell is "less relational" than Brentano's. First, there are two components of the notion of the meaning locus, the entity which is "relational in its own nature." One way to state a "less relational view" is to deny or weaken one of these two conditions. Russell assigns objective scientific status to the view that what the thought means is intrinsic to it; it is determined by its structure. But Russell refuses, on various grounds, to accord objective scientific status to the view that it is intrinsic to the thought that its structure is "meant." That is, he refuses the view that it is "relational in itself."

If the present interpretation of Russell's qualification of the status of the notion of the mental is correct, then (in the brief space of his 1919 essay, "On Propositions") Russell is the modern Hume of the theory of meaning. Russsell has recognized the analogy between the notion of the meaning connection and the notion of a necessary connection between distinct existences, and he has (like Hume) argued that the concept of meaning, which we may have thought to be an objective scientific concept, ultimately has a subjective component. From Russell's 1919 point of view, Brentano is like the pre-Humean philosopher (such as Locke) who formulates the notion of a necessary connection between distinct existences, and who uncritically accords to it objective scientific status. That is, he holds that the notion signifies a real property or power which is present in entities in the world. Russell's 1919 account of the meaning of the proposition is to Brentano's view, as Hume's account of causality is to the prior accounts of causality by philosophers such as Locke.

This analogy between Russell and Hume is not merely of historical interest. In his recent reinterpretation of Wittgenstein's *Philosophical Investigations,* Kripke has emphasized the analogy between the notions of the meaning connection and of a necessary connection between distinct existences.[28] Interestingly enough, he has done this in an attempt to show how important the *rejection* of the notion of the meaning locus is in Wittgenstein's later philosophy. In this respect Kripke's work compliments my own, by tracing out the apparent consequences of rejecting this notion. Kripke's real contribution to the understanding of Wittgenstein and to the theory of meaning can be better understood, and it can be improved, by tracing the conceptual links of his key notion of the meaning locus back to the *Tractatus,* Russell and Brentano. (For more on this theme see section 2.d of the present chapter.)

VI.2   The Notion of the Meaning Locus and the Tractatus

a. The Notion of the Meaning Locus and the Text of the Tractatus

The view that the propositional symbol is intrinsically connected with the relevant state of affairs is stated at 4.03:

4.03 . . . A proposition communicates a situation to us, and so it must be *essentially* connected with the situation.

And the connection is precisely that it is its logical picture. . . .

Wittgenstein is clearly saying at least that what the proposition means in particular must be essential (intrinsic) to it, since he holds that the structure of the propositional symbol perfectly coincides with the structure of the relevant state of affairs. The other component of the meaning locus, that is, the notion of an entity which is such that it is intrinsic to it that its structure is projected, may be intended by Wittgenstein in 4.03. But it is not obvious. Nevertheless, according to 4.03, the sense in which the propositional symbol is intrinsically meaningful is connected with Wittgenstein's notion of a "logical picture." The second more complete formulation of the notion of the meaning locus occurs in Wittgenstein's discussion of his notion of the picture:

2.1513 So a picture, conceived in this way, also includes the pictorial relationship which makes it into a picture.

Wittgenstein's language in this remark is carefully chosen to emphasize that the relevant sort of picture is conceived in a particular way. Wittgenstein's point at 2.1513 is that *the meaning relationship itself*, the "pictorial relationship," is intrinsic to the picture. 2.1513 is a quite Russell or Brentano-like formulation of the notion of an entity which is "relational in its own nature," that is, which is mental in Brentano's sense. (The formulation at 2.1513, in fact, bears a striking resemblance to Husserl's formulation of Brentano's description of a mental entity.)[29] The picture, conceived in the fashion of 2.1513, is a full-fledged meaning *locus*.

Two different notions of pictorial form can be distinguished: (1) A proposition has *pictorial form*$_1$ in the sense that it is composed of proxies which are in the same contingent state in which the subject matter of the proposition may be. And (2) a proposition has *pictorial form*$_2$ in the sense that it presents with itself the possibility that its external subject matter is in the same contingent state in which the proxies in the picture are. The first notion is a purely structural notion of pictorial form, that is, it is the notion of the perfect structural congruence of the picture and the relevant state of affairs. The second notion involves everything the first notion involves, but it also involves the view that the picture *itself* projects its structure on an external subject matter, that it is intrinsic to it that its structure is projected.

The notion of structural congruence is involved in Wittgenstein's notion of pictorial form, and it is that part of his account which Wittgenstein is thinking of when he says that the problems of philosophical logic are "perhaps the most concrete there are" (5.5563). In fact, however, it is the second weightier notion of pictorial form which is present in the *Tractatus*, the notion according to which *the pictorial relationship itself* is intrinsic to the picture. This same idea also appears in other remarks of the *Tractatus* which do not explicitly mention the notion of pictorial form. At 3.02 Wittgenstein writes: "A thought contains *[enthalt]* the possibility of the situation of which it is the thought" (3.02). The latter remark is not merely the claim that the thought has a structure which is congruent with the relevant situation, but that it contains *the possibility that certain objects are structured in a specific way*. The view is that the thought contains the projection of its structure on the external subject matter.

Three distinct notions of a picture have been distinguished. Two of these notions pertain to the sense in which the perceptible propositional sign can be a picture. Both the everyday propositional sign and the artificially constructed sign are pictures in the sense that they are structures which are projected onto the relevant state of affairs by means of supplementary projection rules. The difference between these two types of a picture has to do with the degree of complexity of the accompanying projection rules. But both involve accompanying projection rules of one type or another. If the projection rules are changed, the meaning of these perceptible signs is changed. If perceptible propositional signs are accompanied by no projection rules at all, then they have no meaning at all. The thought, characterized by pictorial *form₂*, is a picture in a sense fundamentally different from both senses which pertain to perceptible signs. The thought "includes its own pictorial relationship," that is, it is intrinsically meaningful in that it is meaningful independently of any accompanying projection rules.

Any propositional sign, whether everyday or ideal is a picture in a sense fundamentally different than is the thought. The former is such that both its particular meaning and its meaningfulness are determined by something extrinsic to it. The thought, by contrast, is characterized by pictorial form in the weighty sense, and it (following 2.1513) *contains within itself the conditions of its particular meaning and of its meaningfulness* (see Chapter IV, section 3 of the present book for the earliest suggestion of this view). In V.2 it is pointed out that Wittgenstein says of the everyday propositional sign that it is a picture "in the orginary sense." The point here is that the notion of a picture which is involved at 2.1513 is a picture in a very extraordinary sense. This extraordinary aspect of the picture in the sense of 2.1513 is the essence of Brentano's account of the nature of the mental.

In V.1 it is argued that the meaning component of the propositional symbol is in fact an imperceptible component, that in fact the everyday propositional signs do not have the refined logical structure of the meaning component. It is now clear why the meaning component of the proposition *cannot* be its perceptible component. No perceptible entity could have *pictorial form₂*. No perceptible entity can have the mental character of intentionality or intrinsic meaningfulness.

There are many important historical precedents for the views which overemphasize the role of the perceptible porpositional sign and which, accordingly, underemphasize the role of the special features of the mental in Wittgenstein's account of the proposition. Russell's introduction to the *Tractatus* has already been mentioned in this regard (see V.3). In another influential historical precedent, Ramsey has interpreted the view at 2.1513 that the pictorial relationship belongs to the picture to mean only that "whenever we talk of a picture we have in mind some representing relation in virtue of which it is a picture."[30] Ramsey's interpretation of 2.1513 is one of those remarkable interpretations in which a view is simply claimed to mean the opposite of what it says. Ramsey's interpretation of Wittgenstein's remark that the pictorial relationship is included in the picture is that the pictorial relationship is *not* included in the picture. Instead a "representing relationship" or projection rule is always had "in mind" when one speaks of a picture. The effect of Ramsey's interpretation is that the intentional entity is viewed as a picture in a sense not fundamentally different from the sense in which a perceptible sign can be a picture.

The general sort of interpretation taken by Ramsey continues to be the dominant interpretation of Wittgenstein's notion of a picture. Ramsey presents an earlier example (Stenius a more recent one[30]) of accounts of Wittgenstein's picture theory. These accounts attempt to reconstruct Wittgenstein's picture theory out of concepts which, from Wittgenstein's point of view, can only characterize the mere perceptible and imperfect "image of the truth."

The textual portion of this inquiry has been completed. The next important question is whether the argument of the *Tractatus* warrants the inference that the genuine propositional symbol involves a meaning locus, whether it warrants the inference that the propositional symbol is characterized by *pictorial form*₂.

b. The Notion of the Meaning Terminus and the Argument of the Tractatus

The fundamental notion of meaning developed in the early stages of the argument of the *Tractatus* is the notion of a presentational symbol. It quickly becomes manifest in the argument of the *Tractatus* that though the notion of the presentational symbol involves the notion of the structure of the propositional symbol, it is not merely the notion of a structure. In IV.3, for example, it is inferred that the genuine propositional symbol must contain proxies for an external subject matter. But it is there pointed out that the relevant notion of the proxy is not simply the notion of a component of a structure: the proxy must perform the "remarkable function" of "presenting with itself the fact that it stands for a subject matter which cannot itself be presented with the propositional symbol." This "remarkable function" is, in fact, the first explicit appearance of the fact that a symbolic entity must be intrinsically meaningful, that it must in itself bear a meaning relationship to its referent. It is in this logical feature of the proxy that the notion of intentionality, that is, the notion of the mental, makes its first appearance in the argument of the *Tractatus*.

The key discussion in this regard is, however, the discussion of pictorial form at IV.4. In that section it is not argued merely that the propositional symbol must have structure which is perfectly congruent with the relevant state of affairs. It is argued that that which is presented with its symbol must determine *both* that it is possible that its subject matter be in a certain contingent state, *and* that it is possible that it not be in that contingent state. That is, the complete description of that which is presented with the propositional symbol involves a "that clause", and the that clause involves reference to the subject matter of the proposition and its possible contingent states. That which is presented with the propositional symbol is not merely its structure. It is better to say that *it is by means of the structure of the symbol* that something about the external subject matter of the proposition is presented with the symbol. This is simply another way of saying that the propositional symbol presents *the projection* of its structure on an external subject matter. The meaning or pictorial relationship is itself presented with the propositional symbol. This is equivalent to the view that the propositional symbol contains the meaning relationship within itself. It is, therefore, a consequence of the argument of the *Tractatus* that the propositional symbol is relational in itself, that it is intrinsic to it that its structure is meant. The notion of pictorial form which is warranted by the argument of the *Tractatus* is not, therefore, merely the notion of structural congruence of the picture and the state of affairs. Instead it is the weighty notion of pictorial form, the notion which includes the mental component. The view that the propositional symbol involves a meaning locus in the full fledged sense of the word is implicit in the argument of the *Tractatus,* at least since section IV.4.

It is now clear that the structural identity of that presented with the propositional symbol with the relevant state of affairs, is only one of the factors in the overall account of the anatomy of the propositional symbol. That which is presented by the propositional symbol is really much richer than a mere structure. *The proposition "shows its sense" (4.022), not its structure.*

The previous most advanced formulation of the notion of the meaning locus is Russell's notion of an entity characterized by both components of the full fledged notion of intrinsic meaningfulness. The argument of the *Tractatus* supports the conclusion that the propositional symbol involves an entity, the thought, which satisfies these two conditions. What the thought means in particular is intrinsic to it in the sense that it is determined by its structure. That the thought is meaningful in the first place is intrinsic to the thought, since the pictorial relationship is itself contained by, and presented with, the thought. More important, however, is the fact that the notion of meaning which is derived in the argument of the *Tractatus* is unique and highly articulated in comparison with Brentano's, and even Russell's, versions.

There are *three* different dimensions to Wittgenstein's account of the symbolic entity. One must distinguish the *structure* of the symbol, the *projection* of the structure of the symbol, and the *presentation*[32] of the projection of the structure of the symbol. Wittgenstein's view is not merely that the propositional symbol "shows its sense" in the sense that it has a structure which is perfectly congruent with that of the relevant state of affairs. Nor is it even enough to say that it "shows its sense"—meaning that it is intrinsic to the propositional symbol that it projects its structure on an external subject matter. It is his view that the projection of the symbol's structure is *itself* presented by the symbol. The sense of the proposition is constituted by the projection of its structure, and it is this, so to speak, "fully constituted" sense which is shown or presented by the symbol.

The view that the propositional symbol presents the projection of its structure on an external subject matter may seem to involve excess verbiage, but this formulation of the thought or meaning locus affords genuine insight into the nature of the symbolic entity. Specifically, this formulation entails that that which is presented by the propositional symbol is presented *as a meaning,* not merely as an inert structure, not merely as another meaningless fact in the world.

The view that that which is presented by the propositional symbol is presented as a meant structure, or *as* a meaning, is a consequence which is of obvious relevance to a series of philosophical problems, (for instance, to the account of consciousness of meanings). However, the present concern is with the logical as opposed to the "epistemological" or other sorts of questions concerning meaning.

One difficulty in giving an adequate account of the logical features of the thought consists in the fact that the thought must (1) present a certain state of affairs, while (2) that which is presented must not be presented as the actualized state of affairs involved. After all, the relevant state of affairs may not even obtain, and that it may not obtain must be determined by that which is presented with the thought. The difficulty in simultaneously satisfying these two conditions is great. One might think that a viable approach to this problem is to hold that that which is presented with the propositional symbol is merely the *possibility* of the relevant state of affairs. But this is unsatisfactory. The thought of *aRb* is not the thought of the possibility of *aRb*. It is the thought of *a*'s being *R* to *b*. The logical gap between that which is presented with the propositional symbol, and the relevant state of affairs, does not concern the *content* of the thought. If it did then the content of the thought would not pertain to just the right thing, i.e., the specific state of affairs involved. The logical gap concerns not the content of the thought but the manner in which that content is presented. In Wittgenstein's view, how the proxies stand in the symbol literally coincides with how the relevant objects in the world may stand. There is no gap on this level between that which is presented by the symbol and the relevant state of affairs. The logical gap consists in the fact that in Wittgenstein's view that which is presented by the symbol is not merely the structuring of the proxies, but *the projection of that structuring of the proxies*. On Wittgenstein's view one can hold both that (1) the content of the thought, which is determined by its structure, literally coincides with that of the relevant state of affairs, while in addition, (2) the relevant state of affairs *is presented as the mere content of a meaning*.

The results of the present subsection must not be underemphasized. The argument of the *Tractatus* warrants the view that the propositional symbol involves a particular version of the notion of the meaning locus, which is more highly articulated than Brentano's or even Russell's best formulations. Wittgenstein's version of the notion makes clear that the thought presents itself as a meant structure, as a meaning. This is not explicitly involved even in Russell's notion of an intrinsically meaningful entity.

c. The Concept of the Meaning Locus and the Awareness of Meanings

In the present section the basic epistemological correlate of these views is developed. Two of the most basic epistemological questions are these: (1) What is the account of the awareness of something as a meaning, and not merely as an "inert" entity? and (2) What is the account of how one is aware of a particular meaning, and not merely of something which is irreducibly ambiguous? The schema of Wittgenstein's answer to the former question is easily constructible on the basis of his account of the logical anatomy of the thought. The thought presents the projection of its structure on an external subject matter. To be aware of the thought is, therefore, to be aware of something which presents itself as a projected structure, that is, as a meaning.

The question of how the object of one's awareness is a particular meaning is the question of how it can be that the object of one's awareness does not admit to a multiplicity of interpretations. In itself, the ordinary perceptible sentence is a structure which may mean anything or nothing. To be aware of a perceptible sentence is, therefore, to be aware of something which does not determine what it means. The situation is not improved by appending to it other perceptible sentences which express some specific projection rule. Such appended sentences, like the original perceptible sentence, do not determine how they are to be interpreted. They must themselves be projected in some way, and they do not determine how they are to be projected. Even the conjunction of the perceptible sentence *and* these interpretative sentences depends on an independent method of projection. Even this conjunction is, in itself, ambiguous among a multiplicity of interpretations. So to be aware of such a conjunction is to be aware of something which does not determine its own meaning.

The thought, by contrast, is a meaning locus. It presents the projection of its structure onto an external subject matter, and this means that the method of projection is intrinsic to it. Thus, a thought has a meaning, but it contrasts with perceptible propositional signs in that whether it has a meaning and what its meaning is in particular, *is not open to interpretation*. The view that the thought is not open to interpretation is the view that it is exempt from the possibility of interpretation *and misinterpretation*. The thought can only be taken in one way, and it itself determines how it is to be taken. To be acquainted with a thought or meaning locus is to be acquainted with an entity which is a completely self-illuminating meaning, an entity which is above interpretation.

The epistemological correlate of the notion of the meaning locus is the notion of the *interpretation terminus*. That is to say, the question of how a given sign is to be interpreted *terminates* at the meaning locus. Wittgenstein refers to the notion of the interpretation terminus in *The Blue and Brown Books*: "What one wishes to say is: 'Every sign must be capable of interpretation; but the meaning musn't be capable of interpretation. It is the last interpretation'" (*BB*, p. 34). To say that an entity has the character of the meaning locus is to say that it determines its own meaning. To say that the meaning locus does not stand in need of interpretation, is to say that to be *aware of* or *acquainted with* such an entity is to be acquainted with something which unambiguously shows the thinking subject what its meaning is. This is the epistemological correlate of the view that the propositional symbol involves an entity which "shows its sense."

d. Recognition of the Significance of these Notions in Contemporary Philosophy

The related notions of the meaning locus and the interpretation terminus have not gone completely unnoticed in commentaries on Wittgenstein, though their real significance has been recognized by only a few. Favrholdt, commenting on the *Tractatus* notion of the thought, writes:

> Whenever we think or have a thought, we inevitably know what the thought pictures or describes. We never have to think of a key of interpretation which indicates how the thought is to be read.[33]

Though there is a certain amount of imprecision in Favrholdt's formulation, he is driving at the notion of an interpretation terminus.

Bruce Goldberg has produced the first fully clear formulation of the notion and of its significance. He writes:

> The conception of thoughts as objects of direct acquaintance is very widespread. . . . Or it might be said: The object of acquaintance stands in an internal relation to an interpretation. Such an object I call a meaning terminus.[34]

Commenting on Wittgenstein's notion of a picture at 2.1513 of the *Tractatus,* he adds:

> In possessing the picture I know what reality it represents. There is no further problem of interpreting it. The lines of projection are already there, in the picture. . . . A picture ["conceived in this way"] is a meaning terminus.[35]

Goldberg's terminology is different from mine. Whereas I find it more accurate to distinguish the logical notion of the meaning locus from its epistemological correlate, the interpretation terminus, Goldberg uses the expression "meaning terminus" to cover both.

Nozick has recognized the significance of Goldberg's interpretation. He refers to the sort of view which "requires" that if there is to be meaning, there must be something which is "intrinsically meaningful."[36] And he points out that Goldberg has both exposed this as the view of the *Tractatus,* and discussed "the far-reaching consequences of its undermining in the *Philosophical Investigations.*"[37] Though Nozick does not himself develop these "far-reaching consequences" any further, Malcolm, Heil, Kripke and Goldberg himself have each attempted to do so.

Malcolm has recently argued that certain types of theories of memory presuppose the existence of an entity with the unique nature of an interpretation terminus. He describes the presupposition of such views as follows:

> To understand the meaning of a physical sentence is to come into the possession of something (not the sentence) the meaning of which *shows* itself—something the meaning of which is transparent, self-revealing, unambiguous. It is something that not only does not require interpretation but cannot be interpreted. It is where interpretation ends.[38]

It would be safe to say that the theories which Malcolm thinks presuppose the existence of the interpretation terminus are *mechanistic* theories, so one of the far reaching consequences of the rejection of this notion is the rejection of mechanistic theories of the relevant human phenomenon. (See the discussion of Katz's theory of communication in VIII.1b.)

Similarly, Heil in his "Does Cognitive Psychology Rest on a Mistake?," argues that Fodor's cognitive psychology rests on a mistaken notion of a 'picture' from the *Tractatus*. It is the notion of a picture which "includes [its own] principle of application."[39] It is the sort of thing for which there will be no "gap between the thing itself and its application to states of affairs,"[40] the sort of thing which stands in some "internal relation to the states of affairs these represent."[41] The notion of such an entity is the notion of a meaning locus and interpretation terminus. (Fodor's view is discussed in its own terms and in more detail in Chapter VI, section 3 of the present book.)

Finally, Kripke has recently argued in his *Wittgenstein on Rules and Private Language* that the author of the *Philosophical Investigations* has produced "the most radical and original skeptical problem that philosophy has seen to date,"[42] a skepticism about the very possibility of "all language [and] all concept formation."[43] The skepticism is based on the view that a certain sort of fact about language users is impossible, a fact which determines what they mean by a linguistic expression.[44] Close attention to the text reveals that Kripke's notion of the fact is the notion of a state, probably a mental state, of the linguistic subject.[45] This state of the linguistic subject must satisfy certain conditions.

> . . . there is a condition that any putative candidate for such a fact must satisfy. It must in some sense show how I am justified in

giving the answer "125" for "68 + 57." The "directions" mentioned in the previous paragraph, that determine what I should do in each instance, must somehow be "contained" in any candidate for this fact as to what I meant.[46]

The notion of an entity which contains directions for how linguistic signs should be applied, which shows one how to go on, and so forth, is the notion of an interpretation terminus. According to Kripke, the far-reaching consequence of rejecting the view that there is a meaning locus, an interpretation terminus, is that one must (apparently) take a certain type of skeptical stand on the very possibility of language and concept formation.

It has not been my present purpose to show either that the notions of the meaning locus and interpretation terminus are correct or that they are incorrect, but to show that some philosophers have recognized both that these notions are pivotol in Wittgenstein's work and that major philosophical questions turn on them. If Malcolm is correct, mechanistic theories of certain human phenomena presuppose them. Heil finds that they are presupposed by cognitive psychology. Kripke even holds that the very sense of saying that there is language and meaning may depend on the decision as to the acceptability of these notions. It should be clear by now that these new approaches are the beginning of a revolution in the interpretation of Wittgenstein.

e. *The Logical Status of the Notion of the Mental*

It has already been noted that in his 1919 essay Russell states that "the possibility of the mental accompaniment makes the essence of the meaning of words." And in an interesting and unexpected remark, Frege writes:

> Neither logic nor mathematics has the task of investigating minds and the contents of consciousness whose bearer is a single person. Perhaps their task could be represented rather as the investigation of the mind, of the mind, not of minds.[47]

Even anti-psychologists like Frege can admit to the intuition that logic and/or the meaning of the proposition has some kind of mentalistic dimension. Often such intuitions are vague. In Wittgenstein's view, however, there is a connection between the notions of logic, linguistic meaning and the mental which can be stated precisely.

The argument of the *Tractatus* is an a priori demonstration that the propositional symbol involves a meaning locus in the full-fledged sense of the word, that is, an entity which is "relational in itself," an entity which is mental in Brentano's sense. Since the argument of the *Tractatus* is based on an interpretation of the nature of the tautologies in accordance with the fundamental idea and a minimum of other purely logical thesis, the view that the propositional symbol involves such a mental entity is a logical view in a strict sense. Similarly, the notion of the mental is a logical notion in a related strict sense. These views and this notion are rigorously derived in the interpretation of the tautologies in accordance with Wittgenstein's fundamental idea.

Wittgenstein's derivation of the views and notions which involve the notion of the mental component of the propositional symbol is that it is founded on an interpretation of the tautologies, the analytic propositions. There could hardly be a more unexpected conceptual connection than this one, between a traditional paradigm of the notion of the mental and the anatomy of the analytic propositions.

The fact that these views and notions are logical views and notions has additional significance. For example, Brentano seems to regard the notion of the mental, that of intentionality, as a notion which has an empirical origin, that is, as one which is, so to speak, "picked up" in an act of perception. Could it be that a notion so fundamental has such a contingent origin? Surely such a fundamental concept must be, in some sense, a necessary concept.

One might give a "transcendental" argument that such a notion is a *necessary presupposition* of our conceptual scheme. A transcendental argument typically treats the existence of our existing conceptual scheme as a hypothesis (in a logical sense), and it is then argued that certain basic concepts or views underlie it. In the particular case at hand, one might argue that if one is to account for the meaning connection between ordinary perceptible sentences and states of affairs (and such a notion is clearly present in our existing conceptual scheme), then one must countenance such basic concepts. Such arguments proceed from the less basic—that is, the more familiar, more developed and diverse conceptual system—to the more basic and less numerous fundamental concepts and views which underlie it. Russell's pattern of argument in his 1919 essay might be viewed as a transcendental argument of this type. Such transcendental arguments do address the feeling that the fundamental views and concepts involved are indeed necessary in a sense. However, Wittgenstein's account of the necessity of the concept of the mental is stronger yet.

Wittgenstein's derivation of the concepts and views which pertain to the notion of the mental does not begin with our full-blown system of concepts and argues to its basic presuppositions. Its order is much the opposite. The argument of the *Tractatus* begins with concepts and views which are *more basic still*, and the demonstration is from these more basic concepts and views to the concepts and views which concern the mental. The concepts and views which pertain to logic and the tautologies are more basic than those which pertain to the mental, and in Wittgenstein's system the latter are derived from the former. The fact that such a deduction exists has great significance.

First, though not all philosophers would immediately grant the need for the notion of the mental, few would deny the need for the notions of the logical propositions. Since the notion of the mental is derived in an interpretation of the logical propositions, this derivation constitutes a *justification* of the former relative to the latter. If the latter are judged to be necessary components of our conceptual scheme, then the former must be accorded the same status. (It is even possible, though it is not argued here, that this derivation constitutes a *reduction* of the notion of the mental to logical notions.)

Second, even those philosophers who accept the need for this notion of the mental take seriously the question concerning the status of that notion vis-à-vis the conceptual edifice of science. We have seen that Russell employs this notion of the mental, but since in his 1919 view, the status of the mental is bound up with that of private feelings, he refuses to accord full scientific status to the concept.

For Wittgenstein, by contrast, the fact that the notion of the mental is a logical notion establishes that its place in the conceptual edifice of science is the place that the logical notions occupy in general. There is no need in Wittgenstein's system for a *special* discussion of the scientific status of the notion of the mental, and it seems clear that the logical notions must be accorded *some* valid status vis-à-vis the scientific edifice.

f. Summary

The view of the *Tractatus* is that the propositional symbol involves a meaning locus, an entity which is intrinsically meaningful, which, for instance, contains its own rule of projection. This meaning locus is also an interpretation terminus: To be aware of such an entity is to be aware of something which unambiguously shows its own meaning, which does not stand in need of interpretation. These are remarkable properties. In fact, it is in terms of just these properties that Brentano's notion of the mental is properly defined. Furthermore, in Wittgenstein's view, this notion of the mental is revealed to be a logical notion, and that has consequences for its status in the conceptual edifice of science. Finally, though the notions of the meaning locus and the interpretation terminus have not yet become themes of general discussion in philosophy, the significance of these notions has been recognized by a number of philosophers, including Malcolm, Nozick, Heil, Kripke and others. In the following section two contemporary psycholinguistic views which incorporate these notions are also discussed.

VI.3 Contemporary Psycholinguistic Versions of the View that the Propositional Symbol Involves a Meaning Locus and Interpretation Terminus

The notion of the meaning locus is present in the theories of languge proposed by Chomsky and Fodor (though with different degrees of explicitness). Chomsky tells us that language is a combination of "sound and meaning."[48] It has an "inner and an outer aspect."[49] The outer aspect is called "the physical signal"[50] and the inner aspect is called the 'deep structure'.[51] The deep structure has a role qualitatively different from that possessed by the surface structure.

> It is the deep structure underlying the actual utterance, a structure that is purely mental, that conveys the semantic content of the sentence.[52]

In addition to saying that the deep structure "conveys" the meaning of the sentence, Chomsky also states that it *is* the meaning of the sentence,[53] that it *specifies* the meaning of the sentence,[54] that it *determines* the meaning of the sentence,[55] and most significantly, that it "incorporates all the information relevant to a single interpretation of a particular sentence."[56] Chomsky's view is, like the view of the *Tractatus,* that the propositional symbol is composed of a perceptible and imperceptible component, where the imperceptible component is, by virtue of its unique nature, suited to be the locus of meaning in the proposition.

Wittgenstein's notion of the meaning locus is the notion of an entity which contrasts with the perceptible propositional sign in that it determines its own meaning and does not, therefore, stand in need of interpretation. Chomsky's view that a deep structure "incorporates all the information relevant to a single interpretation of a particular sentence," expresses the contrast between the two types of entities very well. The reason a perceptible sentence can have more than one interpretation is that it does not incorporate, or contain within itself, the information which is relevant to its meaning. But insofar as the deep structure does incorporate all the relevant semantic information, it does not leave open what its meaning is. Chomsky's notion of the deep structure is the notion of an entity which is suited to be a meaning locus and an interpretation terminus.

It is worth stressing that Chomsky's remarks include the point that the deep structure is "purely mental,"[57] and that it is "a mental accompaniment to the utterance."[58] According to the preceding interpretation, the real meaning of Brentano's account of a mental entity as an intentional entity is that it has just this character of having meaning but does not stand in need of interpretation. Chomsky has not, to my knowledge, directly addressed the question of what he means in characterizing an entity as "mental," but Brentano's intuition about the nature of the mental corresponds very well with Chomsky's descriptions of the unique semantic properties of the deep structure. Chomsky's notion of the deep structure is, in fact, a conceptual descendant of Brentano's account of a mental entity.

Fodor distinguishes between the sentence or 'wave form'[59] and the 'message'.[60] The message is an internal state of the sentence producer; it is an "internal representation."[61] These "internal representations" or "messages" are qualitatively different from mere perceptible entities. Messages are "ambiguity free."[62] Saying that they are ambiguity free is, again, another way of saying that what they mean in particular is not a matter for interpretation. Furthermore, Fodor goes on to say that messages "display . . . the information that utterances convey,"[63] and that they do so "explicitly, in a way that the sentence itself fails to do."[64] Fodor might as well say, with the author of the *Tractatus*, that messages, unlike mere perceptible propositional signs, "show their sense" (4.022). His view is another formulation of the view that the propositional symbol involves an imperceptible component, which differs from the perceptible sentence in that it is a meaning locus, and so does not stand in need of interpretation.

The fact that Fodor employs the notion of a meaning locus comes out in another quite striking fashion in his discussion of the distinction between *real semantics* and *translation semantics*. Though it is already clear that Fodor has the view that the propositional symbol involves a meaning locus, it is illuminating to display the role of this view in his account of the conceptual foundations of "real" semantic theory. Fodor quotes David Lewis, who holds that Fodor's semantics is a translation semantics and that a translation semantics is not a "real semantics" because it fails to deal with "the relations between symbols and the world of non-symbols—that is, with genuinely semantic relations."[65] Translation semantics only involves the translation of sentences from one notation into another notation. In Fodor's case the latter is the notation of semantic markers. But Lewis points out that nothing about the relation between symbols and the world is accomplished thereby, since the semantic markers themselves

> are symbols, items in the vocabulary of an artificial language we might call Semantic Markerese. . . . But we can know the Markerese translation of an English sentence without knowing the first thing about the meaning of the English sentence: namely, the conditions under which it would be true.[66]

In translation semantics one simply replaces one symbolism by another without illuminating the connection between symbols and the world. Fodor writes:

> The real difference between real semantics and mere translation semantics lies in the way in which the two kinds of theory characterize the semantic properties of the object language expressions. Roughly, translation theories characterize such properties by reference to metalinguistic expressions which share them; real semantic theories do not. . . .
>
> Translation theories typically specify, for each referring expression of the object language, some coreferring expression of the meta-language.

The reference of the object language expressions is, therefore, determined but only relative to a determination of the reference of the corresponding meta-language expressions. "Real" semantics, on the other hand, actually *says* what the object language expressions refer to, i.e., it names those referents. In effect, then, real semantics defines a relation of reference, whereas 'mere' translation semantics defines only a relation of coreference.[67]

Fodor's account of how symbols relate to the world lies in the special way in which a real semantic theory characterizes the semantic properties of the symbols of the object language. This special type of characterization of their semantic properties enables one to (1) "actually say" what the expressions of the object language refer to, and (2) define a relation of reference, not merely of coreference. The implicit suggestion is that "actually saying" what the expressions of the object language refer to, and defining a relation of reference, are equivalent and are together opposed to merely defining a relation of coreference. The matter is more complicated than this, however. Fodor actually runs together several different philosophical/ linguistic programs, and he accordingly includes several different kinds of programs under the rubric "real semantics," some of which are more philosophical in nature and some of which belong more properly to the science of linguistics.

One must distinguish the following sorts of sentences:

p1) '*a*' means the same as '*b*'.

p2) '*a*' means (stands for) *a*.

The first sentence states that two expressions corefer, but does not actually say to what either of the two expressions refer. The second sentence actually says to what '*a*' refers. However, what is required for a "real" semantical account of the connection between symbols and the world, is not constituted by sentences such as *p2*, as opposed to sentences such as *p1*. Ordinary speakers "actually say" what expressions refer to all the time, but cannot produce a philosophically illuminating account of the connection between symbols and the world. Nor is the situation improved if one can *systematically*, in a precise canonical notation, "actually say" to what the expressions of some language refer.

What is really needed for the philosophical portion of a real semantic theory is not that one can actually say to what things in the world certain expressions refer, but that one can give an account of what is involved in doing so, that is, of the "relations" of reference or meaning. Fodor's program of "actually saying" to what the expressions of some object language refer is a program for a science of linguistics, which is concerned to describe the reference of the expressions of some actual language. The present inquiry, by contrast, is concerned with the specifically philosophical account of *how* symbols mean something, how they "touch reality."

The important question in the present section is, therefore, Fodor's second question, that is, how does one define the relation of reference?[68] Fodor continues:

> What is certainly true is that a theory of language must say, in some way or other, what the terms of language refer to. For this reason, a real semantic theory would have to be part of a theory of the internal code.[69]

Despite the fact that his conflation of different questions concerning the theory of meaning is present in this remark, Fodor makes the key point nonetheless. His account of the real semantical connection between symbols and the world of non-symbols involves an appeal to the fact that the internal code is involved in the connection between symbols and the world. But this appeal to the internal code can only be effective if the internal code has a nature fundamentally different from that of mere perceptible representations. Recall Lewis's original objection to Fodor's semantics, namely that a translation into "Semantic Markerese" does not illuminate the connection between symbols and the world, since one can be acquainted with the canonical representation of a sentence without knowing the least thing about its meaning. By inference, the relevant property of the internal code appealed to by Fodor can only be that the concept of the internal code is the concept of a kind of representation which, unlike the perceptible semantic markers, is such that *one cannot be acquainted with it without knowing its meaning!* But this is nothing other than the epistemological correlate of the view that the propositional symbol involves a meaning locus. It is the view that the internal code has the nature of an interpretation terminus.

Fodor's own response to Lewis contains the following remarkable passage:

> Since the canonical representation of S is itself a formula in some language, one can know what the canonical representation of S is without knowing what S means: e.g., if one doesn't understand the language in which the canonical representation is couched. But, of course, this will hold for any semantic theory whatever so long as it is formulated in a symbolic system; and of course, there is no alternative to so formulating one's theories. We're all in Sweeney's boat; we've all gotta use words when we talk. Since words are not, as it were, self-illuminating like globes on a Christmas tree, there is no way in which a semantic theory will find its formulae intelligible.[70]

Though Fodor's direct claim is that words are *not* "self-illuminating," the indirect suggestion is that his semantic theory *does* involve the notion of an entity, the units of the internal code, which are self-illuminating. That this indirect suggestion is accurate is born out by the fact that the metaphor of a self-illuminating entity is a particularly apt characterization of Fodor's "message"—given that the message is, as is pointed out in the initial discussion of Fodor's basic views, described as an entity which "displays" its meaning "explicitly, in a way the sentence itself fails to do." Fodor's account of the propositional symbol includes the view that the propositional symbol involves an imperceptible component, a "unit" in the internal code, which is self-illuminating and an interpretation terminus. One cannot be acquainted with such an entity without knowing its meaning.

Fodor's response to Lewis's objection is really the claim that Lewis has incorrectly capitalized on the fact that one must formulate the character of the internal code in mere words. Lewis has emphasized the perceptible semantic marker, and the translation of everyday sentences into Semantic Markerese. But Fodor's view is that a semantic marker is only a kind of perspicuous perceptible image of a unit of the internal code, that is, "psychological reality is usually—if wistfully—claimed for the structures that grammars enumerate" and "it is messages that semantic representations [semantic markers] represent."[71] This is why Fodor initially states that there is a certain unfairness that attaches to Lewis's remarks, if they are taken as a general criticism of translational approaches to semantics.[72] Fodor claims that what makes his own view more than a *mere* translation semantics is that his semantic markers are perspicuous perceptible images of messages which have that unique nature appealed to in the account of the connection between symbols and the world. Lewis's misinterpretation of Fodor's view is an exact parallel to those misinterpretations of the *Tractatus,* which fail to emphasize and develop the unique nature of the imperceptible thought, and instead emphasize its perceptible (and imperfect) image (see V.4).

Fodor, Chomsky, and Katz[73] have all held positions which are more detailed versions of the sort of view held by Russell in his 1919 essay "On Propositions." They hold that the perceptible sign touches reality by "going through" (Russell's expression) an intermediary entity, which itself means the relevant state of affairs, without going through anything else. It is that unique entity which is involved in the account of the "real" semantical connection. Fodor's notion of the message and Chomsky's notion of the "purely mental" deep structure are conceptual descendants of Brentano's notion of a mental entity, a meaning locus.

Though it is clear that Chomsky and Fodor have employed the notion of the meaning locus in their accounts of language, this fact has not, in general, been recognized.[74] Part of the reason for this is traceable to the texts themselves. That is, attention to the texts of Katz, Chomsky and Fodor reveal that the notion of the meaning locus tends to be, as it were, *used* by these philosophers rather than mentioned. They have not made the notion itself an explicit object of philosophical reflection. The exceptions to this seem to be in those places where these theorists are facing serious objections brought on by other philosophers, such as Lewis's objection that he has not provided an account of the connection between symbols and the world. Their relative paucity of explicit attention to the unique nature of the underlying meaning component may derive from the fact that these authors are concerned to work out the *science* of linguistic competence and performance, whereas the notion of the meaning locus is properly located in the *philosophical foundations* of this science.[75]

VI.4   The State of the Contemporary Theory of Meaning

Dummett writes:

> While most of us, myself included, would agree that the concept of meaning is a fundamental and indispensible one, we are unclear even

about the surface structure of statements involving that concept. What kind of sentence, of natural language, should be taken as the characteristic form for an attribution of a particular meaning to some given word or expression? Not only do we not know the answer to this: we do not even know whether it is the right question to ask. Perhaps it is impossible, in general, to state the meaning of the expression: perhaps we ought rather, to inquire by what linguistic means, or possibly even non-linguistic means, it is possible to convey the meaning of an expression, otherwise than by explicitly stating it. Or perhaps even that is wrong: perhaps the question should be, not how we express that a particular expression has a certain meaning, but how we should analyze the concept of meaning in some different way.[76]

Similarly, Putnam writes that "the dimension of language associated with the word *'meaning'*, is, in spite of the usual spate of heroic if misguided attemps, as much in the dark as it ever was."[77] Putnam is even driven to ask, "Why is the theory of meaning so *hard?*"[78] The general point of both of these philosophers is that the theory of meaning is in such poor condition that we do not even know what are the right questions to ask. And this general sort of attitude is not uncommon among philosophers concerned with the theory of meaning. There is, in fact, a crisis in the theory of meaning which is of such proportions that philosophers are even disinclined to make direct reference to the phenomenon of meaning, or perhaps one should say with Putnam, to "the dimension of language associated with the word 'meaning.' "

It is not here claimed that these and like-minded philosophers do not hold that there are many interesting and significant questions raised in connection with the phenomenon of meaning. They have, in fact, offered specific suggestions as to how the poor condition of meaning theory may be improved. Dummett's own suggestion, the one which he himself finds "most fruitful," is the method of determining

what form should be taken by what is called a theory of 'meaning' for any one entire language; that is, a detailed specification of all the words and sentence forming operations of the language, yielding a specification of the meaning of every expression and sentence of the language.[79]

Such a program does not directly confront the question concerning the nature of meaning. It does not raise what Lewis or Fodor would call "real semantical questions," but only involves the program of describing the form which should be taken by a *specification* of the meanings of the expressions of some language. Dummett's program is more concerned with the specification of particular meanings than with the *nature* of meaning. Dummett claims—even stresses—that an analogous proposal has never been suggested as a way of dealing with the problems of epistemology. That is, no one has ever suggested that the way to resolve our philosophical perplexity about knowledge is to give a "detailed specification of everything one individual, or community, could be said to know."[80] This, however, is not quite true.

In Plato's *Theaetetus* Socrates asks the young Theaetetus to "tell me, in a generous spirit, what you think knowledge is."[81] Theaetetus responds:

> I think the things one can learn from Theodorus are knowledge-geometry and all the sciences you mentioned just now, and then there are the crafts of the cobbler and other workmen. Each and all of these are knowledge and nothing else.[82]

Socrates, however, objects to Theaetetus's program:

> You are generous indeed, my dear Theaetetus—so open minded that, when you are asked for one simple thing you offer a whole variety.
> . . .

> The question you were asked, Theaetetus, was not, what are the objects of knowledge, nor yet how many sorts of knowledge there are. We did not want to count them, but to find out what the thing itself—knowledge—is. Is there nothing in that?[83]

It is Socrates's view that the sort of program proposed by Theaetetus is precisely what is *not* of relevance to his *philosophical* question concerning knowledge. Socrates wants to understand the nature of knowledge, and he rejects Theaetetus's attempt to get by with the specification of a mere list of the things, or kinds of things, that one can be said to know.

According to the Dummett/Theaetetus approach, it is not fruitful to inquire directly into the nature of meaning, to ask what *meaning* itself is. Socrates, however, argues that one *must* ask such questions:

Socrates: Take another example. Suppose we were asked about some obvious common thing, for instance, what clay is; it would be absurd to answer: potter's clay, and ovenmaker's clay, and brickmaker's clay.

Theaetetus: No doubt.

Socrates: To begin with, it is absurd to imagine that our answer conveys any meaning to the questioner, when we can use the word 'clay', no matter whose clay we call it—the doll maker's or any other craftsman's. You do not suppose a man can understand the name of a thing, when he does not know what the thing is?

Theaetetus: Certainly not.

Socrates: Then, if he has no idea about knowledge, 'knowledge about shoes' conveys nothing to him.[84]

Similarly, unless we know what meaning itself is, Dummett's expression—"the meanings of every word and sentence in our entire language"—means nothing to us.

Of what would a more direct approach to the problems of meaning consist? Dummett himself, in his book on Frege, writes:

> Many philosophers, Wittgenstein included, have inveighed against the practice of "hypostatizing" or "reifying" meanings—taking meanings to be entities with which words are associated. It is often a little hard to see what conception it is that they find so harmful—what would count as an instance of such an illicit hypostatization.[85]

In his reference to Wittgenstein, Dummett presumably refers to the Wittgenstein of the *Philosophiccal Investigations* ("When I think in language there aren't 'meanings' going through my mind in addition to the verbal expressions. . . ." par. 329). Perhaps if one could specify precisely what notion the author of the *Philosophical Investigations* and others find so harmful, then one would not find oneself forced to support such a limited and indirect approach to the problems of meaning. A direct approach to the problem of meaning is involved in the question: What is the nature of these entities which words are associated with, and which are their meanings, that is, *what is the nature of meanings?*

The notion of a reified meaning which is inveighed against by the author of the *Philosophical Investigations* is, not surprisingly, the fundamental notion of meaning in the *Tractatus*. It is the notion of an entity which accompanies the perceptible propositional sign and which *is* its meaning. The notion of a reified meaning is the notion of a *meaning locus*.

Dummett paints a picture according to which the notion of a reified meaning is an uncommon, or only very obscurely understood one. In an even more sweeping statement, Putnam writes:

> Notice that the topic of 'meaning' is the one topic discussed in philosophy in which there is literally nothing but theory—literally nothing that can be labeled or even ridiculed as the 'common sense view'. . . .[86]

That is, the notion of the reified meaning is neither commonsensical nor common. But in his *Analysis of Mind,* Russell could write:

> Even those [entities], however, which are purely mental will not have that intrinsic reference to objects which Brentano assigns to them and which constitutes the essence of "consciousness" as ordinarily understood.[87]

Earlier in the same book Russell refers to "the apparent simplicity" of Brentano's view "that mental phenomena have essential reference to objects." If Russell is correct, then Brentano's view is the ordinary view, and on some level of understanding it is not a difficult notion. Furthermore, the notion has appeared in various formulations in philosophical and psycholinguistic accounts of language and mind. Brentano, Russell, Wittgenstein, Chomsky and Fodor have all held views which involve it, and recently Goldberg, Malcolm, Nozick, Heil, Kripke and McGinn[88] have noted that significant philosophical questions turn on the acceptability of this notion.

The poor condition of the theory of meaning is to be improved by first recognizing that this notion of the meaning locus is quite fundamental and pervasive, and then by making this notion of meaning the explicit theme of philosophical inquiry. This does not require that altogether new concepts and views be developed, but only that those very concepts and views which played a large role in the beginning of both the analytical and phenomenological movements are reexamined. It is not urged here either that this judgment concerning the validity of the view that the propositional symbol involves a meaning locus ought to be favorable, or that it ought to be unfavorable. The present book is neutral with regard to the soundness of the argument of the *Tractatus* and the truth of its conclusions. The suggestions made in the present section are advanced against the background of the negative judgments on the condition of the theory of meaning, and they concern the means by which this condition may be improved, that is, the means by which *illumination* into the phenomenon of meaning can be achieved.

Unfortunately, the theory of meaning has seen an increasing tendency to overemphasize the perceptible part of language. Just as Plato once tried to remedy the poor condition of the theory of knowledge, by urging that philosophers take seriously the idea of an imperceptible realm of entities which has a unique nature that no mere perceptible entity can have, the poor condition of the theory of meaning can be improved by taking seriously the notion of the imperceptible meaning component of the proposition, the notion of the meaning locus. The reinterpretation of Wittgenstein's *Tractatus* and *Philosophical Investigations* is, therefore, of more than merely historical interest. It could become the basis for a rethinking of the philosophical foundations of the theory of meaning and of the field of psycholinguistics.[89]

CHAPTER VII

The Nature of a Philosophical System and Philosophical Propositions

Wittgenstein is distinguished among analytical philosophers in his concern with the nature of philosophical truth. His views are not merely an aggregate of doctrines, instead they form a philosophical system. Both the system as a whole, and the philosophical propositions which make it up, have some quite unique logical features. These logical features illuminate Wittgenstein's views that finally, there are no philosophical propositions, that one must throw away the ladder after one has climbed it. Furthermore, Wittgenstein's account of the nature of his philosophical system and philosophical propositions is fruitfully compared in some respects with similar accounts in the tradition of German Idealism. Still, Wittgenstein's account contains strikingly original forms of these views, and constitutes an original contribution to reflection on the nature of philosophy.

VII.1   The Self-Contained Philosophical System

I have heard it said that the *Tractatus* is the "least systematic" of philosophical works.[1] This has been said, despite both the rather elaborate numbering system for relating remarks into some kind of systematic whole, and also the remark at 5.4541:

> The solutions of the problems of logic must be simple since they set the standard of simplicity.

> Men have always had a presentiment that there must be a realm
> in which the answers to questions are symetrically combined—a priori—
> to form a self contained system. A realm subject to the law: simplex
> sigillum veri.

If this remark is taken at face value, it would appear to be Wittgenstein's view that the philosophical propositions of the *Tractatus* not only constitute a system, but that this system must meet very high standards.

By saying that a system is "self-contained," one might mean that the system contains a principle which determines whether a certain philosophical "proposition" belongs to the system or not. If there is such a principle, then the system is closed and complete in the sense that, by reference to the principle, it is determined that a given philosophical proposition either does or does not belong to the system.

In Wittgenstein's view, the general proposition form determines "the essence of all description" and "the essence of the world". Since the general philosophical form is that which is presented with the symbols of the tautologies which is relevant to their truth value, the tautology is the single principle by reference to which the answer to all of these philosophical questions is determined. Furthermore, there is a procedure, the *Grundegedanke*-inspired interpretation of the tautologies, which enables one mechanically to derive these features of the general philosophical form. Once this interpretation of the tautologies is settled, then in principle the contents and limits of the philosophical system of the *Tractatus* are settled as well.

To be sure, the contents and limits of the system are settled only in principle. The mere possession of the principle, in this case the tautology, does not ensure either that its significance is recognized or that it is used properly. One requires the proper interpretation of the tautologies. And, of course, one must make the correct inferences in the derivation of the general propositional form.

There is one textual point which lends support to the present interpretation. 5.4541 is, according to the system of the *Tractatus,* a comment on 5.4 where the fundamental idea is stated for the second time in the text. And the fundamental idea is the essential idea in the interpretation of the tautologies which enables one to define the sense in which Wittgenstein's philosophical system is self-contained. A connection which is essential to the present interpretation is verified in the numbering system of the *Tractatus.*

The unified approach to the problems of philosophy, that is, the development of the self-contained system, derives from the unitary method for determining the nature of the proposition. The determination of the nature of the proposition is nothing but the determination of the general propositional form. The general propositional form is not just an arbitrarily collected set of characteristics. There is only one way to determine what belongs to the general propositional form—a method which ensures that the various components have been properly understood, which ensures completeness. And that involves interpreting the logical propositions in accordance with the fundamental idea. It amounts to carrying out the program of 6.12, and thus presenting the argument of the *Tractatus*.

VII.2   The Presuppositionless Starting Point for Philosophy

Another elusive philosophical ideal, one which is connected with that of a self-contained system, is the ideal of an absolutely presuppositionless standpoint for philosophy. There is a sense in which the system of the *Tractatus* is based on a presuppositionless standpoint. Since the argument of the *Tractatus* is a demonstration of that which is presented with the symbols of the tautologies, which is relevant to their truth value and since the tautologies are the emptiest of all propositions, all these philosophical views are really implicit in the tautological symbol. The argument of the *Tractatus* lays claim to having a presuppositionless starting point, not in the sense that it is based on nothing, but in that it is based on a mere analytic proposition, a proposition whose truth presupposes nothing about the world.

The matter is, however, not quite this simple. Though there is one sense in which Wittgenstein's philosophical system has a presuppositionless foundation, there is another sense in which it does not and cannot have a presuppositionless foundation. Also, it is likely that no philosophical system can have a presuppositionless foundation. These two senses correspond to two different perspectives on philosophical truth, and to two different types of philosophical systems. Finally, the non-ordinary philosophical concepts which underlie these types of systems must be made explicit.

*a. The Sense in Which Wittgenstein's Philosophical System Does Not
Have a Presuppositionless Foundation*

In one sense Wittgenstein's philosophical system is constituted by the
argument of the *Tractatus* itself. One clear sense in which an argument
is based on a principle or proposition is that that principle or proposition
is a premise in the argument. The argument of the *Tractatus* is not based
on a tautology in this sense. The conclusions reached in the argument of
the *Tractatus* cannot be correctly described as following from the tautology.
Only tautologies follow from another tautology. The relevant premise in
the argument of the *Tractatus* is the "proposition" that '$P \vee \sim P$' is a
tautology. The argument of the *Tractatus* is not properly described as a
deduction of philosophical views from a tautology, but as a deduction of
these views from the fact that certain expressions are tautologies, *and a
certain interpretation* of the tautologies. This interpretation is constituted
by the various premises in the argument of the *Tractatus,* most notably
Wittgenstein's 'fundamental idea.'

First, the fact that this connection between the tautologies and the
logical form of language and the world is mediated by the interpretation
of the tautologies means that the *apprehension* of the logical form of
language and the world is not immediate upon the understanding and
apprehension of the tautological symbol. This is quite important. There
has been a tendency to understand Wittgenstein's program announced at
6.12 to mean that there is supposed to be some direct connection between
the apprehension of the tautologies and the apprehension of the substantive
views of the *Tractatus.* That is, there has been a tendency to understand
the remark at 6.12 either by using a dogmatic or an overly mystical
model. The dogmatic model is the view that the program of 6.12 involves
immediate inferences from the tautology itself to the views of the *Tractatus.*
The mystical model is the view that there is really no argument or inference
involved at all. One merely apprehends the tautological symbol, and the
"logical form of the language and the world" simply becomes manifest.

The claims involved in these models seem absurd. But even if one
were to grant that there is some direct connection between the apprehension
of the tautology itself and the apprehension of the views of the *Tractatus,*
no philosophical illumination would be afforded by such an immediate
apprehension. The fact that the connection is made by the mediation of
an interpretation of the tautologies is precisely what affords the insight

into the connection between logic and ontology. If the connection between logic and ontology were apprehended in the direct fashion suggested by the dogmatic and/or the mystical model, then the apprehension of the connection could be merely of the fact that there *is* such a connection. The conceptual anatomy of the connection would remain opaque. An epistemological mysticism, like the dogmatism from which it is practically indistinguishable, is not a position within philosophy, but a result of the failure of philosophy to *comprehend* the relevant subject matter.

One reason why the program at 6.12 has not been taken seriously is precisely because it has been wrongly assumed that such dogmatic or mystical models are all that Wittgenstein had in mind in that remark. It is the fact that the connection is not of this direct type, but involves an interpretation of the tautologies, which makes the program of 6.12 a *philosophical* program, as opposed to a dogmatic or mystical pronouncement.

Wittgenstein's own terminology in 6.12, that is, the fact that certain expressions are tautologies *shows* such and such, may itself be thought to suggest these dogmatic or mystical models. The formulation that the tautologies show the logical form of language and the world suggests that the apprehension of the tautologies involves a direct apprehension, modeled on perception, of the philosophical views of the *Tractatus*. Note, however, that Wittgenstein does not write at 6.12 that the tautologies themselves show such and such, but that *the fact that* certain expressions are tautologies shows such and such. The formulation, according to which it is *the fact that* certain expressions are tautologies which show such and such, suggests that the connection between the tautologies and the relevant philosophical views is of the mediated type. It also suggests that there may be somethig like an argument involved. The use of the word *showing* in 6.12 is comparable to its use in the locution, "The fact that Jones tried to conceal the murder weapon shows that he is guilty." Wittgenstein's formulation at 6.12 is a mere shorthand for the view that an argument can be constructed from certain views about the tautologies to the logical form of language and the world.

The second point which must be made about the fact that, not the tautology itself, but an *interpretation* of the tautology is directly involved in the argument of the *Tractatus,* is that this philosophical argument, like any philosophically significant argument, involves presuppositions. It involves premises which can easily be imagined to be denied. The 'fundamental idea', for example, is an assumption about the nature of the logical constants. The preceding point is that the account of the connection between logic and ontology is philosophically illuminating only insofar as it involves an interpretation of the tautologies. The present point is that insofar as it involves an interpretation of the tautologies, it is not without significant presuppositions. Taken together, these two views suggest that the price one pays for philosophical *illumination* is that one cannot have a presuppositionless starting point. Insofar as Wittgenstein's philosophical system is identified with the *argument* of the *Tractatus,* then it must, like any argument, be premised on certain presuppositions.

Still, though the argument of the *Tractatus* does rest on significant premises, or presuppositions, it compares favorably with other great philosophical arguments in the number and the character of its presuppositions. However, the philosophical ideal to which some philosophers have aspired is that of *absolute* presuppositionlessness. In the following subsection it is explained in what sense Wittgenstein's philosophical system does have an absolutely presuppositionless foundation.

b. The Sense in which Wittgenstein's Philosophical System Does Have a Presuppositionless Foundation

There are in the *Tractatus* in general, and in the 6.12's in particular, two entirely different sorts of formulations in which the tautologies are said to be involved in showing something. One must distinguish between (1) the view that tautologies are involved in showing something about the logical form of language and the world, by the fact that certain expressions are tautologies shows such and such, and (2) the view that the tautologies themselves show such and such. The former formulation is a mere shorthand for the view that certain "facts" about the tautologies can be fitted into an argument for the views of the *Tractatus.* The latter formulation occurs in the 6.12's at 6.127 where the tautology itself is said to show that it is a tautology. The formulation that the tautology itself shows something involves the fundamental logical notion of 'showing' in the *Tractatus,* the notion of a presentational symbol. A propositional symbol shows something insofar as that something is presented with its symbol and is relevant to its truth value. The view that a propositional symbol shows something in this sense is not a mere shorthand for the view that some sort of argument is possible, which involves that proposition or views about that proposition. It is a view about the fundamental nature of the symbolic entity.[2]

The view of the *Tractatus* is that the tautologies present with their symbols, or self-guarantee, their own "truth conditions." All the a priori views which constitute Wittgenstein's philosophical system are also implicit in these truth conditions of the tautology. So despite the fact that the conclusions of the argument of the *Tractatus* cannot be said to follow from the tautology, there is a sense in which all these philosophical theses are in fact implicit in that which is presented with the tautological symbol. That is, they are implicit in the symbol of the mere analytical propositions, the emptiest of all propositions.

This means, first, that these views are implicit in the symbols of those propositions which have no factual content or "say nothing." There is a clear sense in which propositions which say nothing do not presuppose anything, that is, they presuppose nothing which might turn out to be false. The formulation that the logical propositions "do not say anything" is, in that form, not far removed from ordinary views and notions concerning logical propositions. The most basic philosophical account of the sense in which Wittgenstein's philosophical system is based on a presuppositionless foundation must, however, involve the basic *philosophical* notions which are developed in the argument of the *Tractatus*.

The account of the a priori character of the logical propositions developed in Chapter II is that the tautological symbol is a presentational symbol in the strong sense, that is, it presents with itself that which determines its own truth value. It is, therefore, a *self-guaranteeing* symbol. Since all the philosophical views concerning the logical form of language and the world are implicit in the tautological symbol, they are implicit in the symbols of those propositions *which presuppose nothing which is not guaranteed by the symbol itself*. Wittgenstein's philosophical system has a presuppositionless foundation in the sense that all the views which comprise his system are implicit in the symbols of those propositions which say nothing (which is significant enough), and which are also the self-guaranteeing symbols.

The connection between the results of the present and the preceding section is this: the account of the sense in which Wittgenstein's philosophical system is self-contained is that all the philosophical propositions which characterize the logical form of language and the world are implicit in that which is presented with the tautological symbol. But it is, in principle, possible that one could have (1) a self-contained but "false" philosophical system, or that one could have (2) a self-contained system which is "true," but whose truth presupposes something external to the self-contained system. But neither of these descriptions characterize Wittgenstein's system. It is the fact that that which is presented with the tautological symbol is that which determines its truth which is the relevant factor in the account of the presuppositionless character of Wittgenstein's philosophical system. That Wittgenstein's philosophical system is self-contained is defined in terms of the fact that all the philosophical views which constitute this system are derivable from a single fundamental principle (the tautological symbol). That this self-contained system is a presuppositionless system is defined by reference to the special logical properties of that fundamental principle, that it has this unique self-guaranteeing charater.

The ideal of a presuppositionless philosophical system is not immediately associated with the view of the *Tractatus,* for it is not, like the notion of a self-contained system, explicitly mentioned in the text of the *Tractatus.* This ideal is, however, part of the meaning of Wittgenstein's remark that "logic must look after itself" (5.473). That view is discussed in the commentaries as the view that logic is "autonomous."[3] If logic is autonomous then it presupposes nothing which is not provided by logic itself. Since Wittgenstein's philosophical system is determined by logic, specifically by the tautological symbol, then if logic is autonomous or presuppositionless this autonomy or presuppositionlessness carries over to the philosophical system.

c. The System of Philosophical Knowledge and the System of Philosophical Truth

One must distinguish between two different notions of the philosophical *system* of the *Tractatus:* (1) If by Wittgenstein's philosophical system one means nothing other than the *argument* of the *Tractatus,* then Wittgenstein's philosophical system, like any argument, involves premises or presuppositions. (2) If, however, by Wittgenstein's philosophical system one means the systematic conceptual connection between the tautologies and the various theses concerning the logical form of language and the world, then these theses are all implicit in the factually empty and self-guaranteeing tautological symbol. That is, one must distinguish the argument, the means by which one comes to know of the intimate conceptual connection between the empty tautological symbol and the logical form of language and the world, and that systematic conceptual connection itself. The former is the system of philosophical knowledge, and its systematic character is conditioned by the limitations which are inherent in the knowing process. The latter is the system of philosophical truth, and its systematic character is independent of all such limitations.

The distinction between these two notions of a philosophical system can be put in terms of the medieval distinction between the 'order of knowing' and the 'order of being'. The a priori order of being, the system of philosophical theses which characterize the logical form of language and the world, is implicit in the tautological symbol. But the tautological symbol is not given to us in such a manner that we make immediate use of it. Though the tautological symbol is in itself rich in "linguistic" and ontological "content," it must, taken by itself, present a blank face to the knowing mind. Arguments, proofs, and so forth are required by philosophers, not because they themselves correspond to anything in the order of being, but because one cannot gain direct insight into the a priori order of being. In order that one can make philosophical use of the tautological symbol, one must gain access to this linguistic and ontological content by means of the *mediation* of an interpretation. And in this interpretation one must make some assumptions or presuppositions. If, however, one makes the right assumptions, or develops the correct interpretations, then one can gain insight into the a priori order of being.

It is the view of the *Tractatus* that the order of being, insofar as this order is a priori, rests on a presuppositionless foundation. Also, insofar as this order is a priori, the order of being, is implicit in the empty and self-guaranteeing tautological symbol. The order of knowing is embodied in the argument of the *Tractatus,* and therefore it involves the necessity of presuppositions which characterize any argument or interpretation. So one is forced to make the distinction between the logical structure of our system of knowledge and logic proper—the latter being the logic of the world. All of the complexity and uncertainty which characterizes philosophical interpretations and arguments pertain merely to the order of knowing, to the system of philosophical knowledge. By contrast, the a priori order of being, whose structure of dependence is reflected in the system of philosophical truth, is as simple and as presuppositionless as the self-guaranteeing tautological symbol which defines it.

VII.3   The Systematic Nature of Philosophical Truth: The Truth Locus for Philosophical Truth

The two most significant dimensions of Wittgenstein's account of the system of philosophical truth, that it is self-contained and presuppositionless, are intimately interrelated. That is, they are both defined in terms of the unique nature of the tautological symbol and the relation of philosophical truth to the tautological symbol. An important perspective on this unique nature of the tautological symbol, a perspective which is both historically and conceptually illuminating, can be gained by tracing the connection between Wittgenstein's account of the tautological symbol and his account of the meaning component of the genuine propositional symbol.

The fundamental notion in Wittgenstein's account of symbols in general is the notion of a presentational symbol. "Genuine" or nonlogical propositions are presentational symbols in the sense that they present with themselves the conditions of their own meaningfulness, that is, they involve a meaning locus. The logical propositions are presentational symbols in a sense which is related to, but is stronger than, that which characterizes genuine propositions. The tautological symbol does not merely present with itself the conditions of its own meaning; it presents with itself the conditions of its own truth. The tautological symbol is not merely self-illuminating; it is self-guaranteeing. One might make the connection explicit in this way: the genuine propositional symbol involves a meaning locus; the tautological symbol involves a *truth locus.*

The tautological symbol is not, of course, a truth locus as regards truth in general. Whether any particular contingent proposition is true or not is independent of the tautological symbol. It is only the truth of the tautology itself which is determined by the tautological symbol. But that which is relevant to the truth value of the tautology is very important, for the "truth conditions" of the tautology are precisely what is of interest to philosophy. The tautological symbol is the truth locus for philosophical truth.

There are two senses in which the tautological symbol is the truth locus for philosophical truth. First, the question of which particular philosophical propositions constitute his system is determined by the tautological symbol, that is, the philosophical propositions demonstrated in the argument of the *Tractatus* are elucidations of that which is presented with the tautological symbol which is relevant to its truth value. Second, that these philosophical propositions are the correct ones is determined by the tautological symbol, that is, these philosophical propositions are elucidations of that which is presented with the self-guaranteeing symbol. The tautological symbol is the locus for philosophical truth not only in the sense that the scope and content of the philosophical system is determined by the tautological symbol, but also that the truth of that content is determined by the tautological symbol as well.

The two essential features of Wittgenstein's philosophical system are defined by reference to these two components of the notion of the truth locus for philosophical truth: (1) The fact that there is a truth locus for philosophical truth—a single principle which is the final terminal point by reference to which the scope and content of the philosophical system is determined—means that philosophical truth forms a self-contained system of philosophical propositions. (2) The fact that the fundamental principle is *itself* the terminal point by reference to which its own truth is determined means that it is a self-guaranteeing principle. It is this feature which makes the self-contained philosophical system a presuppositionless system.

The two most significant notions which have been developed in the argument of the *Tractatus* are those of the meaning locus—which is the key notion in the account of the connection between genuine propositional symbols and the world, and its parent notion, that of the truth locus—which is the key idea in the account of the systematic nature of philosophical truth. In fact, in philosophical thinking about a broad range of issues, which can only generally be characterized here as involving a series of certain sorts, there is the tendency to assume (or to try to prove) that these series must come to an end in some sort of terminal entity. This entity must, therefore, have a unique nature which distinguishes it from the elements of the series. The sort of view which holds that certain types of series must come to an end in some sort of terminal entity, with a unique nature, is quite familiar in connection with cosmological arguments concerning the origin and nature of the world. It is not so common to recognize that similar views are present in philosophical thinking about a broad range of phenomena, including both meaning and philosophical truth itself. The philosophical significance of these notions of "terminal entities" is evidenced by their very pervasiveness.[4]

VII.4   The Holistic Nature of Wittgenstein's Philosophical System

In addition to the view that his philosophical system is self-contained and presuppositionless, it is also a consequence of Wittgenstein's view that his philosophical system is a unified whole in a unique sense. Furthermore, his holism sheds light on his view that there are no philosophical propositions.

The fact that all "true" philosophical propositions are elucidations of that which is relevant to the truth value of the tautological symbol means that there is a sense in which these seemingly separable philosophical propositions are not really separate, and are not really properly considered to be separately true. The point can be made clear by contrasting the case of the genuine propositions with that of the philosophical propositions. Since the philosophical sign of each genuine proposition is the perceptible expression of a meaning locus or self-contained meaning, each such propositional sign is a unit or atom of meaning, that is, each is both meaningful and either true or false in isolation from other genuine propositions. By contrast, the propositional sign of the philosophical propositions is not itself a unit or atom of philosophical significance. That symbol which is the real unit of philosophical significance and truth is the tautological symbol. It, not the separate philosophical propositions, is the *single* truth which is relevant to philosophy, and the multiplicity of philosophical propositions which make up the philosophical system of the *Tractatus* are each only essentially incomplete glimpses of the truth conditions of the tautological symbol. In contemporary terms, the point could be put by saying that whereas genuine propositions must be understood atomistically, philosophical propositions must be understood holistically. The larger whole which is incompletely glimpsed by means of any single philosophical proposition is, in the first instance, the tautological symbol (there are additional insights into the nature of this whole which are discussed in Section 2 of the subsequent chapter).

The key point in understanding why in Wittgenstein's view, his philosophical system must be understood holistically, is that though the philosophical propositions which make up his system are elucidations of that which is presented with the tautological symbol which is relevant to its truth value, the tautological symbol is *not analysable* into any logical combination of these philosophical propositions. The tautology is not equivalent to any conjunction of philosophical propositions, that is, it is not the case that '$P \vee \sim P$' for instance, is logically equivalent to a complex philosophical proposition such as: "Genuine propositions in general are about a subject matter external to their symbol, and they say about that subject matter that it is or is not in some contingent state. . . ." The account of the logical constants developed in Chapter II and III of the present book is that only genuine contingent propositions are conjoinable or disjoinable and so on. Thus, the tautological symbol is not analyzable or atomizable into any logical compound of constituent philosophical propositions. It is not only because Wittgenstein holds that there is a truth locus for philosophical truth, but also because in Wittgenstein's view (1) the philosophical propositions are elucidations of that which is presented with the symbol of the truth locus which is relevant to its truth value, and (2) the truth locus is not analyzable into any logical combination of these philosophical propositions, that Wittgenstein's system of philosophical propositions must have this holistic character. The connection of the tautological symbol with the philosophical propositions which it determines is not like that between molecular proposition and its constituent propositions. It is of an entirely different type. That is, the philosophical propositions are each only essentially incomplete glimpses of the truth "conditions" of the single truth—the tautology—which is relevant to philosophy.

The view that philosophical propositions have an entirely different nature than do genuine propositions, that the former must be understood holistically while the latter must be understood atomistically, is important for a number of reasons. For one thing, it enables one to reconstruct the positive dimension behind some of Wittgenstein's seemingly negative remarks about philosophy and philosophical propositions. For example, the view that philosophical propositions have their significance and truth only in their relationship to a larger whole means that philosophical propositions do not stand on their own. This is behind Wittgenstein's views that there are, strictly speaking, no philosophical propositions. Put negatively, Wittgenstein holds that there *are* no philosophical propositions. Put positively, Wittgenstein's view is that the unit of philosophical significance and truth is larger than the isolated philosophical proposition. The general suggestion is that, according to Wittgenstein's view, (1) there is an oddity to the philosophical propositions which prompts his own negative remarks concerning the philosophical propositions (for instance, his saying that there are none). But (2) this oddity derives from the fact that the philosophical propositions, unlike the genuine ones, must be understood holistically, that is, from the fact that the unit of philosophical significance and truth is larger than the isolated philosophical propositions. This means that (3) the positive account of the philosophical propositions must be developed in terms of their holistic character.[5]

Wittgenstein's view that his philosophical system has this holistic character is the view that the philosophical propositions which make up that system are system-bound. This result is the essential point of contact between Wittgenstein's account of philosophical systems in the first half of the present chapter and the positive account of philosophical propositions in the second half of the chapter. Wittgenstein's view that there is a truth locus for philosophical truth, when properly considered, means that the system of philosophical propositions is a unified whole. This is true in the sense that it, not the individual philosophical propositions which fill his philosophical book, is the indivisible unit of philosophical significance and truth. It is only the whole system of philosophical propositions, commensurate with the truth conditions of that single truth, which is relevant to philosophy. (This, as might be suspected, also sheds light on Wittgenstein's view that one cannot say philosophical propositions. See Chapter VIII.)

VII.5 A Comparison of the Notion of a Philosophical System in the Tractatus and in German Idealism

Wittgenstein's account of the systematic nature of philosophical truth is continuous with views which are present in the tradition of German idealism. The three dimensions of Wittgenstein's notion discussed here are the notions of a self-contained system, of a presuppositionless system, and of a system which is an indivisible whole. The first and third components are claimed by Kant for his system in the first *Critique*.[6] All three components are each present in Fichte, Hegel and Husserl,[7] and in Fichte's case, the fundamental notion in the account of these features of his system is that of a truth locus for philosophical truth.

Wittgenstein's and Fichte's fundamental concepts and views are not identical. There are, of course, basic differences between the two traditions involved which affect the specific form of their fundamental concepts and views. One of the most basic differences between the view of the *Tractatus* and that of the German idealists in general, is that in the *Tractatus* it is the system of philosophical truth which is claimed to be self-contained, presuppositionless and holistic, whereas in Fichte it is the system of philosophical knowledge to which these ideals are claimed to apply. This difference derives from the fact that in the tradition of German idealism the notion of mind and its relation to the world is regarded as the key to all philosophical insight. By contrast, the author of the system of the *Tractatus* holds that this key is the nature of logic and symbols. Thus, Wittgenstein's and Fichte's fundamental concepts and views must bear whatever differences derive from their differing views concerning the priority of the systems of philosophical truth and knowledge. Allowing for this, however, there is a "mapping" of Wittgenstein's fundamental concepts and views concerning the nature of philosophical systems onto Fichte's.

The opening theme in Fichte's *The Science of Knowledge* is that "philosophy is a science,"[8] and that "a science has systematic form [insofar as] all propositions in it are connected in one single fundamental proposition or principle and unite with it to form a whole."[9] Fichte continues: "the separate propositions of the science are not science but form a science only in the whole and through their connection in the whole."[10] Fichte stresses that the propositions which form this whole are not completely separable from the whole unit, within which alone they have their scientific character. To be sure, Fichte's account of the sense in which his philosophical propositions are inseparably united in the whole is not identical with Wittgenstein's analogous view. Whereas Wittgenstein holds that the diverse philosophical propositions do not even have significance or truth apart from their participation in the whole, Fichte only denies that these propositions have *scientific status* insofar as they are not embedded in the whole. This is one of the differences which derive from the fact that whereas Wittgenstein emphasizes meaning and truth, Fichte's emphasis is on mind and knowledge. Abstracting from these differences, however, there is a mapping of the one philosopher's view onto the other.

Fichte also holds that the nature of this whole is bound up with the view that all the philosophical propositions in this system are intimately connected with a single fundamental principle:

> A highest and absolute first fundamental principle must exist as the basis of a complete and unit-system in the human mind. From this first principle our knowledge may expand into ever so many series, each of which again may expand into series, etc., still all of them must

rest from upon one single link, which is not dependent upon another one, which holds itself and the whole system by its own power. In this link we shall possess a globe, holding itself firm by virtue of its own gravitation, . . .[11]

Fichte makes several claims in the present remark about the structure of the complete system of human knowledge,[12] but the relevant point for present purposes is that Fichte's fundamental principle plays a role in his philosophical system which is analogous to the role played by the tautological symbol in the system of the *Tractatus*. The fact that the set of philosophical propositions is based on such a single fundamental principle means that the "science" of philosophy constitutes a unity or system in a special sense. Fichte's image of the fundamental principle as a "globe" which holds the "whole system by its own power" is a particularly apt image of the role of the fundamental principle in determining the self-contained sphere of philosophical truth.

Fichte holds not only that his philosophical system is self-contained, but that it is "unconditioned" or presuppositionless.[13] His account of the unconditioned character of his system is based on the view that his fundamental principle has a unique nature:

This fundamental principle of the science of knowledge . . . is, therefore, absolutely not to be proven; that is, it cannot be deduced from a higher principle, the relation to which might demonstrate its certainty. Since, nevertheless, it is to be the basis of all certainty, it must be certain in itself, through itself and for the sake of itself. . . . All other propositions will have a mediated certainty derived from it but it itself must have immediate certainty. . . . This fundamental principle is absolutely certain; . . . You cannot inquire after its ground without contradiction.[14]

Fichte's view that the fundamental principle must be "certain in itself," that it must be "immediately certain," and so on, are analogous to Wittgenstein's view that the tautological symbol on which his philosophical system is based is self-guaranteeing, or presupposes nothing which is not supplied by the symbol itself. A closely related analogy between Fichte's and Wittgenstein's view is also displayed in the fact that Fichte says the fundamental principle of philosophy is "absolutely not to be proven." In turn, Wittgenstein says at 6.126 that the tautologies on which his philosophical system is based "must show without any proof that they are tautologies" (see Chapter II). Since Fichte's fundamental principle is claimed to determine the scope and content of his own philosophical system, and since that fundamental principle is "unconditioned" or "certain in itself" (because it presupposes nothing which is not given with the principle itself), Fichte's view is that his philosophical system is based on a pre-suppositionless or unconditioned foundation.

Fichte's fundamental principle satisfies the two conditions which characterize the tautological symbol in Wittgenstein's account, and which are the basis for Wittgenstein's notion of the truth locus for philosophical truth. Fichte holds both that (1) the set of philosophical propositions which constitute his philosophical system is based solely on this principle, and also (2) the truth of the fundamental principle itself is immediately connected with it.

The notion of a "science" or system of philosophy is the central theme of Fichte's philosophy.[15] His account of the "scientific" or systematic nature of his philosophical system involves the view that it is a self-contained, presuppositionless and holistic system. Also, his account of these features of his system involves the view that the system is defined by a fundamental principle which has properites analogous to those which characterize Wittgenstein's truth locus for philosophical truth.

Though the three basic dimensions of Wittgenstein's notion of a philosophical system are shared by Fichte's notion, and though the key concept which underlies both systems is a version of the notion of the truth locus for philosophical truth, it is worth pointing out again that Wittgenstein's and Fichte's accounts are certainly not identical. The major difference in the present connection may be that whereas Wittgenstein's key notion in his account of the nature of the foundation of his system is that of a *symbol which is self-guaranteeing,* Fichte's notion of the truth locus seems to be that of a *principle of which one can be immediately certain.* Since Fichte, with the German idealists in general, emphasizes the system of philosophical knowledge as opposed to the system of philosophical truth, his key notions reflect this fact. Thus, the principle which founds his philosophical system is not a logical entity (like the tautological symbol) which contains its own truth "conditions," but it is the notion of a principle which the mind can, in one way or another, immediately know to be certain. The details of Fichte's account of the fundamental principle and of its immediate certainty are not important here. The important point is that Fichte's fundamental principle plays a role in his system of philosophical knowledge which is analogous to the role played by the tautological symbol in Wittgenstein's system of philosophical truth.

The system of philosophical truth in the *Tractatus* lays claim to being self-contained, presuppositionless, and an indivisible whole in an especially strong sense. The fundamental views which underlie these features of Wittgenstein's philosophical system are that there is a truth locus for philosophical truth and that the philosophical propositions which constitute his system stand in a particular relation to the truth locus.

The same set of ideals are present in various combinations and forms in the tradition of German idealism. In at least one philosopher, Fichte, these three ideals are present side by side, and they are grounded in Fichte's version of the notion of a truth locus for philosophical truth. In the tradition of German idealism, the attempts to fulfill these ideals and the forms taken by the fundamental notion of the truth locus are determined by the general framework of the idealistic emphasis on mind. The German idealistic attempts to construct self-contained and presuppositionless philosophical systems have as their uniting idea the view that mind must be able by itself, and by appeal only to what is internally available to itself—to take care of everything which is required for the construction of such systems of philosophical knowledge. This uniting idea could be summed up in the slogan that mind must take care of itself. The theory which backs up this slogan involves the view that it is possible for the mind to fashion the notion of the truth locus for philosophical truth out of the nature, abilities and materials which are internally available to itself, and thereby to take care of everything which is required for the construction of such systems of philosophical knowledge.

Wittgenstein aspired to similar philosophical ideals in the *Tractatus*, and Wittgenstein's general strategy is summed up in his slogan that "logic must care of itself." The theory which backs up Wittgenstein's slogan is that the notion of a truth locus for philosophical truth can be fashioned out of the nature and anatomy of symbols. Wittgenstein's notion of the truth locus for philosophical truth is the notion of the tautological symbol which presents with itself, or shows, that which is relevant to its truth value, where that which is relevant to its truth value is that which determines the scope and content of philosophical truth. Wittgenstein's view that "logic must take care of itself" can profitably be seen as an "analytic" version of the analogous idea and strategy of German idealism.

As is pointed out early in the present book, Wittgenstein transfers the burden of the *a priori* from the self, or mind, to the symbols themselves. That is, Wittgenstein "puts the symbols themselves to work" (see II.5, "The Autonomy of Logic"). Wittgenstein takes over the highest *ideals* of the German philosophical tradition, but his strategy for fulfilling them is taken from the highest *ideas* of the "analytic" emphasis on logic, language and symbols. Wittgenstein is not an idealist, but a logicist. His treatise is not on Reason and Spirit, but on "logical philosophy." Wittgenstein *transforms* the fundamental idealist concepts and strategies into logical concepts and strategies. The differences between Wittgenstein's and the idealist's accounts of the nature of philosophical systems are, therefore, at least as important as the similarities. Wittgenstein's "analytic" strategy allows not only for more precise fulfillment of these ideals, but it also results in genuinely new sorts of philosophical views.[16]

It is especially worthwhile to consider Wittgenstein's account of the unique nature of the system of philosophical truth, and to consider the historical precedents for the notion. First, it is of historical interest since it is the only serious attempt within the analytical tradition to measure up to these ideals of the idealist tradition. Second, such a notion of a philosophical system is not taken seriously in contemporary philosophy. Even the most systematic of contemporary philosophical outlooks would probably be considered mere "aggregates" of philosophical views by Kant, Fichte, and the author of the *Tractatus*.[17] Similarly, the ideals of a presuppositionless philosophical system and a philosophical system which is an indivisible whole in the sense(s) discussed in the present section, are currently not even serious matters for discussion. Wittgenstein's notion of a philosophical system can, therefore, provide a useful counterbalance to contemporary views on the nature of philosophy. Finally, if the fundamental notions in Fichte's philosophical system are indeed analogous to those in Wittgenstein's *Tractatus,* then fresh perspectives on the possible developments of and reactions to the system may be suggested.

VII.6   The "Transcendental" Nature of Logic

The argument of the *Tractatus* is the demonstration of the substantive theses of the *Tractatus,* on the basis of that which is presented with the symbols of the tautologies and which is relevant to their truth value. It seems paradoxical, however, that these substantive philosophical views are implicit in the symbols of the emptiest of all propositions. The very idea that ontology and the account of meaning should be in any sense derivable merely from an interpretation of the tautologies, and interpretation based on a minimum of purely logical theses, seems highly implausible. The resolution of this paradox and the explanation of why Wittgenstein's program is not implausible is connected with the meaning of Wittgenstein's view that "logic is transcendental" (6.13). The feeling of paradox derives from the view that the tautologies are *empty,* while the philosophical theses which are implicit in them are *substantive.* The explanation of the sense in which logic is transcendental involves a qualification both of the sense in which the tautologies are empty, and of the sense in which the relevant philosophical theses are substantive. Whereas the preceding three sections are concerned with Wittgenstein's account of the nature of philosophical systems, the present section is concerned with his account of the nature of both the logical and the philosophical "propositions."

One might think that Wittgenstein's view that logic is transcendental is the view that the *Tractatus* contains a transcendental argument for the substantive theses of the *Tractatus,* or even that the argument of the *Tractatus* developed in the present book is a transcendental argument. However, given the standard notion of a transcendental argument, the argument of the *Tractatus* is not a transcendental argument.[18] Wittgenstein's view that logic is transcendental must be understood differently.

It is helpful in this connection to explain Kant's use of the word *"transcendental."* Kant characterizes transcendental knowledge as knowledge which pertains "not so much to objects but to our mode of knowledge of objects."[19] Kant's view is that transcendental knowledge primarily characterizes our modes of knowledge of objects, but it is consistent with this that transcendental knowledge has ramifications concerning the nature of the objects known by means of these modes or faculties of knowledge. Kant's view is, of course, that transcendental knowledge does have ramification for the nature of the known object, and his account of how there can be synthetic a priori knowledge of objects is based on this view. (Roughly, since one's faculties of knowledge affect the "form" of the known object, then insofar as one can know a priori the nature of one's representational faculties, one can also know a priori the "form" of knowable objects.)

Wittgenstein's most fundamental problems in the *Tractatus* are not problems concerning the nature of knowledge, but instead those having to do with the natures of meaning, truth and symbolic representation in general. Thus, Wittgenstein's notion of the transcendental cannot be identical with Kant's, but it is possible to construct an analogous notion of the transcendental in Wittgenstein's general terms, one defined in terms of the modes of symbolic representation as opposed to faculties of knowledge. A *'transcendental thesis'* is defined as a thesis which primarily characterizes the nature of the symbolic medium itself. As with Kant, it is consistent with this that these transcendental theses have ramifications concerning the nature of the represented entity. It is Wittgenstein's view that logic has ramifications concerning both the nature of the symbolic entity and the nature of the world, that is, the fact that certain expressions are tautologies shows "the logical form" of *both* "language and the world." Wittgenstein's view that logic is transcendental is not to be interpreted as the view that the *Tractatus* contains a standard form of transcendental argument, but as the view that the theses demonstrated in the argument of the *Tractatus* are transcendental theses. They characterize primarily the a priori nature of the symbolic medium and, derivatively, the a priori nature of the world.

The fact that the theses demonstrated in the argument of the *Tractatus* are transcendental theses in this sense is connected with the resolution of the paradox, wherein substantive theses are demonstrated to be implicit in that which is presented with the symbol of the empty tautologies. That is, the fact that the theses demonstrated in the argument of the *Tractatus* are transcendental theses in this sense means that they are *formal* theses in a certain sense. In Chapter II, section 5, two notions of formal theses are distinguished. A thesis is *formal$_1$* if it characterizes the mere perceptible propositional sign (considered in abstraction from "sense or meaning"). A thesis is *formal$_2$* if it characterizes that which is presented with a symbol which is relevant to its truth value, that is, a *formal$_2$* thesis characterizes the symbolic entity where the abstraction from "sense or meaning" is not made. The "transcendental" theses demonstrated in the argument of the *Tractatus* are *formal$_2$* theses, and formal considerations are in general opposed to substantive ones. That is, there is a sense in which the fact that the theses demonstrated in the argument of the *Tractatus* are transcendental means that they are not substantive theses at all, but are *formal$_2$* in nature. It must, however, be further explained in precisely what sense *formal$_2$* theses are not substantive.

It is among the most significant results of the argument of the *Tractatus* that the whole apparatus of the logical constants applies to those propositions whose general form is shown by the tautologies, while this same logical apparatus does not apply to the tautologies themselves. In Chapter III it is demonstrated that affirmation and negation apply only to contingent propositions, that is, to propositions which are only about the contingent structuring of objects. The logical role of negation is to construct out of one proposition another proposition which expresses an alternative logical possibility. Affirmation and negation, and the entire logical apparatus in general, apply only to those propositions which are about, or picture, the *contingent* structure of the world. The class of contingent propositions defines a class of propositions which are substantive in a clear sense. Since these propositions are contingent, each of them has a negation which expresses an alternative logical possibility. These sorts of propositions each rule something in, and rule something out, and what they rule in may or may not be the case, and what they rule out may or may not be the case. These genuine propositions are *substantive* in the straightforward sense that that which is relevant to their truth is only one logical possibility out of a range of logical possibilities. The logical constants apply only to the "genuine" propositions, to those which are about the contingent structure of the world, and it is only these propositions which make a claim in a substantive sense.

The class of philosophical propositions, the class of transcendental theses of the *Tractatus,* are not, by contrast, contingent propositions. They are not about the contingent structure of the world, but are elucidations of that which is presented with the symbols of the tautologies which is relevant to their truth value. Also, the logical constants do not apply to the tautological symbol. These transcendental results of the argument of the *Tractatus* do not, therefore, have a negation any more than does the symbolic entity, the tautological symbol, which they characterize (see III.4). It is illuminating to realize that it is the view of the author of the *Tractatus* that the philosophical propositions are among those which do have a role in the total conceptual edifice of "meaningful" language, but which, to use terminology which became popular many years after the publication of the *Tractatus,* do not have a "contrast." Though the results of the argument of the *Tractatus* have, up to the present section, been referred to as "theses," a more searching appraisal of their logical status suggests that they should be described in some fashion which does not suggest too much similarity to the genuine propositions. Hereafter, they will be referred to as the *"formal₂"* or "transcendental" results of the argument of the *Tractatus*.

The view that the philosophical propositions do not make a claim in the sense in which contingent propositions do is simply another way of expressing a view which Wittgenstein was to hold throughout his philosophical development. He held that the philosophical propositions do not express *theses*, and that the philosophical truth, whatever in particular it is, is not properly conceived as embodied in a *theory* about the world. There is, strictly speaking, no philosophical *point of view*. The idea of a point of view involves the possibility of alternative possible points of view, and since there is no possible alternative to what the tautologies express (even the contradictions express the same thing; see III.4), there is no possible alternative to the transcendental results of the argument of the *Tractatus*. According to Wittgenstein, any suggestion that there is a philosophical or logical point of view fails to comprehend fully the vast difference between the kind of significance possessed by the genuine propositions on the one hand, and the logical and philosophical ones on the other.

It is also important to keep in mind that in addition to these negative views (for instance, that there is no philosophical point of view), there is a positive account of the philosophical propositions. A transcendental result does not express a point of view about the world, but in a sense it expresses the "conditions of the possibility" of there *being* a world (and of any symbolic representation of that world). The philosophical propositions are elucidations of that which is presented with the symbols of the tautologies which is relevant to their truth value; they are elucidations of the logic of language and the world, not theses about the contingent features of the world. One important dimension of the positive account of the philosophical propositions is that, though the philosophical propositions have no negation, they do stand in a special connection with the tautological symbol, and therefore with the *logic* of langue and the world.

For the purpose of the present section it is, however, the negative rather than the positive account of the philosophical propositions which is important. The view that the philosophical propositions are not substantive and do not express a point of view is manifested in many ways in the text of the *Tractatus*. Within the remark at 6.13, for example, the remark that logic is transcendental is preceded by the remark that "logic is not a body of doctrine. . . ." It is also significant that at 6.12 Wittgenstein states that that which is shown by the fact that the logical propositions are tautologies is the *"formal*-logical properties of language and the world" (my emphasis). The use of the word *form* to characterize that which is expressed by the logical and philosophical propositions is indicative of Wittgenstein's view that these philosophical propositions do not express substantive theses or constitute a point of view. That is, the philosophical propositions express only the "formal" properties of the world.

In the Introduction to the present book it is claimed that in the argument of the *Tractatus* all the "substantive" views of the *Tractatus* must be rigorously demonstrated, and this claim is reiterated throughout the book. Since it has now been explained that the philosophical propositions are not substantive, it might appear that this claim must be taken back. There are however, two different senses of the word "substantive" involved. There is a sense in which the point of view in the Introduction to the present book, the point of view one has prior to the production of the argument of the *Tractatus,* is not held in the present section. That is, it is not held after one has completed the argument of the *Tractatus.* The point of view in the Introduction to the present book is, in effect, the point of view of common sense. From that point of view the results of the argument of the *Tractatus* are substantial in the sense that the sentences which express philosophical propositions do not express the beliefs of common sense, nor even the sorts of things which are formulated in the commonsense framework. From that commonsense point of view, the suggestion that these sorts of propositions are even relevant to the understanding of the world is quite *surprising.* These philosophical sentences constitute a clear *addition* to the commonsense framework. This does not affect the fact that one of the consequences of the argument of the *Tractatus* is that there is an important sense in which these propositions are non-substantive and are not theses. One must distinguish these remarks which are made within the self-contained system of logical philosophy from the remarks made from the commonsense point of view. There is no contradiction in the view that those propositions which are substantive in the sense defined by the commonsense framework are nonsubstantive in the different sense defined from within the system of logical philosophy of the *Tractatus.*

If Wittgenstein's view is correct, then the proper way to understand philosophical progress, the progress one makes in the course of the argument of the *Tractatus,* is not that it involves the replacement of one point of view—the commonsense point of view or one particular philosophical point of view—by another point of view. Rather, philosophical progress consists in recognizing that "philosophical truth" is not embodied in a point of view, a set of substantive views about the world, at all. Philosophical progress consists in the recognition that the philosophical point of view is as empty as the tautological symbol which defines it. And so, in comparison with genuinely substantive points of view, it "shrinks to a point without extension." "(See 5.641 where Wittgenstein makes an analgous, and related, point about the 'self' of solipsism.)"

The original paradox which prompts the present discussion is that the argument of the *Tractatus* purports to be a demonstration that certain substantial theses are implicit in the symbol of the empty tautologies. The more careful examination of the nature of these philosophical propositions reveals, however, that they are not substantial propositions or theses at all, but that they are transcendental or *formal*$_2$ in nature. It has only been the error of traditional philosophy that these sorts of propositions have been viewed as substantial, that the philosophical truth has been assumed to constitute a point of view. The very idea that the program of 6.12 is paradoxical, the program of founding a philosophical system on an empty tautological symbol, itself presupposes views about the nature of the philosophical propositions. The paradox is dissolved by the fact that the philosophical propositions are not substantive theses; they do not constitute a point of view on the world.[20]

VII.7   Throwing Away the Ladder

In one of the most famous remarks in the *Tractatus* Wittgenstein writes:

> 6.54   My propositions serve as elucidations in the following way: anyone who understands me eventually recognizes them as nonsensical, when he has used them-as-steps to climb up beyond the them. (He must, so to speak, throw away the ladder after he has climbed up it.)

The view that one must "throw away the ladder after one has climbed up it" is often thought to have a predominately mystical meaning. It is not my purpose to deny that there is a mystical, or a personal, dimension to this remark, but rather to emphasize that there is a logical dimension to this view which has not been recognized. This logical dimension has to do with the specific role of the tautologies in the argument of the *Tractatus,* and with the real status of the tautologies in Wittgenstein's system.

Because the tautologies are so central to the argument of the *Tractatus,* it is disconcerting that Wittgenstein's attitude to the existence of the tautologies seems, at best, ambiguous:

1. "Tautology and contradiction are . . . the disintegration of the combination of signs" (4.466).

2. One "can actually do without logical propositions" (6.122).

3. "There are no such things as analytic *propositions*" (*NB,* p. 21).

On the one hand the description of the argument of the *Tractatus* seems to place great weight on the tautologies, but on the other hand Wittgenstein sometimes seems to deny that there are any tautological propositions. There is a paradox here which lies at the very foundation of the argument of the *Tractatus.* The basic points required for the resolution of this paradox are, in fact, implicit in the account of the logical propositions developed in Chapters II and III of the present book.

The unique status of the logical propositions consists in the fact that they are true (or false, in the case of contradictions) by virtue of that which is presented with their symbols. Those elements which are presented with their symbols are genuine propositions which are not functioning normally, but are acting as exemplars of genuine propositions in general. The effect of this is, however, to shift the emphasis from the logical propositions to the genuine ones. That is, it initially looks as if the logical propositions, specifically the tautologies, are propositions which are distinct from the genuine propositions. They have the unique nature that they are true by virtue of that which is presented with their symbols. However, since that which is presented with the tautological symbol which is relevant to their truth value is the general propositional form, and since the general propositional form is *already possessed by the genuine propositions themselves,* it follows that that which is relevant to the truth value of the tautologies is already possessed by the genuine propositions themselves. The tautologies are not needed, therefore, for any descriptive purpose. A logical propositional symbol is, at best, superfluous for these purposes.

The case against the existence of the logical propositional symbol is, however, even more radical than this. It is pointed out at III.4 that all of the logical apparatus *breaks down* in the case of the logical propositions. It does not even make sense to affirm or negate a tautology or contradiction, or to say that they are true or false. Affirmation, negation, truth and falsity, and so on—all have to do with the genuine contingent propositions, the propositions which say something. Affirmation of a proposition is the affirmation *that* objects in the world are or are not in some contingent state. Truth and falsity are defined in terms of the genuine propositions, that is, a proposition is true if it says that certain objects are, or are not, in a certain contingent state, and they are, or are not, in fact in that state. Such notions as affirmation, negation and truth go to the heart of the notion of a propositional symbol. So there is, strictly speaking, no tautological symbol.[21]

One must distinguish, of course, between the logical propositional sign and the logical propositional symbol. The former is a mere perceptible pattern of noises or marks on paper, and nothing in the preceding discussion constitutes an objection to the existence of this perceptible pattern. The perceptible propositional sign is something which is made by human beings, and it is, therefore, a purely factual question whether there is a logical propositional sign. A symbol, however, is a combination of a sign *and a meaning,* and it is a conceptual truth that there is no tautological meaning, that one can not affirm or negate a tautology. Following III.4, the sense in which tautology and contradiction are cases of "the disintegration of the combination of signs" is that in these expressions propositional signs are combined (for instance, disjoined) in accordance with a pattern which normally results in the production of a more complex propositional *symbol* (a molecular propositional symbol). But in this case, though the combination does result in the production of a molecular propositional sign, *it does not result in the production of any propositional symbol.*

Unfortunately, this result seems to destroy the foundation of the argument of the *Tractatus.* If it is Wittgenstein's view that there really is no tautological symbol, and that it does not really make sense to say that a tautology is true, then how is one to understand the claim that the argument of the *Tractatus* is a demonstration of that which is presented with the symbol of the tautology, and which is relevant to its truth value?

Wittgenstein's interpretation of the logical propositions commits him to the view that there is, strictly speaking, no tautological symbol. Thus, Wittgenstein must give up the view that the argument of the *Tractatus* is correctly described as a demonstration of that which is presented with the symbol of the tautologies which is relevant to their truth value. Contrary to the appearances, however, the argument of the *Tractatus* is not without a foundation. That which is taken away in one form reappears in another.

Since the general form of a proposition is possessed by every genuine proposition there is *a symbol* whose general *formal*$_2$ features are demonstrated in the argument of the *Tractatus*. Only it is not the particular symbol which one initially thought it to be. At first sight it seems that there are two sorts of propositional symbol—both genuine and logical ones. But Wittgenstein's interpretation of the logical propositions shifts emphasis away from the logical propositions and toward the genuine (contingent) propositions. *It is Wittgenstein's final view that talk about the logical propositional symbols is only an oblique way of talking about the logical features of genuine propositional symbols.* The concept of the tautological symbol is a convenient fiction whose real significance is cashed in terms of the general *formal*$_2$ features of the genuine propositional symbol.

Talk about the logical propositional symbol is really an oblique way of talking about the logical features of the genuine propositional symbol. This means that the description of the argument of the *Tractatus* as a demonstration of that which is presented with the symbols of the tautologies, and which is relevant to their truth value, is only an oblique way of describing the demonstration of an aspect of that which is presented with the genuine propositional symbol which is relevant to its truth value. One must take this detour through the fictitious logical propositional symbols since there is no direct way to isolate the general *formal*$_2$ features of the general propositional symbol from its particular representational content, that is, from the representation of the particular state of affairs which is relevant to its truth value.

There is, however, an indirect mode of access to the general form of a proposition. Since the course of the argument of the *Tractatus* itself forces one to conclude that there really is no tautological symbol, one must redescribe this mode of access to the general *formal*$_2$ features of genuine propositions. It is the very fact that genuine propositions "disintegrate" (in the sense explained above) when combined in certain ways which "shows" their general *formal*$_2$ features.

The argument of the *Tractatus* is not itself challenged by the challenge to the existence of the tautological symbol. The point is only that the nature of the foundation of the argument of the *Tractatus* is somewhat different than it at first sight appeared to be. This means simply that the nature of the foundation must be *redescribed*. In fact, 6.12, the guiding remark in the present interpretation of the *Tractatus,* can be *rewritten* in terms of Wittgenstein's own account of the tautologies, as cases of the disintegration of the combination of signs. Instead of saying that the fact that certain expressions are tautologies shows the logical form of language and the world, one must rewrite 6.12 as 6.12':

> 6.12' The fact that certain specific combinations of genuine propositions are cases of the disintegration of the combination of signs shows the formal-logical-properties of language and the world.

The fact that one must rewrite the program of 6.12 in this way once the full account of the logical propositions becomes clear only means that one must give up a certain description of the argument, a description which has proved convenient and which may even have been believed to be accurate prior to and during the actual production of the argument of the *Tractatus*. That is, the employment of the fiction that there is a tautological symbol whose truth conditions are elucidated in the argument of the *Tractatus* is, as it were, a "logical ladder" which is thrown away after one has climbed it.

The logical dimension of the view that one must throw away the ladder after one has climbed it derives from the fact that the argument of the *Tractatus* is initially described as a demonstration of that which is presented with the tautological symbol which is relevant to its truth value. Yet the results of the argument itself force one to conclude that there really is no tautological symbol and that, in fact, one has really been talking obliquely about the general logical features of the genuine propositional symbol.

The view that one must "throw away the ladder after one has climbed it" means that there are two "perspectives" within the *Tractatus,* one prior to, and one subsequent to having thrown away the ladder. So the text must be interpreted accordingly. The existence of these two perspectives correlates with the alleged ambiguity in Wittgenstein's view about the existence of the logical propositional symbol. There is no real ambiguity in Wittgenstein's view about the logical propositions, that is, it is not as if he never succeeded in deciding this question one way or the other. His view is that there simply are no logical propositional symbols, that there is no tautological symbol. Those portions of the text which suggest the contrary are from the perspective prior to having "thrown away the ladder." That is, they involve the employment in the argument of the *Tractatus* of the fiction that there is a tautological symbol, in order to demonstrate the general *formal$_2$* features of genuine propositions. 6.12 is the description of the argument of the *Tractatus* prior to having thrown away the ladder, while 6.12' is the revised description, the description which is more appropriate once the consequences of the argument are made explicit.

Wittgenstein's view that there really is no tautological symbol, and the reasons why this is not a difficulty for the argument of the *Tractatus,* have been explained. There are, however, additional repercussions to this view, illuminating the meaning of the view that there is no tautological symbol. The meaning cannot merely be that one must remove those sentences which express logical propositions from the list of "acceptable" propositions, since the view that there really is no tautological symbol does not mean that the tautological *sign* is not useful or meaningful in some general sense. If the logical dimension of the view that one must throw away the ladder, that there really is no tautological symbol, is not a mere verbal manipulation, then it should involve some important connections with other fundamental views of the *Tractatus.* Specifically, this redescription of the foundation of the argument of the *Tractatus* should have repercussions concerning the redescription of the results of the argument of the *Tractatus.*

What is the real meaning, vis-à-vis the results of the argument of the *Tractatus,* of the fact that there is no tautological symbol and that it does not make sense to say that a tautology is true? A genuine proposition has truth conditions in the genuine sense of the expression, that is, that which is relevant to the truth value of a genuine proposition is the existence or nonexistence of some state of affairs, the being-in-a-contingent-state-of-objects. The view that there is no tautological symbol, and that it does not make sense to say that a tautology is true, means that the results of the argument of the *Tractatus* are nothing like the truth conditions of the genuine propositional symbol. That is, the philosophical propositions demonstrated in the argument of the *Tractatus* do not express anything like facts about the world. But this is the same view which has been developed from another direction in the preceding section, the view that the results of the argument of the *Tractatus* are transcendental or *formal₂* in nature. The fact that there is no tautological symbol means that the results of the argument of the *Tractatus* are nothing like the truth conditions of a genuine proposition, that these philosophical propositions do not constitute a "body of doctrine," a point of view.

Philosophical insight does not consist in the acquisition of some new doctrine or viewpoint, but simply in coming to think logically. Thinking logically does not even mean thinking in accord with the empty tautologies, for there are, strictly speaking, no tautologies. It means simply thinking in the only way in which one can think, the only way because the alternative is empty. There is no alternative. This provides a new way of understanding why Wittgenstein concluded the preface of the *Tractatus* with the remark:

> The second thing in which the value of this work consists is that it shows how little is achieved when these problems are solved.

The fact that there is no tautological symbol is another manifestation of the same conclusion which is reached in the preceding section, that strictly speaking there is *nothing* which one learns in "philosophical enlightenment." The positive way to put this, however, (there is always a positive way) is that philosophical enlightenment leaves one with the form of the world before one: utterly simple, definitely structured, a unified system of possibilities, and presuppositionless, because there is *nothing* else that it could be.

CHAPTER VIII

The Theory of Communication:
The Sayable and the Unsayable

Perhaps the most famous, the most quoted, and the most misunderstood remark in the *Tractatus* is the concluding remark: "Whereof one cannot speak, thereof one must be silent." The "whereof" here is understood to include the philosophical propositions, including those which constitute the argument of the *Tractatus* itself. The concluding remark of the *Tractatus* is, prima facie, a strongly anti-philosophical remark which challenges not only the argument of the *Tractatus,* but philosophy itself. But what does Wittgenstein really mean by saying that one cannot *say* philosophical propositions, that one cannot "put them into words?" In order to understand his view, it is necessary to present Wittgenstein's account of what it is to say something. For he does hold that we can say genuine propositions, that they can be put into words. Wittgenstein's view that one can say genuine propositions is also connected with his view that one can give a *scientific* account of what is involved in such communication. These two related accounts are developed in the first section. In section 2 the positive account of the significance of the philosophical propositions is expanded, since this is a necessary preparation for the discussion in section 3 of why one cannot say philosophical propositions. It is important to emphasize from the beginning that though there is a sense in which one cannot say philosophical propositions in Wittgenstein's account, there is another sense in which one *can* say them, and it is an important part of the present chapter to develop this positive account of philosophical communication.

VIII.1   The Theory of Communication for Genuine Propositions

a. Expressing a Thought in Words

The basic account of how different linguistic subjects communicate concerning matters of fact is built on the account of the genuine propositional symbol in sections 1 and 2 of Chapter V. On that account the propositional symbol is composed of a perceptible propositional sign and an imperceptible thought, the latter being the meaning component of the proposition. The key point for present purposes is that these perceptible and imperceptible structures are connected with each other by means of what are normally very complicated transformation rules. The role of these transformation rules in the process of communication is to act as coding and decoding rules.

A communication between two linguistic subjects is successful if one linguistic subject imparts its thought to another linguistic subject. One cannot directly perceive the other's thought, but one can perceive the perceptible propositional sign produced by the other. This is only helpful though, if the perceptible sign is connected with the hidden thought or meaning in a definite way, and if the different linguistic subjects connect the sign and the thought in the *same way*. In other words, the perceptible propositional sign produced by the other is only helpful to me in reconstructing its thought if the rules by means of which the other *encoded* its thought in the sign are the same rules which I use to *decode* the sign. A shared language is possible only if the different subjects in the linguistic community share the same set of encoding/decoding rules.

There are two points which must be emphasized about the account. First, it is important that these coding rules are the sorts of rules which can be *mechanically applied*. If they could not be mechanically applied, then it would not be the *system* of rules which connects perceptible signs with thoughts which determines how one is to understand a given perceptible propositional sign. In that case, there would be no *explanation* in terms of that system of rules of how these different linguistic subjects manage to transmit their thoughts to each other. And the system of rules is supposed to explain the transmission.

The second point, one which is easily overlooked, is that this theory of communication presupposes the theory of meaning developed in Chapter VI. First, this account of communication presupposes that the perceptible sign and the imperceptible thought are structures, where the meaning is unambigously determined by the structure of the thought. That is, this theory of communication presupposes that the imperceptible structure is a meaning locus. If the imperceptible structure were not a meaning locus, something which determines its own meaning, then the explanation of how I come to construct the correct structure upon observing the other's perceptible propositional sign would not explain how I come to have the correct thought, to grasp the correct meaning.

These two points are connected. What must be explained is how a thought or meaning is transmitted from one linguistic subject to another. This involves a chain which begins in one subject and ends in another. The communication is successful if the end points of the chain are the same thought. The requirement that the coding rules used by each subject be capable of being mechanically applied is the requirement that the relevant links in the chain are determined by the system of rules, not by the decisions, inclinations or whims of the linguistic subjects. The requirement that the end points of the chain are meaning loci is the requirement that the meaning of the imperceptible structure is determined by these structures themselves, not by the decisions or whims of the linguistic subjects involved.

If either the application of the transformation rules or the meaning of the imperceptible structure were not determined by the system, then the system would not *explain* how thoughts or meanings are transmitted from one linguistic subject to another. If, for example, the system requires that the linguistic subject just knows how to apply the rules, or just assigns the correct meaning to the imperceptible structure, then the system needs an homunculus to run it, and that is not acceptable in a genuinely explanatory account.

If, however, the rules can be mechanically applied to produce the same imperceptible structure upon observation of the same perceptible sign, and if the meaning of the imperceptible structure is determined by it itself, then one has an explanation in terms of this system of how thoughts or meanings are transmitted. This is Wittgenstein's view. Every step in the chain—from the meaning of the imperceptible structure in one linguistic subject, through the transformation rules and perceptible sign, to the meaning of the imperceptible structured produced in the other linguistic subject—is determined. There is a mechanical system here.

b. An Account of Communication Within the Limits of Natural Science

The same sort of account is shared by contemporary theoretical linguists. Katz recognizes, indeed emphasizes, that his own views on the nature of communication are similar to the views of the *Tractatus*.[1] He holds that "natural languages have an underlying reality very different from their surface form."[2] This underlying reality, as in the view of the *Tractatus* (see V.1), involves a "structure far richer than any facsimile of the physical structure of sentences."[3] Katz continues:

> The distinction between logical form and grammatical form, between the thought or meaning of a sentence and its overt phonetic or orthographic shape, is an appearance-reality distinction. The distinction is, as I shall try to show, both a tenable one and as central to the understanding of language as the distinction between surface continuity and underlying discreetness to the understanding of matter.[4]

That is, the simplified structure of the perceptible sentence is called its "grammatical form," while the richer imperceptible structure which underlies it is the "thought or meaning." Katz calls this richer structure the "logical form" or even the "logical body"(!) of the sentence.[5] Furthermore, Katz holds that the surface and underlying components are connected by means of complex underlying rules. Katz, with others such as Fodor and Chomsky, is committed to providing an account of these rules, an account of "the principles by which the speakers of a language perform the encoding and decoding of thought in linguistic communication."[6] The complete account includes an account of both the systematic transformation of thoughts into perceptible propositional signs, and also the systematic transformation of perceptible propositional signs into thoughts. What is to be explained in this account is (1) the ability to *express* one's thoughts in perceptible form, and (2) the ability to *understand* the perceptible propositional signs of a language, that is, to assign them the correct meaning, to pair them with the correct thought.

Katz's account of communication is essentially the same as Wittgenstein's. The thought is encoded in a perceptible sign by means of the encoding rules, and another linguistic subject uses the same rules to decode the sign, to produce the thought. The differences are only in the terminology, and in the fact that Katz is less clear about the more philosophical concepts which are presupposed by the account (for example, he is less clear about the details of the notion of the meaning locus).

But Katz is committed not only to the view that this is the correct account of the process of communication. It is also his view that one can provide a "science of language," a scientific theory which includes a perspicuous representation of this process.[7] Katz, along with Chomsky, Fodor and others, is committed to the view that one can give a perspicuous representation of these underlying thought structures, and also a clear and complete statement of the coding rules by means of which thoughts and perceptible signs are "transformed" into one another. In the present section, for simplicity, the focus is narrowed to one part of this "science," specifically, to that part of communication which is involved in constructing the thought or meaning upon observation of the perceptible propositional sign. The same points could be extended to the other parts of this "science."

It is on this point that Katz believes himself to part company with the view of the *Tractatus*. Katz must deal with the fact that Wittgenstein later, in his *Blue Book* and *Philosophical Investigations,* rejected this view that there is an "underlying conceptual reality" to language. Katz argues that there is in fact a flaw in the view of the *Tractatus,* but that the "later" Wittgenstein misperceived its real source. According to Katz, it is the view of the *Tractatus* that the imperceptible thought "is irretrievably concealed behind a phonetic or orthographic disguise," that it is "so successfully hidden by its outward form in speech or writing" that it "become[s] suspicious, taking on the air of queer or occult entities."[8] Katz concludes:

> I think that to have dropped the idea of an underlying conceptual reality in language to which the study of philosophical logic addresses itself was both a tragic mistake and an unnecessary one. It was unnecessary because it was not the only assumption that might have been given up to avoid an admittedly unacceptable occultism. One could retain the idea that language has an underlying conceptual reality and instead drop the view that it is completely inaccessible.[9]

In short, the later Wittgenstein rejected the view that there is an underlying meaning component to language but, according to Katz, that is not the problematic view of the *Tractatus*. The real error of the *Tractatus* is the view that since the meaning component is underlying and "imperceptible," it must be inaccessible. What Katz means by this is that the *Tractatus* held that the meaning component is inaccessible to scientific treatment, not to speakers of the language in ordinary communication.

One must, to be precise, distinguish between two different senses in which a thought is "retrievable." First, a thought is *retrievable*$_1$ if linguistic subjects competent in the relevant language can reconstruct the thought upon observation of the perceptible propositional sign. Second, a thought is *retrievable*$_2$ if it is possible on the basis of empirical data and scientific procedures to produce a representation of the thought, and of the processes by means of which it is transformed into a perceptible propositional sign. The two are not unrelated, that is, the latter involves the scientific account and description of what goes on in the former. Katz himself sees the two as intimately related. In his discussion about whether a "science of language" is possible, Katz writes:

> Still, there is Wittgenstein's claim that overt grammatical form totally disguises the underlying logical body of a sentence. Why should we believe that we can penetrate the disguise? One reason for us to believe we can penetrate phonetic or orthographic clothing is that speakers of a natural language do exactly this when other speakers successfully communicate with them.[10]

It is Katz's view that the imperceptible thought or "logical body" of the sentence is *retrieved*$_1$ by any speaker of a language in ordinary communication, and that this is evidence that the thought can be *retrieved*$_2$ by empirical-scientific means. (If this is evidence at all it is probably *very* weak evidence, but this is not my present concern.)

It is Katz's program to produce an empirically supported scientific theory which includes a description of these rich underlying thought-structures, of the simplified perceptible structures, and of the principles by means of which they are transformed into one another. Katz holds that "it is possible to infer the form of the thought beneath the outward form or surface grammar so long as the inference is of the same sort as that which led to our knowledge of atomic structure.[11] The imperceptible structure of language is no more irretrievably hidden than is the imperceptible structure of physical objects. The same pattern of empirically based theoretical explanations which is applicable in the latter case is also applicable in the former.

It is Katz's interpretation that the view of the *Tractatus* is similar to his own, since they both hold that the meaning of the proposition is embodied in an underlying thought or "logical body" which is structurally richer than the perceptible part of the proposition. But he holds that the view of the *Tractatus* is different from his own view in that Wittgenstein believes the underlying thought is *irretrievable₂*. But is Katz correct that it is the view of the *Tractatus* that thoughts are irretrievable by scientific procedures?

Katz quotes part of 4.002 to support his interpretation that it is Wittgenstein's view that the thought is "irretrievably hidden":

> Language disguises thought. So much so, that from the outward form of the clothing it is impossible to infer the form of thought beneath it, because the outward form of the clothing is not designed to reveal the form of the body, but for entirely different purposes.

This remark, taken by itself, does seem to support Katz's view. But Katz should quote more, or all, of 4.002. His selection is preceded immediately by these remarks:

> Everyday language is a part of the human organism and is no less complicated than it.

> It is not humanly possible to gather immediately from it what the logic of language is.

And it is followed in 4.002 by the remark:

> The tacit conventions on which the understanding of everyday language depends are enormously complicated.

Wittgenstein does not hold that it is completely impossible to infer the form of the thought from the outward form of the clothing. It is only his claim that it is not possible to do so *immediately*. This is a very moderate remark, and it is one with which Katz would certainly agree. Note that Wittgenstein is evidently speaking of *retrieval₂* by scientific means, not *retrieval₁* in ordinary linguistic competence, since the latter is normally immediate. One hears or reads a sentence, and normally one understands it immediately. It is only the construction of a scientific representation and account of the underlying thought which cannot be done immediately.

Second, the final remark in 4.002 suggests that the reason why one cannot immediately infer the form of thought from the outward form of the clothing has to do with the "enormously complicated" conventions which underlie the use of everyday language. But this would suggest that the difficulty of inferring the form of thought from the form of the perceptible sign is the same as that involved in any very complicated phenomenon. That is, it is based not on any *absolute* impossibility, but on the *quantitative* difference in complexity between human language and the sorts of simpler phenomena which are more immediately accessible to scientific theorizing. Wittgenstein's view at 4.002 is only that the process of inferring the form of thought from the "outward form of the clothing," that is, the process of producing a detailed scientific description of the imperceptible component of the proposition, and of the rules which connect it with the perceptible component of the proposition, is very difficult.

It is not customary to view 4.002 of the *Tractatus* as even addressing the question of whether a *scientific* theory language is possible. However, the author of the *Tractatus* is very much concerned with the question of whether such a science of language is possible. The context of 4.002 includes Wittgenstein's discussion of the "limits to the much disputed sphere of natural science" (4.113). The 4.1's also include the remark:

> 4.116 Everything that can be thought at all can be thought clearly.
> Everything that can be put into words can be put clearly.

The context of remarks in the early 4's of the *Tractatus* reveals that it is Wittgenstein's view that an account of how thoughts are put into words falls within the "limits of the much disputed sphere of natural science." It is one of his major claims that a scientific theory of the process involved in communication is possible, and his sketch of the basic form of this process is exactly that proposed by Katz and other contemporary psycholinguists under the different titles of "linguistic competence" and "linguistic performance."

Wittgenstein does not deny that thoughts can be *retrieved*$_2$ by scientific procedures. Rather than differing with Katz in this matter, what Wittgenstein has actually done in the *Tractatus* is to sketch what might be called the *conditions of the possibility* of *retrieval*$_2$. The differences are only that Wittgenstein is more concerned with the *philosophical foundations* of the science of language and of the limits of science in general, while Katz is more concerned with the actual production of the science of linguistic communication.

If the present interpretation of Wittgenstein is correct, then Katz must pay a price. But he gains as well. What he gains is the recognition that Wittgenstein's view in the *Tractatus* is even closer to his own than he had thought. The price Katz must pay is that he must give up his explanation of why the author of the *Philosophical Investigations* rejects the view of the *Tractatus*. It is the desire to find such an explanation of why Wittgenstein came to reject the view of the *Tractatus*, and therefore rejected Katz's type of view, that causes Katz to read a flaw into the *Tractatus*, a flaw which Katz takes pains to avoid in his own view. The explanation of why the author of the *Philosophical Investigations* rejects the view of the *Tractatus* lies elsewhere.

The reasons why Wittgenstein later rejected this account of the *Tractatus* lie, of course, in the philosophical concepts which form the foundation of the account. First, the author of the *Philosophical Investigations* questions the notion of the *mechanical* application of a rule. (See Wittgenstein's discussion of following a rule, *Philosophical Investigations*, par. 85). Second, Wittgenstein came to question the validity of the notion of the "conceptual intermediary" itself. That is, it is not the view that the conceptual intermediary is inaccessible that Wittgenstein came to regard as the mistaken view, but it is the notion of the meaning locus itself which he came to regard as problematic. Unfortunately these criticisms of the view of the *Tractatus* cannot be pursued further here, since the task of the present work is merely to reconstruct the views of the *Tractatus*.[12]

The claim that a purportedly scientific theory is subject to such philosophical criticism may seem odd. This feeling of oddity is, it seems to me, dispelled with the appreciation of the remarkable quantity and nature of the work which has had to be done by theorists such as Katz, Chomsky and Fodor in order to develop the outlines of the *science* of linguistic competence and performance. Quite profound concepts and views have had to be developed in order to make the idea of such a science appear to be anything more than mere speculation. For this is not an ordinary science; it is an attempt to give a scientific account of an area at the very core of the phenomenon of *meaning*. No concept is more philosophically puzzling than this one (see Chapter VI, section 4). If any science could be expected to be so intimately interconnected with fundamental philosophical views, it is this one (see Chapter VI, section 3). Though Katz and others emphasize the philosophical illumination provided by their accounts, it is ironic that they are not so eager to admit that this indicates that their theories are also vulnerable to philosophical (conceptual) criticisms. If the Wittgenstein/Katz theory of communication is true, great philosophical insight into the nature of language and mind is gained. But whether these theories are true or not cannot be decided solely on scientific considerations. The theory presupposes a theory of meaning and what could be called a theory of understanding (a theory of what it is for a person to follow a rule).[13] Whether this theory of communication is true must be decided, at least in part, on these philosophical grounds. Some of the objections to his science of language are not, as Katz would have us believe, misconceived a priori objections to an empirical science.[14] The shoe is really on the other foot. The so-called empirical science of Katz, Chomsky and Fodor is really *a disguised philosophical theory,* and an appreciation of Wittgenstein's view brings this out.

VIII.2 The Significance of Philosophical Propositions

Though Wittgenstein holds that one can say genuine propositions, he holds that one cannot say *philosophical* propositions, that one cannot put them into words. But before his account of the ineffability of the philosophical propositions can be given, it is necessary to expand the positive account of the significance of the philosophical propositions. This preliminary task is the aim of the present section.

It is important to point out at the outset that Wittgenstein's positive remarks on the significance of the philosophical propositions are very sketchy, even by the standards of the *Tractatus.* Perhaps this is because he really did not feel that one could give much of a positive account of them. He does, however, offer some hints which, within the context of other views of the *Tractatus,* suggest the lines along which a positive account could be developed. This account has the added virtue that it makes Wittgenstein's account much more relevant to contemporary discussions in the theory of meaning.

In the account of genuine propositions the perceptible part of the symbol, the propositional sign, has been distinguished from its imperceptible meaning component. A meaningful genuine proposition is composed of both a perceptible propositional sign and an imperceptible thought or meaning locus. It is clear that the philosophical propositions involve perceptible propositional signs; philosophical books and discussions are full of them. But philosophical propositions do not involve an imperceptible thought or meaning locus. This is obvious since philosophical propositions are not about the contingent structure of the world, and the account of the meaning locus involves the view that its pictorial nature involves its *structural identity* with that which it is about. Whatever the positive account of the significance of the philosophical propositions, it is not, as it is in the case of the genuine propositions, that the perceptible propositional sign "goes through" an imperceptible intermediary which itself immediately means or "touches" that which it is about. The philosophical proposition does not involve *both* a perceptible and an imperceptible component. As odd as it sounds, a philosophical propositional sign is not the perceptible expression of a thought. The only component of the philosophical proposition is its perceptible component. The question concerning the significance of the philosophical propositions is, therefore, a question of how the perceptible propositional sign of a philosophical proposition, without the aid of any accompanying intermediary, has "significance." (Because of these differences, we reserve the term "meaning" for genuine propositions.) In the ensuing discussion the perceptible propositional signs of philosophical propositions and genuine propositions are, for the sake of convenience, called, respectively, *'philosophical propositional signs' and 'genuine propositional signs'*.

Wittgenstein's positive account of philosophical propositional signs is implicit in 4.112:

> 4.112 Philosophy aims at the logical clarification of thoughts. Philosophy is not a body of doctrine but an activity. A philosophical work consists essentially of elucidations.

This remark includes several points. First, a philosophical work consists of elucidations. A philosophical proposition is called an elucidation in order to distinguish it from fact-stating propositions. This point is the same as that made in the preceding chapter, that philosophical propositions do not state theses or constitute a point of view. These views are made explicit here in the remark that philosophy is "not a body of doctrine." The chief addition to these now familiar views is that philosophy is an *activity* (presumably the activity of producing elucidations). This view is that the significance of philosophical propositions is constituted by their role in patterns of human activity.

Philosophical propositional signs, in the sense discussed here, include not merely the sorts of propositional signs which occur in the argument of the *Tractatus,* but all propositional signs which are not about the mere contingent structure of the world. That is, they include propositional signs which pertain to ethical, aesthetic, religious and other such matters. If Wittgenstein has any positive account of the "significance" of propositional signs, of propositions other than the genuine propositions, it is that they have a role in the development and/or maintenance of certain characteristic activities.

The account of the significance of the philosophical propositional signs in terms of their embeddedness in patterns of human activity can be illustrated by reference to the case which is of special interest here, the case of the philosophical propositional signs produced in the argument of the *Tractatus.* The production of the argument of the *Tractatus* is itself an activity which can have a significant impact on the course of certain other human activities, that is, on both those activities which are purely philosophical and those other activities (scientific, religious, and so forth) which have philosophical presuppositions. The argument of the *Tractatus* gives illumination into the nature of genuine propositions and, in connection with this, into the nature of facts. Specifically, genuine propositions are about the contingent structuring of objects, and facts are constituted by the existence of this contingent structuring of objects. If the propositions of the natural sciences must have factual content, then the meanings of the propositions of the natural sciences must be cashed in terms of their connection with the mere contingent structure of the world. This sets the "limits" of the "much disputed sphere of natural science" (4.113). In other words, it is a consequence of the argument of the *Tractatus* that one can construct a scientific account of any phenomenon where the subject matter of the purported science consists merely in the contingent structuring of objects. Likewise, one *cannot* construct a scientific account of any phenomenon which does *not* consist in the mere contingent structuring of objects. In the preceding section, one example of these consequences is described in some detail. It is Wittgenstein's view that since the phenomenon inolved in the process of *communication* consists in perceptible and imperceptible structure which are systematically transformed into one another, there can be a scientific account of the phenomenon of communication. Thus the whole set of activities, experimental and intellectual, which are directed toward the production of this science are, in principle, capable of fulfillment. These activities can, in principle, lead to the production of a scientific representation of a real phenomenon in the world.

On the other hand, it is conceivable that the basic concepts which are presupposed by certain other alleged investigations of nature cannot be cashed in terms of this sort of factual content. For example, some philosophers or psychologists might conceive the phenomenon of will to involve entities in the world which are somehow necessarily connected with their effects, that is, other distinct entities in the world. (This particular example is chosen since Wittgenstein makes some relevant remarks on the phenomenon of will at 6.37 and 6.373.) One can imagine debates within this self-proclaimed "scientific" community over the question of whether the *will*, conceived in that way, is an object, an event, or something else, and also over the manner, conceptual or experimental, in which this debate must be resolved. It is, however, a consequence of the argument of the *Tractatus* that all genuine propositions are contingent, and are about the mere contingent structuring of objects. The so-called science of the will is, therefore, not a genuine science at all. Neither side in the debates within this pseudo-scientific community can be correct, since the basic concepts which they share in common are empty of factual content. All of the activities of this pseudo-science are absolutely incapable of any successful fulfillment. These sorts of examples illustrate how the activity of producing the argument of the *Tractatus* can impact on other activities in a variety of ways, how certain activities can be warranted, and others undercut, by the results of the argument of the *Tractatus*. The important point here, however, is that the significance of the philosophical propositions does not involve representations or pictures of the world, but is instead defined in terms of their role in or impact on certain types of activities.

Wittgenstein's account of the significance of the philosophical propositional signs in terms of the activities in which they are embedded must be more precisely defined. Different philosophers could accept the view that the significance of the philosophical propositional signs involves their role in certain activities, but disagree completely about what their role, or significance, is in particular. Wittgenstein has a very specific view about the significances of the philosophical propositions. That is, the "true" philosophical propositions, those warranted by the argument of the *Trac-*

tatus, tie into human activity in a very definite way. Since the philosophical propositions produced in the argument of the *Tractatus* are elucidations of the mere empty tautological symbol, this emptiness must characterize that level of human activity which embodies the significance and truth of the philosophical propositions. Thus, the argument of the *Tractatus* does not warrant any particular activity or other. The philosophical truth, according to the argument of the *Tractatus,* is very abstract, and this abstractness must characterize that level of human activities which embodies the "significance and truth" of philosophy. The "truth" of philosophy, the significance of philosophical propositional signs, consists in nothing more or less than their support for *consistent activity.* The relevant notion of a consistent activity is a very specific *philosophical* notion. It is not the ordinary notion of an activity which is consistent, in the sense that the activities of practicing for a performance in a particular way, and then performing the activity in that way is consistent, or in which the activity of hitting a home run and then running the bases in the wrong direction is inconsistent. The relevant philosophical notion of a consistent activity is the notion of an activity which is consistent with a priori natures of language and the world. The activities associated with the production of a science of linguistic competence and performance are consistent with the a priori nature of language and the world. This is true insofar as the fundamental concepts which rationalize these activities are concepts which are warranted by the account of genuine propositions and facts in the argument of the *Tractatus.* The activities of the above-mentioned pseudo-science of the will are inconsistent in this philosophical sense with the nature of the world, since they are guided by concepts which are empty of factual content (or, perhaps, they are not guided by genuine concepts at all).

The present positive account of the significance of the philosophical propositional signs fills in the positive dimension of this view. That is, the view that (1) the significance and truth of philosophical propositions do not involve representations, but instead involve roles in human activities, and that (2) it is not even any particular activity but only *consistent* activity which is warranted by the argument of the *Tractatus,* are a further development of the view that the philosophical propositional signs do not constitute a point of view on being. Nevertheless, it is extremely important to make the fundamental concepts which underlie this view fully explicit.

The fundamental concepts and views which define the relevant difference between the genuine and the philosophical propositional signs are developed in the first two sections of Chapter V, and are repeated in the preceding section. The genuine philosophical sign has a meaning insofar as it is *systematically* connected with a thought or meaning locus. This is insofar as it is itself a structure which is mechanically mapped onto a perfect picture—a perfect representation of that which it is about—by means of some mediating projection or transformation rules.

The view that the genuine propositional sign has this special systematic (mechanical) connection with its meaning is a central view of the *Tractatus.* Also, the view that the philosophical propositional signs do *not* satisfy these conditions for a systematic connection with their significance is the basic substratum of the account of the significance of the philosophical propositions. The present positive account of the significance of the philosophical propositional signs is only properly understood if it is synthesized with this most basic view. The complete positive account of the significance of the philosophical propositional signs is a synthesis of the view that their significance is constituted by their role in certain activities with the view that they are not connected with their significance by means of a system of rules which can be mechanically applied.

Because there is a set of transformation rules which mechanically connect the genuine propositional sign with its meaning, it is possible to isolate the genuine propositional sign from the whole pattern of activities within which it exists, without isolating it from its meaning. The meaning of the genuine propositional sign is a function of its structure, plus these transformation rules. This is why it makes sense to say that the genuine propositional sign is a unit or atom of meaning, and it is also why it makes sense to call it a representation of what it is about.

The fact that the significance of the philosophical propositional sign is not a function of its structure, plus any mechanically applicable transformation rules, means that the philosophical propositional sign is not a representation; it is not a unit or atom of significance. The significance of the philosophical propositional sign must be understood *holistically.* The essence of the holistic view is that one cannot isolate an individual meaning or significance for the relevant proposition, but must understand its significance only in terms of its embeddedness in a larger whole.

The important questions are, therefore: What is the unit of significance in the case of the philosophical propositions? And what is the manner of connection of the philosophical propositional sign with that which embodies its significance? If anything can be considered to be the unit of significance in the case of the philosophical propositions, it can only be the whole pattern of relevant activities within which the philosophical propositional signs are embedded. The point of saying that it is *embedded* in the pattern of activities is that it has its significance only insofar as it fulfills its role in this context of activities. Outside the context of this embeddedness it does not have the relevant significance, because there is and can be no system of rules by means of which it can be connected with its significance. This is an important theme in subsequent discussions.

The connection between a propositional sign and its significance according to the holistic conception can be illustrated by analogy. In Wittgenstein's view, the connection between a philosophical propositional sign and its significance is not like that between a genuine propositional sign and its meaning (its meaning locus), but it is more like the connection between a note in a musical theme and its beauty. A note which is beautiful within the context of a developing musical theme may not be, by itself, beautiful. The musical note may be the concrete building block of a musical piece, but it is not the unit of aesthetic value. Even if it is, within the context of some actual musical piece, said to be beautiful, it is in its surroundings that it has this beauty. The musical note only has its beauty within the context of the developing theme. This note, in that context, contributes to the beauty of the whole, and in that context it is *itself* heard as beautiful. But there is no system of rules which connects it with its beauty for the reason that its beauty is *not a function of* it itself, or of its structure, but it is a function, as it were, of the note only when it is taken together with the developing whole.

One can isolate the philosophical propositional sign from the relevant flow of activities, but it is a mistake to think that in this isolation it has any philosophical significance. This contrasts with the genuine propositional sign which, because there is a set of transformation rules which mechanically connect it with its significance, *can be isolated from the flow of activities within which it occurs, without thereby losing its connection with it meaning.* The type of mistake one makes in isolating a philosophical propositional sign from the relevant flow of activities is analogous to that which one makes if one is overcome by the beauty at some point in a musical piece, and one tries to recapture the moment of beauty by playing the note which occurred at the moment of beauty, by itself, over and over again.

The beauty of a musical piece, like philosophical significance and truth, lies in the flow, not in the frozen moment. The philosophical propositional sign, like the note in a developing musical theme, only has its significance, or its beauty, insofar as it is a dissolving stage in the flow.

It is important to recognize that in addition to the merely negative stage of Wittgenstein's views concerning the philosophical propositions (that there are no philosophical propositions, that one must throw away the ladder, and so forth), there is a positive dimension to these views. His negative account involves, for example, the view, that the philosophical propositions do not involve representations, that they do not constitute a point of view, and that they are not systematically connected with their significance. The positive account of their significance involves the view that they are essentially embedded in certain relevant patterns of activity where it is the whole developing activity, not the sign itself, which is the unit of significance. For example, Wittgenstein's *positive* reconstruction of the view that there are no philosophical propositions is definable in these terms. The formulation according to which there are, strictly speaking, no philosophical propositions seems very negative, but it is in reality the view that the unit of significance in the case of the philosophical propositions is altogether larger than and different in nature from the unit of meaning in the case of the genuine propositions.

The positive account of the sense in which one must throw away the philosophical propositions after one has used them is definable in similar terms. The view that the philosophical propositional signs are embedded in the relevant context of activities, without being systematically connected with them, means that the philosophical propositional sign, by itself, is not an indicator of its significance. Its role is, instead, discharged insofar as it is a mere passing stage in the flow of activities. One must "throw away" the philosophical propositional sign after one has used it, just as one must let go of a note in a musical theme after one has heard it. The philosophical propositional sign and the musical note are not the relevant units of significance, but they serve their purpose only insofar as they promote, without interrupting, the flow which surrounds them and within which only they have significance.

Most commentators have recognized that it is insufficient simply to dismiss the philosophical propositions as "nonsense," if this is supposed to mean that they have no significance of any type. Thus it has been said that if the philosophical propositions are nonsense, then they are very "important" nonsense. Though this sort of positive *value judgment* is in the right spirit, it is not philosophically illuminating. Such a value judgment only indicates the need for a philosophically illuminating positive account of the significance of the philosophical propositional sign. This positive account is constituted by the synthesis of the views that its significance is constituted by its role in certain patterns of activity, and that it is not systematically connected with that which embodies its significance. The synthesis results in the view that the significance of the philosophical propositional sign must be understood holistically, where the relevant whole is in the whole developing pattern of relevant human activities. The holistic conception of the philosophical propositions means three things—that one cannot speak of the *individual* meaning of the philosophical propositional signs, that their significance is derivative and incomplete, and that this is what is behind the negative remarks that there are no philosophical propositions or that one must throw them away after one has used them. The appearance of a negative tone in Wittgenstein's remarks concerning the philosophical propositions does not indicate that they have no significance in any sense. Instead, it corresponds precisely with the contemporary views, perhaps the central theme in Dummett's reflections on meaning, that if a language is correctly characterized holistically, one cannot give a certain type of systematic account of the significance of the propositional signs of that language.[15]

The proper way to understand Wittgenstein's program to place *limits* on language (that is, to enclose genuine propositions within certain limits, and to place philosophical propositions outside those limits) is not that it is concerned to exclude dogmatically certain sorts of propositions from significant language, and certain "things" from "the world." Instead it is to delimit those sorts of language which can be *regimented* in certain ways from those sorts of language which cannot be regimented in these ways. Wittgenstein's program is to separate those parts of language (and life) whose meaning is amenable to a certain kind of systematic account, from those parts whose significance is not amenable to that sort of account. In short, he has a positive account of the meaning of the genuine propositions, and it is the sort of account which is appropriate to that sort of proposition whose meaning is characterized atomistically. Also, he has a positive account of the significance of the philosophical propositions, and it is the sort of account which is appropriate to that sort of proposition whose significance is correctly characterized holistically.

The notion of "holism" has appeared twice in the account of the philosophical propositions. In VII.4 Wittgenstein's philosophical system is called "holistic" in the sense that the various philosophical propositions which constitute his system cannot be separately regarded as significant or true. The reason given for this view at that point is that, since the tautological symbol is the unified truth which determines the scope and content of the philosophical system, the philosophical propositions which express that which is presented with the symbol of the tautology, which is relevant to its truth value, are each only essentially incomplete glimpses of that single unanalyzable philosophical truth. That is, that there is some whole within which only the philosophical propositional signs have significance is clear at VII.4, but it is not there determined what positive nature this whole has. In the present section the positive account of the significance of the philosophical propositional signs is given, and this positive account consists in the view that their significance is embodied only in the whole pattern of relevant activities. The present section provides the account of the concrete embodiment of the whole which is glimpsed, as it were, under another description at VII.4. Thus, the whole system of philosophical propositions is not, as it might have been wrongly conceived at VII.4, a whole system of representations. Rather, the relevant whole is the whole system of relevant human activities.

It is important to point out that the view that the philosophical propositions must be understood holistically is based on the a priori account of the tautologies. However, the view that the concrete embodiment of this whole is human activities is not a priori. The latter is Wittgenstein's hypothesis about the particular nature of the relevant whole. That it has this particular character is not demonstrated from any more basic logical views.

The train of development in the present section is this: It is first pointed out that whereas the meaning of genuine propositions involves representations, the account of the significance of the philosophical propositions involves their embeddedness in certain sorts of activities. But it is then urged that if this contrast is to be properly understood, one must make explicit the fundamental concepts which underlie it. It is pointed out that the fundamental concepts and views which underlie the view that genuine propositions involve representations of that which they are about, are those concepts and views which characterize the atomistic conception of language. The view of the *Tractatus* is generally regarded as atomistic, so this is no great surprise, though the connection of the atomistic conception with the view that the genuine proposition involves a meaning locus and other elements is not generally recognized. The more novel suggestions made in the present section are that (1) the fundamental concepts and views which underlie Wittgenstein's positive account of the significance of the philosophical propositions are those which characterize the holistic conception of language, and (2) the relevant whole is the whole developing pattern of human activities within which the philosophical propositional signs are embedded.

The notion of holism has clearly become, according to the present interpretation, a major concept in the reconstruction of Wittgenstein's views. The problem with the present account as an interpretation of the *Tractatus* is that though atomism is recognizable at an early stage in the pages of the *Tractatus,* there is no place in the *Tractatus* where Wittgenstein even mentions holism. Since the positive interpretation of the significance of the philosophical propositions is constructed on the basis of this view about the holistic character of the philosophical propositions, it may be that the present interpretation presents too positive an interpretation of this portion of the *Tractatus.* That is, it may be that Wittgenstein developed the views that the meaning of genuine propositions must be understood atomistically, and that this means one can develop a certain kind of positive account of their meaning. It could be that though he had a vague idea that philosophy and the significance of philosophical propositional signs, has to do with the activity of philosophizing, he simply had not at that time thought very hard about this portion of his view, and he had not explicitly formed the conception of a holistic view of language.

This point may very well be correct. Nevertheless, it is worth developing this holistic interpretation of the philosophical positions for several reasons. First, it affords insight into Wittgenstein's struggles concerning the differing natures of genuine and philosophical propositions in terms of a contemporary discussion in the theory of meaning. It also enables one to develop a positive reconstruction of Wittgenstein's distinction between sensical and nonsensical propositions in terms of the contemporary distinction between (1) language which must be understood atomistically and (2) language which must be understood holistically.

Second, Wittgenstein's view of language in the *Philosophical Investigations* is that it is homogeneously holistic in nature. This view cannot be argued in detail here, but the key view which underlies the holistic conception of the meaning of propositions is that the philosophical propositional sign is not connected with its meaning by means of any system of rules which can be mechanically applied. This view is one important dimension of Wittgenstein's view in the *Philosophical Investigation,* that "uttering a sentence is not operating a calculus according to definite rules" (*PI,* par. 81; see also par. 80). The view of the *Philosophical Investigations* that the meaning of linguistic expressions is bound up with this role in a form of life is the view that language is holistic, where the relevant whole is the form of life within which linguistic expressions are embedded.

The claim is not that the views of the *Tractatus* and the *Philosophical Investigations* are the same. Quite the contrary, according to the view of the *Tractatus,* genuine propositions involve a meaning locus and must be understood atomistically, while the view of the *Philosophical Investigations* is that language must be understood holistically. The point is only that the view of the *Tractatus* may have a place for a holistic conception of a very narrow class of propositions, the philosophical ones, and in the *Tractatus* the treatment of the philosophical propositions suffers by contrast with that of the genuine propositions.

Despite these qualifications concerning just how explicitly Wittgenstein in the *Tractatus* grasped the fundamental concepts which underlie his positive account of the significance of the philosophical propositions, it is clear that he regarded their significance as bound up with the activities of life, not with representations. This is why in the closing pages of the *Tractatus,* in the discussion of various philosophical, religious and ethical matters, the notion of life suddenly becomes prominent (see, for example, 6.4312, 6.521). This sudden concern with the problems of life, and the point that such problems cannot be solved by natural science, is not a mere personal statement of the author which is unconnected with the detailed conception of language developed in the book. The fact is that Wittgenstein regards himself as having separated those propositions whose meaning involves representations, from those whose significance is constituted only in the activities of life. The odd twist in Wittgenstein's view is that whereas the meaning of genuine propositions involves true or false representations of the world, the significance and "truth" of philosophy is not embodied in true representations, but in a "true" life, a life which is in harmony with the logic of the world.

VIII.3   Wittgenstein's Doctrine of Silence

One of the primary purposes of the present book is to counter the interpretation that Wittgenstein holds a strongly negative view about the nature of philosophical propositions and activity. One of those remarks, one however which seems most difficult to square with the positive interpretation of the *Tractatus*, is the concluding remark of the book:

7   Whereof one cannot speak, thereof one must be silent.

This remark expresses what might be called Wittgenstein's "doctrine of silence." That is, it is not merely Wittgenstein's view that one must discard philosophical propositions after one has used them, but that one must be *silent* about such matters. Philosophical matters "cannot" even be "put into words" (6.522). Wittgenstein's doctrine of silence is a doctrine concerning the possibility of the communication of philosophical matters by means of words. This is why the positive account of the doctrine of silence is not automatically given with the positive account of the significance of the philosophical propositions in the preceding section. Even if one admits that philosophical propositions are significant in that sense, it appears that the significance of philosophical propositions cannot be communicated from one individual to another.

Wittgenstein's doctrine of silence is one of the most famous doctrines of the *Tractatus*, and it has had more to do with the interpretation that Wittgenstein's view is anti-philosophical in some deep sense, than any other single view of the *Tractatus*. Carnap and others have, for example, held that it is inconsistent with this doctrine to write philosophical books or engage in philosophical discussions.[16] Wittgenstein's view does not, however, have these negative consequences concerning the practice of philosophizing, but it is actually connected with a very positive view about the nature of philosophical activity. The positive account of the doctrine of silence is described in the present section, and it is built upon the positive account of the significance of the philosophical propositions described in the preceding section. The two key points in that discussion, that the significance of the philosophical propositional signs is bound up with human activity, and that the philosophical propositional sign is not connected with its significance by means of any system of rules, are also key points in the present section. The connection of the doctrine of silence with the view that the significance of the philosophical propositions is bound up with their embeddedness in human activity is discussed first. But, as in the preceding section, the later discussion reveals the key view that philosophical propositions are not connected with their significance by means of any system of rules.

The significance of the philosophical propositional signs is constituted by their role in the development or maintenance of certain relevant patterns of characteristic activities. Therefore, since there is a sense in which one's activities are one's own alone, one can no more communicate philosophical illumination to another than can one perform his activities for him. One can give another one's words, but not one's actions. And since philosophical illumination is embodied only in the relevant activities, one cannot transmit to another one's philosophical understanding. Another individual can, of course, participate in the same activities, and one individual might even stimulate another to enter into the philosophical activity. But then whatever illumination the latter achieves is a result of his own activity and is embodied in his own activity. The significance of a philosophical propositional sign cannot, therefore, be *transmitted* from one individual to another.

Just as one level of Wittgenstein's account of the significance of philosophical propositional signs is derivative from their intimate interconnection with human activity, so also the fact that one level of his account of the reason philosophical significance cannot be communicated is derivative from this same connection with human activity. The real meaning of this view is not, however, fully appreciated unless the fundamental concepts and views which underlie it are made fully explicit. These fundamental concepts and views can be made fully explicit by answering the following question: "Even if the significance of philosophical propositional signs is constituted by their role in certain activities, and there is a sense in which one's actions are one's own alone, why cannot acquaintance with someone's relevant patterns of activity or with the products of this activity—philosophical propositional signs—convey certain 'semantic information' which is relevant to the significance of philosophical propositional signs?" The key ideas which are needed in order to answer this question are developed in the account of how a thought is communicated by means of words in the first section of the present chapter.

The most important point for our present purposes is that there is a *systematic* connection of a specific type between the genuine propositional sign and its meaning. The systematic connection between the genuine propositional sign and its meaning involves the views that (1) the meaning of the genuine propositional sign is embodied in a structure (the structure of the meaning locus), (2) the perceptible propositional sign is itself a structure, and (3) there is a set of rules which mechanically transform the former into the latter and vice versa. The account of how meanings are communicated by means of perceptible propositional signs is built upon the account of this systematic connection. Because the connection between the perceptible sign and its meaning is captured in a set of transformation rules, a linguistic subject who possesses these rules can "retrieve," or understand, the perceptible propositional sign produced by another linguistic subject. That is, upon observation of a perceptible propositional sign produced by another individual, one employs one's own set of transformation rules to construct one's own meaning locus. The communication is successful if one's own meaning locus has the same structure, and therefore embodies the same semantic information, as the other's meaning locus.

The philosophical propositional signs are not, by contrast, about the mere structure of the world, and this means that their significance cannot be embodied in an underlying thought structure. The conditions required for a systematic connection between the philosophical propositional sign and its significance are not satisfied, and so the conditions required for the communication of this significance are not satisfied. That is, since the account of how a thought is "put into words" and is "retrieved" by a linguistic agent competent in the relevant language involves the view that this linguistic agent possesses a set of rules, which constitute the systematic connection between the perceptible "words" and the underlying thought, no such $retrieval_1$ is possible with regard to philosophical propositions. It is not, therefore, possible for one individual to retrieve "philosophical meanings" upon observation of the perceptible philosophical propositional sign produced by another individual. The philosophical propositional sign is simply not a usable perceptible indicator of its significance in the way in which the genuine propositional sign is a usable perceptible indicator of its meaning. The employment of perceptible propositional signs to communicate meanings is possible in the case of fact-stating propositions, but not in the case of philosophical propositions. This means that *there cannot be a common language of philosophy in the sense in which there is a common language concerning mere matters of fact.* There is no set of rules whereby different philosophers can systematically decode the propositional signs produced by other philosophers. The appearance that philosophical "insights" are communicated or transmitted by means of philosophical propositional signs is, therefore, an illusion.

Wittgenstein opens the *Tractatus* with the remark:

> Perhaps this book will be understood only by someone who has himself already had the thoughts that are expressed in it—or at least similar thoughts—so it is not a textbook.

The claim that the *Tractatus* will only be understood by one who has himself had similar thoughts is not a mere personal remark which is unrelated to the detailed account of language in the *Tractatus*. It is a consequence of the view that philosophical propositional signs are not systematically connected with their significance, and that, therefore, one is *on one's own* in understanding these philosophical propositional signs in a way in which one is not on one's own in understanding the propositional signs of the factual sciences. To understand a book of philosophy, to achieve philosophical insight, one must do the work, that is, engage in the philosophical activity oneself. Wittgenstein's view that one cannot put philosophical matters into words does not mean that one should not write philosophical books. It only means that since philosophical significance is not systematically connected with the philosophical propositional signs, these philosophical books cannot be conceived as textbooks. In other words, they cannot be conceived as books which contain information which can be mechanically retrieved if one is in possession of the relevant transformation rules. There are, and can be, no such sets of transformation rules. Wittgenstein's view is not anti-philosophical, but it is the view that philosophical understanding is of necessity a very personal achievement.

It is now clear that Wittgenstein's doctrine of silence does not commit him to the view that the normal sorts of philosophical activity are fundamentally incoherent in any way. But even this account does not do full justice to Wittgenstein's view of the positive nature of philosophical activity. This view that philosophy is a personal matter in the sense described above is consistent with the view that *there is an intersubjective dimension to philosophical activity*. It must, however, be an intersubjective dimension which is qualified in an important way. The view that one cannot communicate philosophical significance is developed upon the basis of a very specific account of the nature of communication. Wittgenstein's view that one cannot communicate philosophical significance by means of words involves the view that there is no system of rules which connect the philosophical propositional sign and its significance. Let us call this notion of communication, which involves this sort of connection between a propositional sign and its significance, "*communication₁*." It does not follow from the fact that one cannot *communicate₁* with another individual that one individual cannot have a philosophical *influence* on their individuals. That is, if there can be certain types of connections between human lives which are not that sort of systematic (mechanical) connection, then one can define a second notion of communication. It is consistent with Wittgenstein's doctrine of silence that one can communicate philosophical significance in this second sense.

A subject S_1 *communicates₁* with a subject S_2 if (1) S_1 possesses a certain meaning locus M_1 and transformation rules R, (2) S_1 transforms M by means of R into a perceptible sign P, (3) S_2 observes P and possesses the same rules R which are used to transform P into M_1. Communication involves a chain which begins in the one self and ends in the other, and the communication is successful if the end points of the chain—the meaning loci—are identical. The means by which the same meaning locus is generated in the "receptive" self involves a perceptible sign which is produced by the "productive" self. This same general schema must apply to *communication₂*, but the nature of the end points and of the connection of the end points with the perceptible sign is entirely different. In *communication₂*, one subject influences another by means of a perceptible propositional sign. But the end points of the successful communication are not a pair of meaning loci within the two selves, *they are relevantly similar patterns of activity in which the two selves participate.*

Second, the account of how one subject generates a similar pattern in the other does not involve reference to any set of rules which each possesses and which mechanically connect the two meaning loci involved. Instead it involves reference to *the similarity of kinship of the two free selves involved.* ("One touch of nature makes the whole world kin." *Troilus and Cressida*). The account of how *communication₂* is possible rests not on systems of encoding and decoding rules which the various selves possess, but on the fact, which can not be explained in terms of any more basic system, that these selves just tend to react in similar ways. ("Explanations come to an end somewhere," *PI*, par. 1). The two selves are *free* in *communication₂* insofar as they are not bound by any mechanical system of coding rules and structures which determine what they mean. The two selves understand each other because they are what they are (react as they do), and they are similar. There is no mechanical system in *communicating₂*.

It is the view of the *Tractatus* that there are two fundamentally different types of language—one atomistic and one holistic—and that there are, therefore, (1) two fundamentally different types of communication, and (2) two fundamentally different types of account of the conditions of the possibility of communication. If a language is properly understood as atomistic in nature, then it is possible to *communicate₁* the meanings of the propositions of that language. If, however, a language is understood holistically, then it can only make sense that the significance of the propositional signs of that language are *communicated₂* from one self to another. The account of the conditions of the possibility of *communication₂* must be developed without reference to any system of rules which connect the propositional sign with its significance, and thus is what makes the account of the conditions of the possibility of *communication₂* such a challenge. The whole problem with understanding how significance is communicated if a language is understood holistically is based on the incommensurability of the propositional sign with its significance in such a conception. Since there is no systematic connection between the propositional sign and its significance in a holistic conception of language, it is difficult to see how the relevant significance can be transmitted from one self through the propositional sign to the other self. In fact, the metaphor that meaning or significance is passed from one self to the other *through* the propositional sign is an appropriate metaphor for *communication₁*, but not for *communication₂*. The key insight needed to understand how *communication₂* is possible is that the incommensurability of the propositional sign with its significance must be made up for by the commensurability, or similarity, of the two selves with each other. The two selves, without guidance by any rules, just react to that propositional sign in similar ways.

It is imperative to emphasize that the reason why one must develop entirely different sorts of accounts of meaning or significance and communicability for genuine and philosophical propositions ultimately derives from the fact that what they are "about" is entirely different. It is because the genuine propositions are about the mere structure of the world that their meaning can be embodied in a structure, in a meaning locus, and it is because its meaning can be embodied in a structure that there can be a systematic connection between its propositional sign and its meaning. It is because of the facts that the philosophical propositions are not about the mere structure of the world, and that they thus do not satisfy the conditions which are required for a systematic connection between the propositional sign and their significance, that the accounts of significance and communicability which apply to them must be entirely different from that which applies to the genuine propositions. In short, the account of both meaning or significance and communicability, which one must adopt, are not independent of the most fundamental philosophical questions concerning the nature of the "world" or "being." The view of the *Tractatus* that language is heterogeneous in nature (and all the consequences which derive from this) is derivative from his view that *"being"*, what we must talk about, is heterogeneous.

It is pointed out in the concluding remarks of the preceding section that the account of the significance of the philosophical propositional signs in terms of the holistic view of language may be too positive as an interpretation of the *Tractatus* itself, as it was actually conceived by Wittgenstein at the time of its writing. The same might be said of the positive portion of the account of the communication of philosophical propositional significance developed in the present section. There are, however, several reasons for developing the outline of the notion of *communication₂* here.

First, as it was pointed out in a related context in the preceding section, Wittgenstein's "negative" remarks concerning the philosophical propositions are not to be understood to mean that he wishes to deny dogmatically that the relevant phenomena have any sort of validity at all. These remarks are concerned with segregating those phenomena which can be regimented in a certain way from those which cannot. Wittgenstein's remarks that philosophical propositions have no sense and that they cannot be communicated must, therefore, be subscripted. The fact that philosophical matters cannot be *communicated₁* does not mean that one cannot develop an account of how they can be communicated in some other sense. The different subscripts do not distinguish between a completely coherent and a completely incoherent account (a sensical and a nonsensical account), but between an account which is scientific in a certain sense and one which is not. The important questions are, therefore: In what sense can philosophical matters be communicated? How much can one say about this type of communication? and Do the fundamental concepts which underlie this type of communication require that it is other than a scientific type of account? The fact that in the holistic conceptions of language there is no systematic connection between the philosophical propositional sign and its significance only means that one cannot give a certain type of account of how philosophical significance can be communicated. Whether one can give any type of account at all, and if so, what form it must take, involve one in questions concerning the nature of the fundamental concepts which underlie the notion of a scientific account, and in the question of whether science, conceived in that way, is the measure of all things. As is now clear, Wittgenstein's negative remarks in the *Tractatus* concerning the philosophical propositions are best viewed as promisory notes for the development of the fundamental concepts which underlie the accounts of those sorts of phenomena lying outside the "limits of the much disputed sphere of natural science." The sketch of the conditions of the possibility of *communicating₂* in the present section is, from the point of view of the *Tractatus,* a sketch of such nonscientific accounts of a type of phenomenon. It is an account which must be nonscientific since it is about a type of phenomenon which cannot be regimented in the way required by a scientific account.

Second, even if Wittgenstein did not in the *Tractatus* explicitly grasp the notion of *communication₂* or explicitly hold that philosophical matters can be *communicated₂,* his account in the *Philosophical Investigations* of how all communication is effected is more in harmony with the account of *communication₂* than it is with that of *communication₁.* It is obviously beyond the scope of the present section to develop the view of the *Philosophical Investigation* in any detail. However, there are two key views which underlie the account of *communication₂,* and these are present in the *Philosophical Investigations.* The first is the view that there is no set of rules which can be mechanically applied and which connect a propositional sign and its meaning. In the *Philosophical Investigation,* Wittgenstein writes:

> All this can only appear in the right light when one has attained greater clarity about the concepts of understanding, meaning, and thinking. For it will then also become clear what can lead us and did lead me to think that if anyone utters a sentence and *means* or *understands* it he is operating a calculus according to definite rules. (par. 81)

Here the author of the *Philosophical Investigations* rejects the view which he had held in the *Tractatus* with regard to genuine propositions: that the account of how one means or understands a perceptible propositional sign involves a systematic connection, constituted by definite rules which can be mechanically applied, between that propositional sign and its meaning (see also par. 80).

The second idea which underlies the account of *communication₂* is that instead of operating such a calculus, the various selves just tend to react in similar ways, and this idea is found in several ways and places in the *Philosophical Investigations*. In the discussion of how a teacher communicates the application of a mathematical formula to a pupil Wittgenstein writes that "the effect of any further *explanation* depends on his reaction" (par. 145). It is also the idea which is behind the view of the *Philosophical Investigations* that the foundation on which language and communication are built "is not opinions but a form of life" (par. 241; see also par. 242). Even if it is true that Wittgenstein did not, in the *Tractatus,* have the concept of a holistic conception of language, there may be a path from (1) the view of the *Tractatus* that the significance of the philosophical propositions is constituted by the activities of life which surround them, to (2) the view of the *Philosophical Investigations* that the significance of *all* propositions is constituted by their role as a form of life. That is, it may be that subsequent to the completion of the *Tractatus,* Wittgenstein recognized that it is not sufficient to dismiss the philosophical propositions as nonsense. He was then led to develop the holistic conception of the philosophical propositions, and whether correctly or incorrectly, and for whatever reason, he was then led to extend the holistic conception to language in general. If the present interpretation is correct, then the author of the *Philosophical Investigations* found himself in the difficult position of having to fashion an account of the philosophical foundations of all communications, out of the conditions about which in the *Tractatus* he had said "one must be silent."

Wittgenstein's doctrine of silence concerning philosophical matters is, essentially, a doctrine about the impossibility of communicating philosophical significance by means of words. But this is not the purely anti-philosophical doctrine that it may appear to be. It certainly does not mean that one should not produce philosophical sentences or books. That activity can have great significance for the ones who engage in the philosophical activity themselves. Nor does it mean that one cannot influence another by one's philosophical words. The point is only that since the conditions of the possibility of *communication₁* are not satisfied, there is no *mechanical* system here.

This positive account of the possibility of philosophical communication explains why Wittgenstein is consistent when he presupposes that, in fact, some sort of philosophical communication is possible. He claims in the preface to have been stimulated by the "great works" of Frege, and by the "writings" of Russell, and his doctrine of silence quite rightly does not prevent him from writing a more positive remark concerning the significance and communicability of philosophical matters:

> Here I am conscious of having fallen a long way short of what is possible. Simply because my powers are too slight for the accomplishment of the task.—May others come and do it better.

Wittgenstein not only assumes that others can be stimulated by his writings, but he even calls upon others to redo the system of the *Tractatus*. The negative tone of the remarks with which Wittgenstein concludes the *Tractatus* might be brought into line with the more positive tone with which he opens the book, had he concluded the book with the following remark (which is consistent with his views):

> 7.001 Whereof one must be silent, thereof one must oneself do a great deal of work.

Summary of the Central Views of the *Tractatus*

It would be impossible to state all of the important results of the argument of the *Tractatus*. But it may be useful to single out some of the more important ones here. The following remarks are not intended as substitutes for the formulations in the text, but only as reminders of some of those formulations.

1. The logical operations are given a new definition by means of the 'fundamental idea'. Namely, they are those operations on propositions which result in propositions, but do not result in the production of any new sense (my $sense_1$).

2. The multiplicity of logical constants are reducible to the structural features of genuine propositions in general, that is, the general propositional form is "the sole logical constant."

3. The logical propositional symbol is a presentational symbol in the sense that it presents with itself that which determines its own truth value. (In the final analysis, however, there is, strictly speaking, no logical propositional symbol. See section VII.7).

4. Since that which is relevant to the truth value of the logical propositions is the general form of genuine propositions, and since the statement of that general form both constitutes the "whole philosophy of logic," and determines the answer to any logical question, it is possible, in principle, to answer all such questions "without more ado." In other words, unlike physics and psychology, for instance, which are always subject

to revision in the light of new data, it is possible in principle to bring philosophy to a close, to solve "all the problems" (preface, *Tractatus*) and to determine that they are *all* of the problems. The tautological symbol is a truth locus for logical (philosophical) truth.

5. The subject matter of genuine propositions is external to its symbol, and this means that it is not possible to represent what that subject matter is in itself. That is, what that subject matter is in itself is beyond the limits of representation.

6. The genuine propositional symbol has pictorial form, that is, it involves a thought which is perfectly structurally identical with the relevant state of affairs. Though it is not possible to represent what the subject matter of propositions is in itself, it is possible to represent how that subject matter is structured. How things are in the relevant state of affairs is literally internal to the propositional symbol, and so it is within the limits of representation.

7. The genuine propositional symbol is a presentational symbol, but not in the same sense as the logical propositional symbol. The thought component of the genuine propositional symbol presents with itself the conditions of its own meaningfulness. The thought is a meaning locus.

8. The perceptible component of the genuine propositional symbol is merely the perceptible manifestation of the thought or meaning. So all accounts of the meaning of the proposition which, like Russell's view in both the "Lectures," and in the introduction to the *Tractatus,* emphasize the perceptible dimensions of language, are merely accounts of the perceptible "image of the truth."

9. Since the perceptible propositional sign is connected to the meaning locus by means of a system of rules which can be shared by different linguistic subjects, and which can be mechanically applied, it is possible for different linguistic subjects to communicate matters of fact by means of perceptible propositional signs.

10. Whereas the account of the meaning of genuine propositions is atomistic, the account of the significance of the philosophical propositional signs is holistic.

11. Since philosophical propositional signs do not satisfy the conditions mentioned in 9, they cannot be communicated by means of words in that sense. However, the possibility remains open for alternative accounts of philosophical communication.

12. The limits of natural science include any accounts of phenomena which can be cashed in terms of the warranted notion of factual content. For example, important parts of both the phenomenon of meaning and of the communication of thoughts can be given scientific accounts. But other parts of the phenomenon of meaning and of the communication of philosophical propositions cannot be given such a scientific account, since they do not involve merely contingent structurings of objects in the world.

13. It is not the least important fact about Wittgenstein's views that they are deduced on the basis of the *Grundegedanke*-inspired interpretation of the tautologies, for this means that they have the status of *logical* views. For example, that the genuine propositional symbol has pictorial form, that the genuine propositional symbol is a *picture* in this sense, is a logical view in a non-trivial sense. Similarly, what *form* must be taken by any account which falls within the limits of natural science is also determined by logic.

14. Since these views are logical views in the sense defined in the text, philosophical truth does not constitute a body of doctrine or a point of view on the world. It is, for example, a matter of logic that the general form of meaning and the world is as it is. There is no possible alternative to its being as it is.

15. Since the core of Wittgenstein's system is an elucidation of that which is presented with the tautological symbol which is relevant to its truth value, the system is self-contained, presuppositionless and an indivisible whole in a logically significant sense.

Concluding Remarks

The *Tractatus* is distinguished among works on analytical philosophy in its concern with the nature of philosophical truth. Wittgenstein's conception of philosophical truth is the foundation of the system of the *Tractatus*. Since the philosophical truth is not "at hand," like "genuine" truths and falsehoods, one cannot even determine what the philosophical truth is unless one develops first a special mode of access to it. Pre-twentieth century logic was not clearly distinguished from psychology, mathematics or even metaphysics itself, so it could not in that form be the key to philosophical truth. But just prior to the writing of the *Tractatus*, logic had been cast into a new and perspicuous form (primarily by Frege, Russell and Whitehead), a form which enabled one clearly to distinguish logic from these other areas, and to deal with logical truth and falsehood in a simple mechanical fashion. To some philosophers this seemed to make logic impotent for philosophical purposes. But Wittgenstein conceived that logic had just been put into the form which revealed its true shape as the key to philosophical truth. The significance of the title, *Tractatus-logico-philosophicus,* is not merely that the book is a treatise on a kind of philosophy which is in some sense "logical," but that philosophical truth bears a special relation to logical truth.

Given this new form of logic, it seemed to be plausible that the centerstage in logic is held by the logical propositions, and that central among these are the tautologies in the truth-functional sense. The other sorts of logical propositions seemed to Wittgenstein to be less basic than these. A virtue of these tautologies in the truth-functional sense is that they are relatively simple sorts of logical propositions, and there are relatively simple sorts of procedures for manipulating them. Their most important components are the logical constants, and the procedures for working with them are determined by the meanings of the logical constants. Thus the "proper interpretation" of logic and so, from Wittgenstein's point of view, the key to philosophical truth in general, reduces to the question of the proper interpretation of the logical constants.

With his 'fundamental idea'—that the logical constants are not representatives—Wittgenstein argues that the logical propositions themselves have no representational content, that they do not represent anything in the world. Instead, they are true by virtue of that which is presented with their symbols. Since that which is presented with these symbols which is relevant to their truth value is the general form of genuine propositions in general, a link is made between the tautological symbols and the general form of propositions about the world. Since this general form of genuine propositions is rich in linguistic and ontological content, the tautological symbol determines a domain of philosophical truth, the core of the views of the *Tractatus*.

This core of views is a priori since (1) it is implicit in that presented with the tautological symbol which is relevant to its truth value, and (2) it can be mechanically derived from a minimum of a priori views (that '$P \vee {\sim} P$' is a tautology, that the logical constants are not representatives, and so forth) as is done in the argument of the *Tractatus*. The core of views is also correctly characterized as belonging to philosophical logic for the same reasons. Though not all of the remarks in the *Tractatus* conform to these descriptions, the core views do. Those views which do not directly conform to it nevertheless presuppose those which do in various ways. For example, Wittgenstein's theories of communication and of the limits of science presuppose his theory of meaning, and that theory does conform to these descriptions.

Philosophical logic, the a priori part of the theory of symbolism, is therefore central to Wittgenstein's philosophical program. The key notion in his philosophical logic is the notion of a presentational symbol, and of it there are two types. The tautological symbol is a presentational symbol in the strong sense that it presents with itself the conditions of its own truth. The genuine propositional symbol is a presentational symbol in the weaker sense that it only presents with itself the conditions of its own meaningfulness. The former is the key notion in Wittgenstein's account of philosophical truth. The latter is his key notion in his account of the connection between symbols and the world.

The importance of these two notions should not be underestimated. This is evidenced by the significant historical connections with Wittgenstein's views. The central notion in his theory of meaning is traced back to an important beginning in the German philosophical tradition (Brentano), and versions of it are also relevant to the more recent work by Fodor, Kripke, Malcolm, Goldberg, Dummett and others. The notion is relevant to a whole range of contemporary debates—from the nature of the mental, the possibility of language and meaning, the theory of communication, the nature of memory and the limits of science—to many others. The more perspicuous formulation of this key notion exposes the strengths, and the weaknesses, of many current positions.

Second, Wittgenstein's account of the sense in which the tautological symbol is a presentational symbol plays the central role in his account of a philosophical system and philosophical truth, and his account has important parallels with views in the tradition of German idealism. Though Wittgenstein's account of the nature of philosophical truth does not tie into contemporary debates to the same degree as does his theory of meaning, this does not invalidate its importance for contemporary philosophy. Though the nature of philosophical truth is not much of an issue in contemporary philosophy, it should be. One of the measures of the philosophical depth of a tradition is in its recognition of and reflection on the unique nature of philosophical truth. In this, the current traditions are found wanting. Wittgenstein, along with Plato, Aristotle, Kant, Hegel and others, is opposed to the current tendency to model philosophy on one of the subsidiary sciences. Though one may not accept Wittgenstein's specific views on the nature of philosophical truth, the argument of the *Tractatus,* properly conceived, focuses attention on the issue, and in this respect it points the way for contemporary philosophy.

This argument as to the importance of Wittgenstein's philosophical system does not require that Wittgenstein's views are true, certainly not tht they are true in their present form. The aim of the present work is expository and diagnostic. The more complete and clear exposition of the views of the *Tractatus* facilitates a more penetrating diagnosis of the state of contemporary philosophy. But can one be content with a mere exposition and diagnosis? The aim of philosophy is the *truth,* not who held what or whose position is similar to whose. What is of ultimate importance is not that Wittgenstein's theories of meaning, communication and so forth, have striking parallels with more contemporary positions, but instead the question: Are Wittgenstein's interpretations of the logical propositions, and his theories of meaning, communication, and philosophical truth, true?

The truth of Wittgenstein's theories cannot be decided here, but it is worthwhile to make some remarks in this connection. There is evidence from many quarters that the views of the *Tractatus* are not, as they stand, true. One of these quarters is Wittgenstein's own evaluation of the truth of the *Tractatus* in his later writings. In the preface to the *Philosophical Investigations,* for example, Wittgenstein refers to the "grave mistakes" of the *Tractatus.* Though it is, of course, possible that Wittgenstein's later works are in error in this respect, such an evaluation of a work by its own author must be taken seriously. One issue which must be settled is the actual connection of Wittgenstein's earlier and later philosophies. And it is reasonable to expect that in the clearer resolution of this issue, something about the truth must become clear as well.

The author of the *Tractatus* apparently believed, at the time of its publication, that his conclusions follow from his premises, and that these premises are true. But though Wittgenstein's later writings seem generally critical of the Tractatus, we do not find him explicitly criticizing the basic premises of the argument of the *Tractatus,* or drawing attention to the invalidity of some specific key inference in the argument. This suggests the possibility that Wittgenstein came to believe that the argument of the *Tractatus* contains a suppressed premise—or alternatively, that the inference and also the conclusions of the argument of the *Tractatus* depend on an underlying way of looking at things—where it is this suppressed premise or way of looking at things which Wittgenstein came to recognize and reject.

In the sequel to the present work, I argue that Wittgenstein came to believe both that the argument of the *Tractatus* does depend on an underlying way of looking at things and that this way of looking at things is wrong. The main tasks of the sequel are the formulation of this underlying way of looking at things, the clarification of its connection with the views of the *Tractatus,* and the evaluation of the truth of the argument of the *Tractatus.* (In this regard not only Wittgenstein's own post-*Tractatus* writings are employed, but the works of other philosophers as well.)

Once this is accomplished, it is possible to settle the vexing controversy over the actual relationship between Wittgenstein's earlier and later writings, to state precisely the extent of the similarity and differences between the two philosophies. Second, and more important, it is possible to decide whether it is the *Tractatus* or whether it is Wittgenstein's later critique of the *Tractatus,* and his "alternative" to it, which is true.

The criteria for this choice require that one can decide whether the argument of the *Tractatus* does depend on an underlying way of looking at things, and whether that way of looking at things is correct. One of the fundamental differences between the *Tractatus* and the *Philosophical Investigations* can be made clear in this connection. Though the view may sound strange at first hearing, it should be agreed that the author of the *Philosophical Investigations* holds that there is something more basic than logic and the philosophy of logic as it was conceived in the *Tractatus,* including "grammar", "forms of life" and so forth. (Of course, these must be carefully defined.) Like the *Tractatus,* the *Philosophical Investigations* is founded on a conception of the nature of philosophical truth, but the *Philosophical Investigations* takes a different stand on the matter. It is the view of Wittgenstein's later writings that the way of looking at things underlying the view that logic (as it is conceived in the *Tractatus*) is the key to philosophical truth, is wrong. The *Philosophical Investigations* rejects the way of looking at things which underlies the philosophical argument and philosophical system of the *Tractatus,* and for that reason, among others, it rejects that argument and system. The *Philosophical Investigations* admits that logic is important for philosophy, but denies that there can be a "logical philosophy" in the strong sense of the *Tractatus.* It denies that logic can be the key to philosophical truth.

Obviously, however, an adequate treatment of these issues requires a fresh effort devoted solely to the critique of the argument of the *Tractatus.* The tasks of the present work must be limited to characterizing the views of the *Tractatus* as Wittgenstein conceived them at the time of its writing, and to indicating the relevance of those views to contemporary philosophy. This alone is sufficient to make the present project timely and worthwhile. But most importantly, it is a necessary step in the process of determining the nature of philosophical truth, and derivatively, of establishing the truth about logic, meaning, mind and communication.

Notes

Introduction

1. Black, *A Companion to Wittgenstein's Tractatus,* (Ithaca, NY: Cornell University Press), p. 173.

2. Ibid., p. 330.

3. Ibid., pp. 332–336.

4. Stenius, *Wittgenstein's 'Tractatus,'* (London: Basic Blackwell, 1960), p. 201.

5. Russell, "Lectures on Logical Atomism," in *Readings in Twentieth Century Philosophy,* ed. by Warren Alston and George Nakhnikian (New York: The Free Press, 1964), p. 298.

6. Ibid.

7. Carnap, "On the Character of Philosophical Problems," in *The Linguistic Turn,* ed. by Richard Rorty (Chicago: The University of Chicago Press, 1975), p. 60. In the following pages of this introduction, Carnap's views are employed as representative of the positivist point of view. This is obviously an over-simplification. But Carnap's views are probably the clearest and most influential, and Carnap does provide explicit commentary on the *Tractatus.* Nevertheless, the logical positivist movement is not always credited with the internal diversity that it possessed, and it is hoped that this simplification does not contribute to this mistaken attitude.

8. The positivists, of course, did not agree with the *Tractatus* that propositions about the logical form of language are nonsensical. In place of Wittgenstein's "radically negative" view, the positivists, primarily in the person of Carnap, sought to provide a "positive account of propositions about the structure

of language," an account in which propositions about language "make sense."
See Carnap, p. 56.

9. Other commentators have also sought to provide a more positive account
of those problematic propositions (see Anscombe, *An Introduction to Wittgenstein's
Tractatus,* (Philadelphia: University of Pennsylvania Press, 1971), pp. 161–163.

Chapter I

1. Russell, "Lectures," pp. 325–328. Russell's "Lectures" do not purport
to present a clear or complete view. As lectures, they are intended for use by,
and the stimulation of the student, and will be treated accordingly. But, since
they are based on ideas Russell "learnt" from Wittgenstein, they provide useful
points of comparison and contrast with Wittgenstein's final view.

Similarly, it is obvious that the *Notebooks 1914–16* do not present a
complete or final view. Therefore, the ultimate court of appeal must always be
the *Tractatus* itself. Nevertheless, some of the remarks in the *Notebooks* prove
particularly fruitful when coupled with the fundamental ideas of the *Tractatus.*
Wittgenstein, *Notebooks 1914–16* (New York: Harper and Row, 1965).

2. Russell, "Lectures," p. 298.

3. Ibid., p. 325.

4. Black, *Companion,* p. 173.

5. Russell, "Lectures," p. 326.

6. Ibid. The original article by Demos is in *Mind,* April 1917.

7. Actually, in Demos's view '$\sim p$' goes proxy for another proposition 'q'
which asserts the existence of a positive fact. But this simplification is not
harmful in this context.

8. Russell, "Lectures," p. 326.

9. I am assuming that one proposition is not reducible to the terms of
the other, for example, "R_1" to "R_2". One example might be where "a_1" =
"b_1" = "the chalk," and "R_1" = "is white" and "R_2" = "is red." Assuming
that "being white" is not analyzable in terms of "not being red," we have
irreducible, distinct, but logically incompatible propositions: "The chalk is white"
and "The chalk is red."

10. Russell, "Lectures," p. 326.

11. Ibid., p. 325.

12. Ibid., p. 323.

13. Ibid.

14. Ibid.

15. Ibid.

16. Ibid., p. 328. Note that he would not even admit the question, "How would you define a disjunctive fact?," but would say that the meaning of disjunction is entirely captured by the truth table. The truth table for negation, however, does not exhaust its meaning, that is, '$\sim p$' is true when 'p' is false . . . and so forth, does not exhaust the meaning of negation. There is, therefore, some ultimate content left over which pertains to the fact which makes '$\sim p$' true.

17. Ibid., p. 325.

18. Ibid., p. 328.

19. That is, in theory the distinction is clear even if one has no criterion for determining in practice exactly which propositions are the genuine negative ones, that is, which ones would be made true by the existence of a negative fact.

20. It is important not to jump to conclusions about the role of the logical object referred to by '*not*'. For even if '*not*' refers to an object, that object may be a constituent of the corresponding negative fact, or not. That is, it is in principle possible that one of the terms of the negative proposition refers to this logical object, but that the corresponding fact not be composed of $n+1$ objects. If the objects which compose the negative fact simply are the n objects which are referred to by the terms of the positive proposition, *plus* the logical object (negativeness) then the negative fact consists of $n+1$ objects. But '*not*' may refer to an object and have a different function in the negative proposition than to signify the mere addition of one more object to the relevant fact. The function is the following: The function of '*not*' is to combine with some of the signs in the positive proposition in such a way that the references of those signs in the negative proposition are distinct from their reference in the corresponding positive proposition. For example, if 'p' is 'aF', then '$\sim p$' is '$\sim aF$'. But it could be, for instance, that '*not*' combines with 'F' in such a way that 'not-F' refers to a different object than is referred to by 'F' in the positive proposition.

Russell suggests this view in his response to one of Demos's objections to the existence of negative facts. Russell writes:

His third point I do not entirely agree with: that when the word 'not' occurs,
it cannot be taken as a qualification of the predicate. ("Lectures," p. 325)
Russell suggests that 'not' can, at least sometimes, be taken as a qualification
of the predicate and suggests that this is connected with his view that there
are negative facts. That is, *'aF'* "refers" to *a* and *F,* and *'∼aF'* refers to *a*
and a quality distinct from *F,* namely that referred to by *'not-F'!*

21. Russell, "Lectures," p. 305.

22. This idea that there are *distinct* "possible facts," or states of affairs
which are relevant to the truth value of a proposition, is none other than the
view that propositions and states of affairs belong to a logical space in which
there are necessary connections between distinct existences. Demos explicitly and
Russell implicitly accepts such a view. As we shall see, in the *Tractatus,*
Wittgenstein is fundamentally opposed to the existence of a logical space of
this type.

23. Stenius, *Wittgenstein's 'Tractatus,'* p. 171.

24. Ibid., p. 172.

25. Anscombe, G.E.M., *An Introduction to Wittgenstein's Tractatus* (Philadelphia: University of Pennsylvania Press, 1971) p. 67.

26. Black, *Companion,* p. 71.

27. An enormous amount of confusion has surrounded discussion of Wittgenstein's views concerning negative facts. One of the reasons for this confusion
is that commentators tend to regard the *Tractatus* as containing a correspondence
theory of truth. This dogma is, in part, the result of the fact that Russell
apparently holds a correspondence theory in the *Lectures,* and Russell's views
are often taken as the measure of Wittgenstein's.

Russell states the correspondence theory in a number of ways and places.
Sometimes he speaks of propositions, other times of beliefs, but he seems to
move from one expression to the other almost indiscriminately.

> There are also beliefs, which have reference to facts, and by reference to facts
> are either true or false. . . . When I speak of a fact . . . I mean the kind
> of thing that makes a proposition true or false. ("Lectures," p. 301; see also
> pp. 305–306.)

For Russell, all propositions are made true or false by virtue of correspondence
with facts.

But according to the *Tractatus,* a negative proposition asserts the non-
existence of a state of affairs. It is true when the possible fact which is relevant
to its truth value does *not* exist. It would be a correspondence theory in name
only which held that negative propositions are made true by virtue of corre-

spondence with negative *facts*₁, that negative propositions are true when they correspond to non-existent states of affairs. A genuine correspondence theory of truth must hold that negative propositions, when true, correspond with an *existent* state of affairs, that they are true when some fact exists instead of that which would exist if the positive proposition were true.

Black cites 2.223 of the *Tractatus* as evidence that Wittgenstein accepts something like a correspondence theory of truth (p. 71). Further, he states that this involves a correspondence with facts. (p. 172) But at 2.21 Wittgenstein only writes that "a picture agrees with reality or fails to agree; . . . ." There is no mention of facts here, and likewise at 2.223 Wittgenstein only mentions "reality." Reality is defined at 2.06 as "the existence and *non-existence* of states of affairs" (emphasis mine). Since a fact is defined as an existent state of affairs (2.06), correspondence with reality does not necessarily imply correspondence with facts.

According to the interpretation advanced in the preceding sections, giving up the dualism which "can't exist" requires that one give up the correspondence theory of truth—unless one is willing to give up the view that there are any negative propositions.

Wittgenstein does not take this route ("The positive *proposition* necessarily presupposes the existence of the negative *proposition* and vice versa" (5.5151). Black, however, argues that Wittgenstein is actually committed to doing without negative propositions (Black, *Companion,* p. 71). But his argument is based upon elevating the mere terminological definition of negative facts at 2.06 into the privileged position, and forgetting Wittgenstein's basic definition of a fact in proposition 2.

Black, *Companion,* p. 171.

29. Fogelin, *Wittgenstein,* (Boston: Routledge and Kegan Paul, 1976), p. 28.

30. Ibid.

31. Black, *Companion,* p. 224.

32. It may appear that Wittgenstein's views are mostly negative, that they tell us that there are *no* negative *facts*₂, and so forth. There is some truth to this point but it is not completely true. In addition to saying that negation, and the logical constants in general, do *not* contribute to the *sense*₁ of a proposition, Wittgenstein also tells us that they have the positive function of projecting that "finished" sense into reality. And in addition to saying that the negative proposition does not affirm the existence of any state of affairs, he also says that negation *excludes* reality. The idea that there is a fundamental logical function of *excluding existence* is the beginning of a positive account of negation.

Chapter II

1. Black, *Companion,* p. 320.

2. Russell, "Lectures," p. 346.

3. Ibid., p. 347.

4. Ibid., p. 349.

5. Ibid.

6. Ibid., p. 313.

7. Ibid., p. 349.

8. In the first lecture Russell does suggest that the logical propositions are "about nothing," with less hesitation. But even there his statement is ambiguous. "Then there are . . . the completely general facts of the sort that you have in logic, where there is no mention of any constituent whatever of the actual world, no mention of any particular thing or particular quality or particular relation, indeed strictly you may say, no mention of anything. That is one of the characteristics of the logical propositions, that they mention nothing. . . . All the words that come in the statement of a pure logical proposition are words really belonging to syntax. They are words merely expressing form or connection, not mentioning any particular constituent of the proposition in which they occur." ("Lectures," p. 303).

Even so, it is not completely obvious that this passage is in harmony with the view of the *Tractatus.* For, first, it seems clear that Russell here understands a constituent of a proposition as a *"particular,"* that is, "any particular thing or particular quality or particular relation." This means that a logical proposition may still be about something in the world as long as that something is not a particular, as long as it is general in nature ("the completely general facts of the sort you have in logic"). Thus, there is a further ambiguity in the use of the term *"constituent"* in Russell's "Lectures." If a constituent is something "in the world," it may be (1) something particular, or (2) something general. But in both cases it is still something external to the propositional symbol. Russell cannot shake the view that the logical propositions are about something "in the world." When he says that the logical propositions merely express "form or connection," he *seems* to be saying that they are about nothing in the world of any kind. But how does he understand the notion of form or connection? Is it perhaps understood as the most general structural features of the world? In the lectures, Russell continually returns to that interpretation. He cannot free himself from the view that the logical proposition must be about a fact which is "in the world."

9. Ibid., p. 329.

10. Ibid., p. 348. Note that the language which Russell uses to describe the logical propositions ("peculiar quality") is strikingly similar to that at 6.113 where Wittgenstein says it is the "peculiar mark" of the logical propositions that one can recognize their truth from the symbol alone.

11. In one of his early letters to Russell he emphasizes a point which is important in my interpretation: "Logic is still in the melting-pot but one thing gets more and more obvious to me: The propositions of logic only apparently contain variables. . . ." (See *Letters to Russell, Keynee and Moore*, ed. G.H. von Wright, [Ithaca, NY: Cornell University Press, 1974] p. 10.)

12. Since that which 'is true' must already contain a verb, and since the tautology does not contain a verb, it follows that in an important sense the tautologies are not true, do not have a truth value at all. This is connected with a number of themes in the *Tractatus* which are discussed in the following chapter and can only be briefly mentioned here. Among these themes are that "tautology and contradiction" are the "disintegration of the combination of signs" (4.466) and the fact that one can "actually do without logical propositions" (6.122). The very same fact which enables one to comprehend how the truth of the tautologies is "recognizable from the symbol alone" is also connected with the fact that a tautology is the disintegration of the combination of signs. This means that it has no verb, that strictly speaking it does not have a truth value in the sense in which genuine propositions do.

It is, however, necessary to treat the tautology as if it were actually true. Ultimately, the illumination that derives from the tautologies consists in seeing how treating them as true only forces one to admit that they are the disintegration of the combinations of signs. (See VII.7)

13. Black, *Companion*, p. 320. Of course, Black may not understand this view in exactly the same way I do (see his discussion of the autonomy of logic on pp. 272–274 of the *Companion*).

14. Carnap, "Philosophy and Logical Syntax," in *Readings in Twentieth Century Philosophy*, ed. by Warren Alston and George Nakhnikian (New York: The Free Press, 1969), p. 436.

15. For a classic attempt to account for meaning in terms of a $formal_1$ theory of language, see Carnap, *Philosophical Problems*, p. 56. "According to prevalent conceptions the connotative questions of the logic of science are much

richer and more fruitful than the formal [my *"formal₁"*]. . . . Though the formal do belong to the logic of science they are at most a small and insignificant section. But this opinion is wrong. . . . It is possible in the case of purely formal procedures, that is from a viewpoint in which one does not reckon with the meaning, finally to arrive at an answering of all those questions which are formulated as connotative questions."

16. Black, *Companion,* p. 272.

17. Ibid.

18. For such a standard view see Carnap, "Philosophy and Logical Syntax" in *Readings in Twentieth Century Philosophy.*

19. Nakhnikian, George, Introduction to "Logical Positivism," in *Readings in Twentieth Century Philosophy,* p. 386.

20. It must be admitted that there is still a level of obscurity in Wittgenstein's account. The views and arguments of the *Tractatus* ultimately rest on an underlying interpretation or way of looking at things. For example, the ideas that thoughts *present* such and such, *represent* such and such, and even the idea of the *structure* of a thought are involved in this underlying interpretation. These ideas may even be metaphorical in nature. Whatever their nature, such notions are widespread in philosophical and psychological literature. The questions of whether they can or should be replaced, and by what, are very large philosophical questions. In the present book Wittgenstein's view has been pressed to the limit of its dependence on this underlying way of looking at things. In addition, these notions have received considerable additional clarification (most particularly in Chapter VI). Still, much more work remains to be done. This more critical posture is taken in the sequel to the present book.

21. This is connected with Wittgenstein's further view that tautologies and contradictions are cases of the disintegration of the combination of signs. Normally a logical combination of propositions is a molecular proposition which is merely a compound of the component propositions with a sense. The *Grundegedanke*-based definition of the logical operations is that the logical operations are precisely those operations which do not enter into the representational content of the proposition in which they occur. But then '$P \vee \sim P$' should be a mere logical combination of the propositions with a sense 'P' and a sense '$\sim P$'. But '$P \vee \sim P$' has no representational content at all. This shows that the signs for the logical constants are not functioning normally in this context, that they have "disintegrated." (For further discussion, see Chapter III, section 5.)

22. Though in his first "Lecture on Logical Atomism" Russell does not explicitly formulate the notion of a presentational symbol, he does, in his discussion of the non-logical propositions, come very close to such a notion. He writes:

> For each fact there are two propositions, one true and one false, and there is nothing in the nature of the symbol to show us which is the true one and which is the false one. If there were, you would ascertain the truth about the world without looking around you. ("Lectures," pp. 305–306)

Russell here denies that genuine or fact-stating propositions are true or false by virtue of that which is presented with their symbols, and Wittgenstein would agree. But Russell does not consider the possibility that this very characteristic might be the mark of the logical propositions which he is seeking. Wittgenstein does identify this at 6.113 as the "peculiar mark" of the logical propositions.

Chapter III

1. This tautology is chosen in part because of Wittgenstein's abiding interest in this "law" in his later writings. See, for instance, pars. 352 and 356 of the *Philosophical Investigations* (Oxford: Basil Blackwell, 1958) and pars. 199 and 200 of *On Certainty* (New York: Harper and Row, 1972).

2. Wittgenstein's assumptions must be made clear here. Affirmation sounds like an elocutionary act, something *people* do. The opposite of the elocutionary act is denial, also something people do. However, Wittgenstein is not talking about these elocutionary acts but about logical operations. For Wittgenstein, affirmation and its opposite, negation, are logical operations, not human operations. I am assuming that Wittgenstein holds that, for example, '$P \mathbin{v} {\sim} P$' is true independently of whether the human elocutionary acts of affirming and denying ever take place, or even whether human language and human beings exist at all. (Perhaps this must be argued, but it seems to me that Wittgenstein is right about this independence of logic from human practices.)

3. The argument is carried out by assuming that 'P' is other than true, and then arguing that there is only one truth possibility which is other than true. A formally rigorous account would also include arguments that (1) if '${\sim}P$' is other than true, then there is only one other truth value it can have, (2) if 'P' is other than false, there is only one other truth value it can have, and (3) if '${\sim}P$' is other than false, there is only one other truth value it can have. But those arguments are exactly analogous to the one presented here, and it is not necessary to present them here.

4. It is highly important that one need not content oneself with mere historical explanations of why Wittgenstein holds that the genuine proposition must involve a picture (for instance, that he saw a model of an accident in a law court), nor even with an explanation of the logical properties of propositions *if* they include such a picture. There is nothing hypothetical in Wittgenstein's argument. His view is built on the *Grundegedanke* inspired interpretation of the logical constants, that is, the view is derivative from his most basic way of understanding logic.

5. Wittgenstein's recognition of the problematical character of *ex falso quodlibet* anticipates later logicians who avoid it by modifying or rejecting modern classical logic by the construction of relevant or paraconsistent logics, a school which stretches from Belnap and Anderson (*Entailment* [Princeton: Princeton University Press, 1975]) to Graham Priest ("Semantic Closure," *Studia Logica* 43, 1979 and "Logic of Paradox Revisited," *Journal of Philosophical Logic* 13, 1984). Relevant Logics avoid *ex falso quodlibet* by the requirement that if 'Q' follows from 'P' then 'Q' is relevant to 'P' in some sense (usually in the sense of semantical or propositional "overlap"—a condition not satisfied if "The world is flat" is alleged to follow from "It is both raining and not raining"). Paraconsistent Logics avoid it by the claim that the requirement that it is impossible that "$(C \cdot \sim Q)$" is true (where "C" is a contradiction and "Q" is any proposition) is not satisfied if "C" is a certain kind of contradiction, the kind which is *both* true and false. ("The Russell set both is and is not a member of itself" is arguably such a case of a contradiction which is both true and false.) If this is so then the truth of these contradictions is compatible with the falsehood of the proposition 'Q,' and so 'Q' cannot be said to follow from the contradiction.

It is important to stress that while Wittgenstein in his *Tractatus* period is in accord with the relevant and paraconsistent logicians in the recognition that *ex falso quodlibet* must be rejected, he differs from both of them in that he does not think that this requires the construction of non-classical logics. Wittgenstein's strategy involves two levels, the second being the more fundamental one. First, since in his view, tautologies cannot be applied to contradictions at all, then one cannot deduce any proposition from a contradiction. Second, although there can be a perceptible sign for a contradiction, there are strictly speaking *no self-contradictory symbols,* and, hence, no self contradictory symbols from which all propositions follow. Wittgenstein's response differs from that of these non-classical logicians in that whereas they retain the existence of self-contradictory symbols to which logical laws apply, and must, therefore modify those laws to accommodate this fact, Wittgenstein *does away with the problematical symbols altogether,* and so he can leave the classical logical laws intact. It is important to recognize that Wittgenstein, in his *Tractatus* and *Notebooks* period, develops the generally unacknowledged first formulations of the problems with *ex falso quodlibet* which stimulated the development of Relevant and Paraconsistent Logics.

One final note: Though in his *Tractatus* period he remained faithful to the tenets of classical logic, there are hints of paraconsistency in his later writings, notably in the *Remarks on the Foundations of Mathematics* where he talks of those who are "Free of the superstitious fear and awe . . . of contradictions" (p. 53) and those "glad to lead their lives in the neighbourhood of a contradiction" (p. 105), and also in the much earlier *Philosophical Remarks* where he talks of the time when "people will actually be proud of having emancipated themselves from consistency" (p. 322).

Obviously this whole note linking Wittgenstein to the development of these non-classical logics is only the sketch of a fascinating development of ideas, which deserves a much more detailed treatment. (My thanks to John N. Williams who provided me with much of this information on non-classical logics.)

Chapter IV

1. Russell states in his first lecture that the data with which the philosopher should begin are "truisms" and are in fact "ludicrously obvious." (Russell, "Lectures," p. 302). Russell continues by saying that

> The first truism to which I wish to draw attention—and I hope you will agree with me that these things that I call truisms are so obvious that it is almost laughable to mention them—is that the world contains facts . . . and that there are also beliefs, which have reference to facts, and by reference to facts are either true or false. (Ibid.)

It is not my concern to question Russell's "truisms," but only to point out how much more minimal, by comparison, are Wittgenstein's. Wittgenstein assumes only that there is something by virtue of which the truth value of propositions is determined. He does not assume that this "something" is a fact. In actuality, it turns out that the subject matter of propositions which is external to their symbol belongs not to the category of facts but to the category of things. Facts, as we shall see in IV.4, turn out not to be wholly external to the propositional symbol (see my discussion of pictorial form). But the important points at present are that the logical categories which are needed in an account of genuine propositions (objects, facts, contingent states, and so forth), and how they are to be integrated with each other into a unified theory, are *theorems* which are demonstrated in the argument of the *Tractatus,* not assumptions at its foundation. Wittgenstein must, of course, make *some* assumptions, but they are few in comparison with Russell's.

It is worth pointing out that minimal as Wittgenstein's assumption is, it has been denied, and denied by significant philosophers and movements. Carnap, for example, distinguishes "two different viewpoints" which are possible in "logical analysis." He calls these "connotative" *(inhaltlich)* and "formal." The first viewpoint makes reference to "the meaning of concepts and propositions." It poses questions such as: "What meaning *(Inhalt, Gehalt)* does this proposition have?" The formal viewpoint dispenses with such notions of meaning and makes reference only to "arrangements" of "words" and the like. That is, the formal viewpoint dispenses with the notion of that which propositions are about, the notion of that which is relevant to the truth value of propositions. Using Carnap's terminology, we could say that Wittgenstein's view is "connotative." In fact, the development of the positivists' "formal" viewpoint is in large measure a reaction against this view, which they felt was the primary source of the problems with the *Tractatus*. (See Carnap, "Philosophical Problems," p. 56).

2. See III.4.

3. In that case, that '*P*' and '∼*P*' have the same subject matter would have to be determined by some other factor. There are numerous candidates for such alternative accounts. The determining factor might be (1) a rule determining the use of the proxies involved, (2) a "definition" of the proxies, (3) a reference to the context in which the proxy is used, and so forth. (And, of course, there would be problems concerning whether any of these views are adequate.) It is illuminating to realize that the author of the *Philosophical Investigations* rejects the view of the *Tractatus* that what a symbol means is determined by that which is presented with its symbol, and adopts some combination of the above-mentioned views. In fact, the great difference between the views of the *Tractatus* and *Philosophical Investigations* can be traced to the rejection in the latter of the notion of the presentational symbol so central to the former.

4. Russell, "Lectures," p. 314.

5. In 3.203 Wittgenstein makes this point about signs, and the structure of the sign language. In the present interpretation, however, we are concerned with the symbol. This discrepancy is only apparent, and is dealt with in detail in a subsequent chapter. However, the broad lines of the solution consist in the fact that Wittgenstein is interested in describing the structure of an artificial sign language, constructed by philosophers for the primary purpose of providing a perspicuous perceptible representation of the logical structure of symbols. Symbols, we remember (II.5), are a compound entity composed of a perceptible

sign and an imperceptible thought. Thus, the artificially constructed sign language is intended to be a perspicuous perceptible representation of the structure of thought. There will, therefore, be a parallelism of structure between the artificially constructed sign, *not* the signs of "everyday language," and the thought. That this interpretation of 3.203 is correct is borne out by the fact that 3.203 is a comment on proposition 3.2: "In a proposition *[Satzel]* a thought can be expressed in such a way that the elements of the proposition correspond to the objects of the thought." (The fuller treatment of this matter is developed at V.3.)

6. In order to avoid prolixity I have stated the argument in terms of a particular proposition '*S* is *F*' and the corresponding particular instance of excluded middle '*S* is *F* or it is not the case that *S* is *F*'. But, of course, that which is relevant to the truth value of the tautology is the general form of a proposition. Thus, though the particular subject matter *S,* or the particular contingent state *F,* is apparently involved in the argument, it is not really involved. What follows in the argument has nothing essential to do with any particular subject matter or contingent state. What follows is only that whatever the subject matter and whatever the contingent state involved, that which is presented with the symbol of the tautology must determine the possibility of that subject matter being, or not being, in that contingent state.

7. Urmson, J.O., *Philosophical Analysis: Its Development between the Two World Wars,* (New York: Oxford University Press, 1969) p. 79.

8. The view that the genuine propositional symbol presents with itself the "conditions of its own meaningfulness" may sound like a very strange and infrequently held view. We shall, however, see in Chapter VI that such views are presupposed by many psychological, linguistic and philosophical theories.

9. Fogelin, *Wittgenstein,* p. 28.

Chapter V

1. Ludwig Wittgenstein, *Tractatus-logico-philosophicus,* Russell's Introduction (London: Routledge and Kegan Paul, Ltc. 1966), p. x.

2. There are other sorts of arguments which can be given, and which have been given, for the view that the meaning component of the proposition is an underlying (imperceptible) structure. See for example, Jerrold Katz's *The Underlying Reality of Language* (New York: Harper and Row, 1971). Katz's view

does not, however, involve exactly the same description of this underlying structure.

3. Wittgenstein, *Tractatus,* Introduction, p. x.

4. The present discussion does not purport to exhaust the topic of logical issues concerned with the vagueness of everyday language.

5. Wittgenstein, *Tractatus,* Introduction, p. x.

6. Obviously this does not mean that everyday propositional signs may not be altered as the practical situations of daily life change. On the contrary, it is such gradual and specific changes which keep everyday language well suited for practical purposes. What is ruled out is only the wholesale alteration of everyday language in the service of some philosophical ideal such as Russell's.

7. Russell, "Lectures," p. 304.

8. The reason that this is a philosophical fantasy, and not merely factually incorrect, is that the meaning component of the proposition must have the unique nature of the mental, a nature which no mere perceptible entity can have. This is the theme of the subsequent chapter. See Chapter VI.

9. One important remark in this series forces one to broaden the interpretation in a significant way. Immediately after having told us at 4.011 that "at first sight, a proposition—one set out on the printed page, for example—does not seem to be a picture of the reality with which it is concerned, . . ." Wittgenstein adds:

4.012 It is obvious that a proposition of the form 'aRb' strikes us as a picture.

In this case the sign is obviously a likeness of what is signified.

That is, the point of constructing this particular type of idealized sign is not that it is a picture, whereas the everyday propositional sign is not. Rather, the everyday sign is a picture, but it does not *strike us* as such. The rules which project the everyday sign onto reality are so complicated that the everyday sign need not itself look much like a fact, or a picture. This does not interfere with its performing its everyday function, but it can mislead the philosopher who takes it as a guide in an account of linguistic meaning. (At 3.143 Wittgenstein cites Frege as a philosopher who has been mislead by the fact that the everyday propositional sign does not strike us as a picture.) Note, however, that there is no mention of *thought* at all at 4.012, and the point seems rather to be that the ideal sign is a perspicuous image of the everyday sign. It is the everyday sign which philosophers, like Frege, have failed to recognize as a picture. The ideal sign is designed to remind us of the structure of the everyday propositional sign. This point must be admitted, but it does not follow from this that the ideal propositional sign is not intended to be a perspicuous perceptible image of the imperceptible thought. The key point is that although the everyday sign is itself an image of the imperceptible thought, it is a blurred image (blurred for practical purposes). Thus, insofar as the ideal sign is intended to remind us of the fact that the everyday sign is a picture, it can simultaneously remind us of the fact that the thought is a picture. On the present interpretation it is not claimed that the ideal sign reminds us of the structure of thought to the exclusion of everything else. Instead, it reminds us of the structure of the thoughts by means of reminding us of the structure of the everyday propositional sign.

One of the difficulties in discussing the role of the ideal propositional sign is that there are a range of possible uses for it. This is because the construction of the perceptible part of language is not, like the structure of thought, a priori. That is, it is influenced by the shifting of human purposes, whether these are practical or "reflective." The use singled out in the present interpretation is central to Wittgenstein's concerns, and many of the additional uses of the ideal propositional sign can be understood as derivative from this basic use. My present aim is, therefore, only to shift the emphasis to what is, I believe, the central use for the ideal propositional sign.

10. Urmson, *Philosophical Analysis,* p. 79.

11. The reader is reminded that in Wittgenstein's view, but not necessarily in Urmson's interpretation or Russell's view, there is an "as if" quality to the use of the ideal propositional sign. Urmson seems to attribute to Wittgenstein the program of constructing a perfect language (see also p. 81 of Urmson's *Philosophical Analysis*).

12. Perhaps the expression "a certain relation" in 3.1432 can be read as "a certain particular relation, that is, the same one in which objects may be." If Wittgenstein meant this more determinate view, he should have said so. However, even the context of 3.1432 suggests that he did not intend that view. At 3.2, for example, he only says that the "elements of the propositional sign" can "correspond to the objects of the thought." The context (the 3.2's) makes clear that by the elements he only means the names, not the relation between the names, which can be made to "correspond" to the objects of the thought. This suggests that Wittgenstein understands the ideal propositional sign as a structure which is merely *isomorphic* with the relevant thought and/or state of affairs.

13. See Urmson's discussion of the distinction between same and new level analysis, and its connection with Wittgenstein's and Russell's views about the

metaphysical significance of their analytic programs. (*Philosophical Analysis,* Chapter III)

14. Urmson, *Philosophical Analysis,* p. 40.

15. The early "analytical" programs were, however, intimately connected with the desire to gain ontological insight into the world. In fact, in the early stages of the "analytical" movement it was felt that analysis stood in need of justification, and that the fact that ontological insight is achieved through analysis is a justification of the analytic program. Urmson is, in contrast with the most recent commentators, more sensitive to the radical nature of Wittgenstein's conception of analysis. There is no doubt that a radical new-level analysis of everyday propositions of the sort which I have here ascribed to Wittgenstein is difficult to work out and defend, but this is true of *any* new-level or reductive analysis.

Furthermore, such a new-level analysis may be relevant to the solution of certain current discussions in philosophy and theoretical linguistics. Putnam characterizes Katz's theory of meaning as follows: "1) each word has its meaning characterized by a string of 'semantic markers.' 2) These markers stand for concepts. . . . Examples of such concepts are: *unmarried, animate, seal.* 3) Each such concept is a 'linguistic universal,' and stands for an *innate* notion—one in some sense-or-other 'built into' the human brain. . . ." Putnam criticizes this view. "For example, 'seal' is given as an example of a linguistic universal . . . but in no theory of human evolution is contact with seals universal. . . . Thus we may take it that Katz means that whenever such terms occur they could be further analyzed into concepts which really are so primitive that a case could be made for their universality. Needless to say this program has never been carried out, . . ." (H. Putnam, *Mind, Language and Reality,* Vol. 2, pp. 144–145).

In the view which has been attributed to the *Tractatus,* the concepts involved in everyday language are analyzed into concepts which are of such a nature that a case might be made for their universality. That is, all concepts involved in everyday propositions are reducible to concepts of logically simple objects and to "logical" relations. These sort of concepts and relations are altogether different from concepts of seals, and so forth. The matter is quite complicated, but the general point can be made that these sorts of concepts and relations are concepts of the sorts of entities which are implicit in the symbolic medium itself, that is, they are not obtained by experience.

When Wittgenstein suggests in the *Notebooks* that "all relations must be logical in order for their existence to be guaranteed by that of the sign," he is making the first primitive step towards the view that the real concepts and relations involved in the representation of the world are those which are *inherent in the symbolic medium itself.* We now know that Wittgenstein eventually came to the view that the real representational medium is the medium of *thought.* Thus, the suggestion is that the real relations in which objects in the world may be represented are those same relations which are inherent in the medium of thought. They are the relations into which the components of thought may enter—whatever the medium of thought turns out to be (the brain medium?). This view lends itself to the traditional doctrine of *innateness.* Katz himself need not take precisely this route. The point is only that the view here ascribed to the *Tractatus* is a version of the sort of view which Putnam suggests Katz must take. The sort of radical new-level analysis here attributed to Wittgenstein may seem remarkable, but such an analysis may be relevant to the programs in contemporary psycholinguistics.

Chapter VI

1. Russell, "On Propositions: What they are and how they mean," in *Logic and Knowledge,* ed. by Robert C. Marsh (New York: G.P. Putnam's Sons, 1971).

2. Ibid., p. 289.

3. Ibid., p. 290.

4. Ibid.

5. Ibid., pp. 299–300.

6. Ibid., p. 308.

7. Ibid., p. 302.

8. Ibid., p. 309.

9. Ibid.

10. Ibid., p. 315.

11. Ibid., pp. 315–316.

12. Russell, "On Propositions," p. 316.

13. One significant difference between Russell's 1919 view and the view of the *Tractatus* is that Russell only *explicitly* states that propositions involve an imperceptible component with pictorial form in one special kind of case, that is, propositions involving "visual memory images." Wittgenstein's view is that it is a priori true that all genuine propositions involve an imperceptible

component with pictorial form. That is, for various reasons Wittgenstein holds that there is a greater unity in the phenomenon of linguistic meaning than does Russell. Russell may hold that cases which do not easily fit the model of pictorial form must simply be treated in some other way.

14. Brentano, F. *Psychology From an Empirical Standpoint,* (London: Routledge and Kegan Paul, 1973) p. 88 and p. 271, respectively.

15. Bertrand Russell, *Analysis of Mind* (London: George Allen and Unwin, Ltd., 1971), p. 15.

16. Ibid., p. 26.

17. Ibid., p. 306.

18. Even this structural dimension of the notion is not beyond question. In his discussion of Wittgenstein's notion of a picture, Urmson writes: "A more serious point is this. If a law of projection is all that we require for similarity of structure, then the fact that we can find a law of projection connecting any drawing with any object reduces the significance of the demand for identity of structure almost to a vanishing point. So the metaphysical content of saying that sentence and fact must have identity of structure becomes trivial. [I]t is clear that [Wittgenstein] read more into the notion [of a picture], something like intuitively recognizable similarity of structure." But how is this nontrivial "metaphysical content" of the notion of a picture to be explicated? Urmson continues, "[T]here is a special difficulty here, apart from the general impossibility of there being any significant philosophical sentences. It is peculiar to the doctrine of picturing, interpreted as involving a recognizable likeness, as we have suggested Wittgenstein did in practice interpret it. . . . Clearly the likeness [between picture and fact] cannot be represented, . . . We can draw pictures of things and the likeness must show itself. I can draw things having a certain structure but I cannot draw the structure on its own. This is the special difficulty Wittgenstein finds here. This is why it is especially hard to produce even bogus elucidations of the notion of similarity of structure." (*Philosophical Analysis,* pp. 90–91). Urmson concludes: "[The doctrine of picturing] . . . is a puzzling doctrine. Some of the puzzles connected with it we have already tried to remove, . . . But others, more fundamental, can only be removed by and in the light of a better doctrine of the relation of language to fact" (*Ibid.,* p. 93).

In fact, Urmson leaves out the key notion in Wittgenstein's account of the connection between symbols and the world, the notion of pictorial form. But bringing in that notion only enhances Urmson's point. Urmson's general point is that, though the notion of structural identity between the picture and the fact may appear to be a quite straightforward or commonsense notion, it is, in fact, a not unproblematic *philosophical* notion, a notion which is supposed to have "metaphysical content." The notion of the structure of an entity, and that of the structural identity of two entities, are notions which might easily escape scrutiny, but which are deserving of serious philosophical commentary. Several recent discussions of these issues, and of their relevance to certain philosophical problems connected with psychology, are: (1) Norman Malcolm's *Memory and Mind,* especially Chapter X, (New York: Cornell University Press, 1977), (2) Howard Bursen's *Dismantling the Memory Machine,* especially Part III, (Dordrecht: Reidel Publishing Company, 1978), and (3) John Heil's "Traces of Things Past," in *Philosophy of Science,"* March 1978 and his "Does Cognitive Psychology Rest on a Mistake?," in *Mind,* July 1981.

19. Russell, "On Propositions," p. 306.

20. Ibid.

21. Ibid.

22. Ibid., p. 305.

23. Ibid., pp. 309–310.

24. Russell, *Analysis of Mind.,* pp. 161–162, 168, 186.

25. Brentano, *Psychology,* for instance, pp. 6 and 29.

26. David Hume, *A Treatise of Human Nature,* Book I (London: Oxford University Press, 1973). Hume writes that when we talk of a necessary connection between distinct existences, we may do so with "no distinct meaning" but that "tis more probable that these expressions do here lose their true meaning by being *wrong applied,* than that they never had any meaning; . . ." (p. 162). So Hume tries to find the "primary impression" from which our idea of a necessary connection between distinct existences arises (p. 75). However, he finds that "there is no object which implies the existence of another if we consider these objects in themselves, . ." (p. 86). That is, we have no "objective" notion of a necessary connection between distinct existences. If, therefore, we do have any notion of a necessary connection between distinct existences, it must be a mere "subjective" notion, that is, a notion derived from some "internal impression" (p. 165). But from what internal impression is the notion of necessary connection derived? Sometimes he states that this idea is derived from the "determination" of the mind to move from the appearance of the object to the idea of its effect (p. 156). But in one place Hume writes:

> But if we go farther and ascribe a power or necessary connection to objects;
> this is what we can never observe in them, but must draw the idea of it from
> what we feel internally in contemplating them (p. 169)."

It is hard to say how seriously Hume intends one to take this reference to a feeling. If, however, it is to be taken seriously, then Hume and Russell each consider an idea of necessary or intrinsic connection between distinct existences (though they are not the same ideas), and each argues that though there is a basis for the relevant notion, this basis is only a subjective feeling. Russell's account of the mental dimension of the intrinsic meaning connection bears a thought provoking similarity to Hume's account of the notion of necessary connection between distinct existences.

27. It is often recognized that though it is tempting to view meaning as a relation between propositional symbols and states of affairs, there are good reasons why meaning cannot be viewed as a "relation" in the ordinary sense. Several of these reasons have emerged in this discussion. First, since the meaning locus can be about that which does not exist, the meaning connection cannot involve a real relation to an existent. This is why Brentano calls the intentional connection "quasi–relational." The remarkable nature of the meaning locus consists in this capacity to seem just like a relational entity, without actually being related to anything existent. Second, *if* the intentional connection involves a purely private dimension, as in Russell's view, then the intentional connection does not really reach to the relevant objective state of affairs, but stops at the inner limits of consciousness.

The meaning locus is, as it were, a *monad of meaning* which both represents the relevant portion of the universe, while also remaining completely self-contained and untouched by it.

28. Saul Kripke, *Wittgenstein on Rules and Private Language* (London: Basil Blackwell, 1982), p. 62.

29. Husserl, Brentano's most thorough heir, writes: "It must not be overlooked that époche with respect to all worldly being does not at all change the fact that the manifold *cogitationes* relating to what is worldly bear this relation *within themselves,* e.g., the perception of this table still is, as it was before [before the époche], precisely a perception of this table. In this manner, without exception, every conscious process is in itself conscious of such and such, regardless of what the rightful actuality status of this objective such and such may be, . . ." (*Cartesian Meditations,* trans. by Dorion Cairns [The Netherlands; Martins Nijhoff, 1970], p. 32). Wittgenstein's notion of a picture which contains within itself the pictorial relationship which makes it into a picture is strikingly similar to Husserl's description of his cogitationes, which bears within themselves their meaning relationship to what is worldly. 2.1513 of the *Tractatus* is a quite Brentano/Husserl-like formulation of the notion of an intentional (mental) entity.

30. Ramsey, "Review of 'Tractatus' ", in *Essays on Wittgenstein's 'Tractatus'* ed. by Copi and Beard, (New York: Macmillan, 1967) p. 10.

31. In a section titled "Picture and Thought," Stenius writes:

> Pictures of facts concerning red flowers or green leaves need not have the colors 'red' or 'green' as elements—as has been repeatedly stated above, there must only be a structural similarity between a picture and its prototype. We need only take this fact into consideration to give an account of 'thinking' as a sort of depicting which proceeds as easily on a completely physiological as on any other basis for psychology. . . .
>
> Thinking, according to thesis 3 [that is, Wittgenstein's view that the logical picture of facts is a thought], consists of the formation of such mental pictures—or perhaps also of the formation of pictures in a more 'public' material.
>
> A thorough analysis might expose many difficulties here. In the present investigation, however, we shall accept it as description of something that might be considered true: all 'thinking' that is relevant to our inquiry is assumed to show the essential features of isomorphic representation (*Wittgenstein's 'Tractatus,'* pp. 113–114).

First, Stenius's emphasis on the idea of pictures as isomorphic representations leaves out the fact that, according to the text of the *Tractatus,* some pictures satisfy at least the conditions of pictorial $form_1$. They are structures which are not merely isomorphic with the relevant state of affairs, but are perfectly structurally congruent with it. Second, and more important here, is that Stenius has not taken account of the mental or intentional dimension of Wittgenstein's notion of the thought-picture. Thus, he fails to distinguish the nature of the thought-picture from that of an ordinary sort of picture, from the sort which is (to use his own words) formed in "some more public material." Here Stenius manifests the fact that his paradigm notion of a mental entity is that of a private entity. For Stenius, thoughts are, unlike perceptible pictures, *private* pictures, but they do not differ in their pictorial character. Stenius's account omits the mental or intentional character of Wittgenstein's notion of the thought-picture.

It is for this reason that the notion of a key of interpretation is so central to Stenius's account of Wittgenstein's notion of a picture. Stenius writes

> An articulate field F is called a picture (true or false) of the articulate field G if there is a key of interpretation C according to which the elements of F are considered to stand for the elements of G. . ." (p. 96).

It is Stenius's view that an articulate field is a picture if it is *accompanied* by a key of interpretation by means of which the elements of the one field are "considered" to stand for the elements of the other. This is like Ramsey's view that the pictorial relationship is not intrinsic to the picture, but is merely had in mind when one calls something a picture. The whole point of Wittgenstein's remark at 2.1513 is, however, that a picture "conceived in this way" need not be accompanied by any key of interpretation. But it is the independence of thoughts from the need for a supplementary key of interpretation which distinguishes them from mere perceptible pictures.

Stenius does recognize that a "more thorough analysis might expose many difficulties" with his account of the notion of thinking and thought-pictures. He recognizes that he has taken a particular stand on the deep philosophical issue concerning the nature of the mental, a stand which is not without alternatives. The present chapter defends an interpretation which takes seriously the possibility that Wittgenstein's notion of the thought involves a different stand on the nature of the mental.

32. The most basic dimension of a symbol is neither its structure, nor its projective capacity, but its *presentational* dimension. The presentational dimension of the symbol is what, in the *Tractatus,* is referred to as the "showing" dimension of symbols. The showing or presentational character of symbols is commonly acknowledged, but seldom isolated and made an explicit subject of inquiry. For example, Russell, in his 1919 essay refers to mental entities as presentations: "The view to be taken on this question [the question, what is the content of a belief?] depends, to some extent, upon the view we take of 'ideas' or 'presentations. . .'" ("On Propositions," p. 305). Russell does not focus on the notion of presentation itself. This is because the notion of presentation, like all fundamental concepts, is quite difficult to isolate and make into an object of reflection. It is worthwhile to review here the means by which the presentational dimension of the symbol is, in the present book, isolated from the other symbolic dimensions.

In Chapter II it is argued that in the tautological symbols the representational content of the symbol drops out as irrelevant to the truth value of the symbol. This means that the particular *structure* of the symbol and the *projection* of that structure are not relevant to the truth value of the tautological symbol. But though the tautological symbol is not a *projective* or *representational* symbol, it is a symbol nonetheless. Thus, it is inferred that that which is relevant to its truth value is presented with its symbol. It is in the interpretation of the logical propositions, the *purely* presentational symbols, that the most basic dimension of symbols is isolated! But in what does this most basic dimension of symbols consist? Is the notion of the presentational dimension of symbols a primitive concept, or can some further analysis or illumination be given?

(1) Since the logical propositions have a truth value but are neither projective symbols, nor symbols whose particular structure is relevant to their truth value, the presentational dimension of the symbol is thereby isolated as the most basic dimension of the symbol. This dimension determines that something is relevant to the symbol's truth value. The most basic anatomical feature of symbols is

that one must distinguish the symbol from its "content" in this most abstract sense of "content." (2) The logical propositions are distinctive in that they *present with themselves* that which is relevant to their truth value. That is, the whole expression "present-with-itself" must be considered as a unitary expression. What this means is that the view that a symbol presents such and such is the view that the symbolic entity *itself* presents such and such. In other words, the presentational dimension of symbols is the most basic dimension of the intrinsic meaningfulness of symbols. Synthesizing these two results, one arrives at the view that the presentational dimension of symbols is the most basic feature by virtue of which they have an intrinsic "content"—something which is relevant to their truth value.

There are, however, limits as to how much illumination about the presentational dimension of symbols can be achieved. It is the content of the symbol, and the fact that the symbol has a content, which are all that is needed to understand the logical properties of the symbol (that is, these are *presented* by the symbol). But the Tractatus does not indicate *how* it is to be understood that something has a content in the sense which is relevant to logic, meaning and truth value, or *how* it is to be understood that something presents such and such or is a symbol in the first place. Philosophical logic, or the interpretation of the tautologies, leads one *to* the basic conditions of logic but not *into* them. If it is possible to go into these conditions, a different kind of inquiry—one more fundamental than any envisaged by the *Tractatus*—is required.

33. D. Favrholdt, *An Interpretation and Critique of Wittgenstein's 'Tractatus'* (Copenhagen: Munksguard, 1967), p. 84.

34. Bruce Goldberg, "The Correspondence Hypotheses," *Philosophical Review* (October 1968).

35. Ibid., p. 449.

36. Robert Nozick, *Philosophical Explanations* (New York: Oxford University Press, 1981), p. 747 n. 13.

37. Ibid.

38. Malcolm, *Memory and Mind,* p. 140.

39. Heil, "Does Cognitive Psychology Rest on a Mistake?"

40. Ibid., p. 333.

41. Ibid.

42. Kripke, *Wittgenstein on Rules and Private Language,* p. 60.

43. Ibid., p. 62.

44. Ibid., p. 66.

45. Ibid.; see, for instance, pp. 51, 52 and 63.

46. Ibid., p. 11.

47. G. Frege, "The Thought: a Logical Inquiry," in *Philosophical Logic,* ed. by Peter F. Strawson (New York: Oxford University Press, 1967).

48. Noam Chomsky, *Language and Mind* (New York: Harcourt Brace Johanovich, Inc., 1972); p. 17.

49. Noam Chomsky, *Cartesian Linguistics* (New York: Harper and Row, 1966), p. 32.

50. Chomsky, *Language and Mind,* p. 29.

51. Chomsky, *Cartesian Linguistics,* p. 35.

52. Ibid. Chomsky uses the expression "deep structure" ambiguously, sometimes to refer to a structure which is produced at some intermediary point in the transformational process, and other times he uses it to refer to the final product itself. When he uses the expression to refer to the intermediary structure, the final product is referred to as the semantically interpreted deep structure. Whatever the terminology, it is the final product—the entity which determines its own meaning—which is the meaning locus.

53. Chomsky, *Language and Mind,* p. 103.

54. Ibid.

55. Ibid.

56. Noam Chomsky, *Aspects of a Theory of Syntax* (Cambridge, MA: M.I.T. Press, 1970), p. 16.

57. Chomsky, *Cartesian Linguistics,* p. 35.

58. Ibid., p. 34.

59. Jerry Fodor, *The Language of Thought* (Cambridge, MA: Harvard University Press, 1979), p. 151.

60. Ibid., p. 111.

61. Ibid., p. 198.

62. Ibid., p. 121.

63. Ibid., p. 151.

64. Ibid., p. 114.

65. Ibid., p. 120.

66. Ibid.

67. Ibid., p. 121n. 16

68. Ibid.

69. Ibid.

70. Ibid., pp. 120–121.

71. Ibid., p. 125.

72. Ibid., p. 120.

73. See Jerrold Katz's *The Underlying Reality of Language and Its Philo-sophical Import* (New York: Harper and Row, 1971). Katz writes: "We shall argue that natural languages have an underlying reality very different from their surface form" (p. 4). Further, Katz refers to the "later" Wittgenstein who is said to "berate the tendency to assume a conceptual structure intermediary between signs and facts, between words and the world," and the context makes clear that Katz identifies himself with this berated view (p. 13). Finally, in the closing pages of his book, Katz again refers to Wittgenstein's reasons for abandoning the idea that "concepts are to be understood as the meanings that give 'cognitive life' to otherwise dead pieces of orthography. . ." (pp. 177–178). It is Katz's view that there are concepts or conceptual structures intermediate between words and the world. These have a nature which contrasts with mere perceptible signs, and which suits them to be the meaning component. They can give "cognitive life" to the otherwise meaningless perceptible signs.

74. The exception to this is Bruce Goldberg's "Mechanism and Meaning," which is to appear in *Knowledge of Mind,* ed. by Carl Ginet and S. Shoemaker. Goldberg recognizes that these philosophical psycholinguists do employ a version of the notion of the meaning locus. He calls these views which accept this notion "Internal Structure" theories of meaning (p. 208), where the internal structure is the meaning locus. According to Goldberg, the meaning locus in these views plays a role in the mechanistic account of how sentences are disambiguated. That is, ordinary perceptible sentences are ambiguous among a multiplicity of interpretations, yet they have a particular meaning. Thus, according to these "Internal Structure" views, the ordinary perceptible sentence is merely the perceptible accompaniment of an internal structure which determines its

particular meaning. The internal structure must, therefore, have a nature unlike the mere perceptible structure, otherwise it would itself be open to a multiplicity of interpretations. This sort of view is now familiar. Goldberg is, however, concerned to criticize such views. An outline of his view is the following:

A meaning locus is, as we have seen, a completely self-contained meaning. And as such, that it has meaning and what its meaning is in particular, are independent of the relevant linguistic context. The meaning locus is, by its very nature, a context independent meaning. But the idea of a context independent meaning is, according to Goldberg, "unintelligible." His reasoning for this view cannot be presented here. Goldberg does, however, propose an account of disambiguation which does not involve an internal structure with the unique properties of the meaning locus. He writes, "There is an alternative [to Internal Structure Theories of Meaning]. It would be to see sentences as becoming disambiguated, as acquiring the meaning they have, because of, among other things, the relation in which they stand to an ongoing flow of human behavior. That is, to see disambiguation as *positional*. A particular remark in a given situation will be taken a certain way. But this does not require that a structure be attached to it" (p. 206). Goldberg sums up his view as follows: "The moral is this. The notion of sentence meaning cannot be rendered intelligible unless sentences are seen, essentially, against the background of and embedded into the flow of characteristic patterns of human behavior" (p. 208). In short, Goldberg suggests that rather than holding that the account of meaning involves the notion of a self-contained or context independent meaning, one must understand the meaning of a sentence in terms of its position in the relevant linguistic context.

Goldberg's view is a development of the view Wittgenstein presents in his *Philosophical Investigations*. In the *Philosophical Investigations* Wittgenstein criticizes the notion of a self-contained meaning:

You say to me: "You understand this expression, don't you? Well then—
I am using it in the sense you are familiar with."—As if the sense were an atmosphere accompanying the word, which it carried with it into every kind of application.

If, for example, someone says that the sentence "This is here" (saying which he points to an object in front of him) makes sense to him, then he should ask himself in what special circumstances this sentence is used. There it does make sense. (par. 117)

A detailed exegesis of this passage cannot be presented here. It is clear, however, that the author of the *Philosophical Investigations* criticizes the view that the meaning of the proposition consists in an entity (here he uses the image of an "atmosphere" to indicate such a meaning entity). He instead emphasizes that it is the "circumstances" in which the sentence is used which are the important factor. There has been much debate concerning the relation of the views of the *Tractatus* to those of the *Philosophical Investigations*. Many have held that there is a continuity in the views of these two works, that these views are, similar at core, and that they differ only in detail or scope. If the present interpretation is correct, however, the views of the *Tractatus* and the *Philosophical Investigations* concerning the meaning of propositions are entirely different and incompatible. The reason this has not been seen is that the fundamental notions of meaning in the *Tractatus* have not been clearly visualized. Once it is recognized that the fundamental notion of meaning in the *Tractatus* is the notion of a meaning locus, the relation of the two books can be precisely defined. The *Tractatus* accepts the view that the perceptible propositional sign has meaning insofar as it is accompanied by an entity which has the nature of a meaning locus, a context independent meaning. The *Philosophical Investigations* holds that the notion of a context independent meaning is unintelligible. The views of the *Tractatus* and the *Philosophical Investigations* on the issue of the meaning of language *could not be more different*.

75. It might be pointed out that these texts by Chomsky, Fodor and Katz are older texts, and that the authors may not accept the same views at present. This may be true, but it does not diminish the interest of understanding these stages in their development, and it is my main purpose here only to show that the occurrence of the notions of a meaning locus and interpretation terminus are far more common than is commonly recognized.

But even if one's interest is in Chomsky's Fodor's or Katz's present views, the present inquiry is still important. For if these authors no longer hold that the meaning of sentences is determined in these ways, then we must ask how it is determined. What effects do the changes in their positions, if there are any, have for their goal of giving an *explanation* of overt linguistic behavior *in terms of the internal states of the linguistic subject*. That is, if they had a role for the meaning locus and interpretation terminus in their earlier views, and if they have given up those notions, then what if anything performs the function formerly assigned to those notions? If something else performs this function, then we must be told what it is. If nothing takes over that function, then we must be told what portions of their original goals they have given up. Specifically, if they no longer accept these notions, then do they give up or qualify their claims that they can give an *explanation* of the linguistic behavior of subjects? It would be a refreshing change if the leaders in this tradition would directly and clearly confront their basic philosophical presuppositions and changes of position. *That* would tell us something about their current views.

76. Michael Dummett, "What is a Theory of Meaning?," in *Mind and Language,* ed. by Samuel Guttenplan (New York: Oxford University Press, 1975), p. 98.

77. Hilary Putnam, *Mind, Language and Reality,* Vol. 2 (New York: Cambridge University Press, 1979), p. 215.

78. Ibid., p. 139.

79. Dummett, "Theory of Meaning," p. 97. It is worth pointing out for the sake of completeness that this program of specifying the meanings of the expressions of one entire language is not unproblematic. It presupposes that the meanings of the expressions of the language are recursively specifiable. This, it may be argued, presupposes that there are certain atomic concepts and operations, and that the meanings of the expressions of the language are a function of these. Dummett's program presupposes, therefore, in the terminology which he uses in that essay, that the "atomistic" as opposed to the "holistic" conception of language is true. He does not claim to know that holism is not true. He writes, "I do not know that holism is an incorrect conception of language. But I am asserting that the acceptance of holism should lead to the conclusion that any systematic theory of meaning is impossible. . .; my own preference is, therefore, to assume as a methodological principle that holism is false" (Ibid., p. 121).

80. Ibid., p. 97. There are two points. First, Dummett suggests that the reason an analogous proposal has never been suggested for epistemology is that "our grasp on the concept of knowledge is rather more secure than our grasp on the concept of meaning" (Ibid.). It seems to me that there is an important point to saying that this must be an illusion. That is, there is a real point to saying that the concept of knowledge presupposes the concept of meaning, and any problems which pertain to the latter transfer automatically to the former. For example, when Dummett says (to take just one example) that we are unsure whether it is possible "to *state* the meaning of an expression" (Ibid., p. 98), we should automatically doubt our security that is is possible to *state what one knows.* This point that our insecurity about the concept of meaning ought to transfer automatically to our concepts of knowledge, may not be regarded as obvious. It is, however, a manifestation of a particular point of view on the history and progress of philosophy. That is, it seems to me that twentieth century philosophy is distinctive in its attention to problems connected with meaning, as opposed, for instance, to problems connected with knowledge. But this should not to be regarded as a manifestation of the fact that we have become clearer about the concepts of knowledge, and have moved on to different problems. On the contrary, the insights and attitudes which guide the interests

of contemporary philosophy are based on the view that the concepts of meaning are *fundamental* concepts. This is so in the sense that nothing can be secure until these concepts are. It is not that problems of knowledge have been so sufficiently illuminated that we can move on to other problems, but that problems of knowledge have been shelved until those more fundamental problems which underlie everything can be solved. Contemporary philosophy is distinguished by the fact that it has penetrated to the point at which the most basic problems lie.

The second point is that Dummett is wrong in saying that a similar approach has never been suggested for the problems of epistemology. To take just one example, the question of whether knowledge must involve a systematic character, or whether there can be, so to speak, "atoms of knowledge," acquired individually, is a question about the correct form of a complete specification of everything an individual, or community, could be said to know.

81. Plato, "Theaetetus," in *The Collected Dialogues of Plato*, ed. by Edith Hamilton and Huntington Cairns (Princeton: Princeton University Press, p. 851).

82. Ibid.

83. Ibid.

84. Ibid., pp. 851–852.

85. Michael Dummett, *Frege: Philosophy of Language* (London: Duckworth, 1981), p. 92.

86. Putnam, *Mind*, p. 216.

87. Russell, *Analysis of Mind*, p. 26.

88. Just as this book was to go into print a copy of Colin McGinn's recent book, *Wittgenstein on Meaning*, a response to Kripke's *Wittgenstein on Rules and Private Language* was given to me by my friend Antonio Chu. McGinn's book goes even further than Kripke's in highlighting the importance of the notion of the meaning locus in Wittgenstein's philosophy, specifically, by stressing the importance of the denial of the soundness of this notion by the *Philosophical Investigations*. McGinn writes, "What is more surprising and challenging about Wittgenstein's critique of the interpretational conception is the application to the idea of *mental* signs, signs whose medium is not marks and sounds but the mind itself. For it seems that there is a standing temptation to endow such alleged mental signs with the power of generating their own meanings—to think of them as self-interpreting . . . I refer to the doctrine that there is a 'language of thought' which determines linguistic comprehension. It is hard to see this particular theory of understanding as anything other than

the idea that there are privileged signs which *terminate* questions of meaning—special signs which are such that of translation is made into them then meaning is determined." (p. 118) McGinn goes on to characterize mental items on this conception as "intrinsically meaningful", and he argues that the Wittgenstein of the *Philosophical Investigations* rejects all such language of thought views, and is right to do so. (p. 119)

What McGinn has done in the brief passage is to (1) indicate several different formulations of the notions of the meaning locus and interpretation terminus, (2) implicate Fodor in such theories, (3) suggest some connection of such notions with the nature of the mental and (4) stress the importance of all of this for the contemporary theory of meaning. McGinn's book deserves more careful discussion, but unfortunately, this cannot be undertaken here.

89. The present chapter develops the full fledged notion of the meaning locus, the notion which involves *both* a structural and a mental dimension. There are, however, purely "materialistic" versions of the notion. These are views which hold that semantic information is embodied in material, usually neurophysiological, structures. Materialistic trace theories of memory hold that the memory trace is a structure which is stored in the brain or body and which, given the appropriate stimulus, can cause a memory event of a past experience, that is, the experience which originally left the trace. In order to fulfill this function, the trace must have a structure which is identical with the original experience; otherwise the "trace" would not be a trace of just that experience. The purpose of the present chapter is, however, to develop Wittgenstein's fundamental notion of meaning and to describe its connections with a long tradition concerning the nature of the mental. It is, however, important to recognize that a notion of the meaning locus can be found in a materialistic form (Fodor, for example, sometimes speaks as if his view is ultimately intended, or hoped, to have a materialistic interpretation: "We have been supposing that the nervous system 'speaks' an internal language . . ." (*Language of Thought,* p. 122). Also see Howard Bursen's illuminating study, *Dismantling the Memory Machine* (Dordrecht: D. Reidel Publishing Company, 1978).

Chapter VII

1. Anonymous reviewer, and others.

2. The fact that Wittgenstein uses the word *showing* in such a variety of ways is one of the most misleading features of the *Tractatus,* and it may even have mislead Wittgenstein himself. Wittgenstein may have confusedly oscillated between the formulation according to which the tautologies themselves show

such and such, and the formulation according to which the fact that certain expressions are tautologies shows such and such. As a result, he may have failed to grasp clearly the fact that the construction of the argument of the *Tractatus* is a possible project. Wittgenstein's loose usage of key terminology may have prevented him from seeing the full possibilities of his own project.

3. See, for example, Black, *Companion,* pp. 272–275.

4. Other notions are the notion of a 'value locus or terminus' and the notion of an 'action terminus'. The notion of an entity which is good or evil, beautiful or ugly in-itself or intrinsically, is the notion of a value locus (such as Plato's Forms) and on some accounts, pleasure and pain).

The notion of an act of will or intention is often conceived as an 'action terminus'. An action terminus is that entity in the mind or body which can be identified as the ultimate source of the action.

5. The account of truth which must be developed on a holistic conception of propositions must be quite different from that which is developed on the atomistic conception of propositions. This is, in fact, a part of the theme with which Russell opens his "Lectures on Logical Atomism," though Russell is himself only concerned to work out the details of the atomistic view:

> The logic which I shall advocate is atomistic as opposed to the monistic logic of the people who more or less follow Hegel. When I say that my logic is atomistic I mean that I share the common sense belief that there are many separate things; I do not regard the apparent multiplicity of the world as consisting merely in phases and unreal divisions in a single indivisible reality. It results from that, that a considerable part of what one would have to do to justify the sort of philosophy I wish to advocate would consist in justifying the process of analysis. One is often told that the process of analysis is falsification, that when you analyse any given concrete whole you falsify it and the results of analysis are not true. I do not think that is the right view." (pp. 298–299).

The theme of this remark is the general conflict between the generally atomistic, and "monistic" or holistic world views. The choice between these world views involves differing conceptions of the natures of truth, facts, propositions, analysis, and so on. It is important to remember that Russell had at an earlier time been a Hegelian, a holist in some sense, and that his early analytic efforts are attempts to work out an alternative to these holistic conceptions of truth. From the very beginning, Russell identified the *analytic* outlooks with the *atomist* one, that is, he held that analysis is bound up with an atomistic metaphysics. Russell wants to work out a view according to which individual propositions are separable atoms of truth or falsity and of meaning, but it is important to recognize that Russell regards this sort of view as a consequence of a more basic choice between the atomistic and the holistic world view. In the holistic view, the most basic unit of truth or falsity and meaning must be some larger whole, and truth or falsity and meaning apply to the isolated proposition, if at all, only derivatively, or only against the background of their embeddedness in the larger whole. There is obviously a great deal more which must be said if the various dimensions of the holistic view and the various versions of the holistic view are to be made clear. This is, unfortunately, beyond the scope of the present discussion. This atomistic conception which Russell regarded as bound up with the decision between world views has, unfortunately, become a tacit presupposition of most contemporary philosophizing. It is only more recently, with the recognition of the real difficulties in working out the details of the generally atomistic world view (for instance, the crisis in the contemporary theory of meaning) that philosophers have begun to consider seriously the possibility of the holistic conception of meaning, truth, and other issues.

6. Kant's general discussion of the self-contained character of his system is presented in the concluding pages of the first *Critique* ("The Architectonic of Pure Reason"). Kant writes:

> In accordance with reason's legislative prescription, our diverse modes of knowledge must not be permitted to be a mere rhapsody, but must form a system. . . . By a system I understand the unity of the manifold modes of knowledge under one idea. The idea is the concept provided by reason—of the form of a whole—in so far as the concept determines *a priori* not only the scope of its manifold content but also the positions which the parts occupy relatively to one another. . . . The unity of the end to which all the parts relate in the idea of which they all stand in relation to one another, makes it possible for us to determine from our knowledge of the other parts whether any part be missing, and to prevent any arbitrary addition, or in respect of its completeness any indeterminateness that does not conform to the limits which are thus determined *a priori*. The whole is thus an organized unity *(articulatio)*, and not an aggregate *(coacervatio)*. It may grow from within *(per intussusceptionem)*, but not by external addition. Kant, *Critique of Pure Reason* (London: MacMillan & Company Ltd., 1961), p. 653.

It is Kant's view that the set of justifiable philosophical propositions do not constitute a mere set of propositions, a mere *aggregate* of propositions, but that they form a system in a certain sense. The set of philosophical propositions belong together; they form a special kind of whole or unity. One important part of Kant's account of the systematic or holistic nature of philosophical knowledge is connected with the view that his set of philosophical propositions is self-contained in a certain sense. This idea of a self-contained system of philosophical knowledge is indicated by Kant in the remark that our diverse modes of knowledge form a unity or system insofar as it may grow from within but not from without.

7. This is not meant to imply that the notions of such a system are exactly the same in all these philosophers. For purposes of illustration I consider briefly only one aspect of these philosophical systems, their self-contained character, and only two philosophers of the idealist tradition—Husserl and Hegel.

Husserl claims in the *Cartesian Meditations* that it is his purpose to show "the concrete possibility of the Cartesian idea of a philosophy as an all-embracing science grounded in an absolute foundation" (p. 152). But "the idea of an all-embracing philosophy becomes actualized-quite differently than Descartes and his age, guided by modern natural science, expected: Not as an all-embracing system of deductive theory, . . . but in an *all-embracing self investigation*" (p. 156). Husserl continues: "This system of the all-embracing a priori is therefore to be designated also as the systematic unfolding of the all-embracing a priori innate in the essence of a transcendental subjectivity . . . or as the systematic unfolding of *the universal logos of all conceivable* being. . . . But a priori science must not be naive; on the contrary, it must have originated from ultimate transcendental-phenomenological sources and be fashioned according to an all-round a priori, resting on itself and justifying itself by itself" (pp. 155–56). Husserl's ideal of a self-contained system of philosophy does not even purport to involve the rigorous deduction of the components of the system from a single principle, but it is instead connected with his view concerning the nature of phenomenology, that is, with the idea that the whole system is "innate in the essence of a transcendental subjectivity." A detailed discussion of this is beyond the scope of the present inquiry.

The ideal of a self-contained philosophical system is also to be found in Hegel, but Hegel's view is even more difficult than Husserl's to characterize briefly. Some idea of Hegel's view can be gleaned from the following remark. Hegel writes, "the identity of the Idea with itself is one with the process; . . . by virtue of the freedom which the notion attains in the Idea, the Idea possesses within itself also the *most stubborn opposition,* its repose consists in the security and certainty with which it eternally creates and eternally overcomes that opposition, in it meeting itself." [*Phenomenology of Spirit,* trans. by A. V. Miller [New York: Oxford University Press, 1979], p. 759]. The viewpoint which is expressed here can, for present purposes, be characterized as the view that though there is apparently an "opposition," something external to the realm of the "the Idea," this opposition is continually overcome and "the Idea" finds that this apparent opposition is really its own self, that is, there is nothing that is not included in the self-contained realm of the Idea. Like Husserl, Hegel's notion of the self-contained realm is not to be construed on a deductive model. Hegel's notion is also different from Husserl's in many ways. Hegel's self-contained realm must be explained in terms of the mediating "process" in which "the Idea comes to comprehend itself . . . etc." The important point for the present purpose is only that there are various notions of self-contained philosophical systems in German idealistic philosophy, and though they all differ from each other, they are all alike in identifying the mind as the ultimate self-contained entity, and the self-contained philosophical system is thought to be in one way or another derivative from the self-contained nature of mind.

8. J. G. Fichte, *Science of Knowledge*, p. 11. It is important to stress here that no special kinship between Wittgenstein's and Fichte's philosophies, beyond the specific *analogy* described here, is asserted. It is also worth pointing out that it is this author's opinion that both Fichte's method and content leave much to be desired. However, if it is one's goal to identify certain currents in 19th century German philosophy, Fichte is quite useful, and it is this which is done here.

9. Ibid.

10. Ibid., p. 14.

11. Ibid., p. 29–30.

12. That is, one must distinguish the philosophical system from the complete system of human knowledge (though on Fichte's view the two are intimately connected), and the fundamental principle plays a role with respect to both the former and the latter. Fichte's view is straightforward, and moreover it parallels a view of the *Tractatus*. Fichte's view is that the contents of the philosophical system determine the *form* of the subsidiary sciences which fall under it. This view can be illustrated by reference to the view of the *Tractatus*. We have seen that Wittgenstein's philosophical system includes consequences concerning the account of the notion of a fact, and this has ramifications concerning the form of any science which purports to have factual content. To take a specific example, since a fact, in Wittgenstein's view, consists in a mere contingent structuring of objects, there can be a science of communication only if its fundamental concepts can be defined in terms of the notions of mere contingent structurings of objects. The form of the science of communication is thus determined: communication involves the transformation of structures into structures by means of rules which can be mechanically applied. Thus, in Wittgenstein's view, as in Fichte's, there is a sense in which the tautological symbol determines not only the scope and content of philosophical truth, but also the form of the "complete and unit-system [of factual knowledge] in the human mind."

13. Fichte, *Science of Knowledge*, p. 63.

14. Ibid., pp. 21–22. One of the fundamental problems which dominated early analytical philosophy is the general problem of self-reference. One form

this problem takes is based on the fact that, though there seems to be no immediate reason why self-reference should not make sense, if one allows that propositions can refer to themselves, specifically to their own truth values, then contradictions follow. One program is, then, to modify or eliminate the view that self-reference is possible in order to eliminate the contradiction. This, it is thought, illuminates the nature of language. It is interesting to recognize that another notion and another problem of self-reference is present in the German philosophical tradition, and in the *Tractatus,* and that it is connected with the fundamental nature of logic and of both philosophical systems and philosophical truth. It is important to Fichte that the fundamental principle which grounds his philosophical system is "absolutely not to be proven," that it is "certain in itself," and that it must even be a "contradiction" to "inquire after its ground." What lies behind these descriptions of the unique properties and independence of his fundamental principle is that it has something like a special self-referential property. That is, the reason it is contradictory even to inquire after the "ground" of the fundamental principle is that it must in some sense determine its own certainty or truth. The point is even clearer with respect to the analogous view in the *Tractatus.* The "unique status" of the logical propositions is accounted for in Chapter II of the present book in terms of the view that the logical propositions are presentational symbols. This is true in the extreme sense that they present with themselves that which is relevant to their own truth value, or "every tautology itself shows that it is a tautology" (6.127). The unique status of the logical propositions which found Wittgenstein's philosophical system consists in nothing other than the fact that the logical propositional symbol has this unique self-referential property. That is, in Wittgenstein's *Tractatus,* as in Fichte's philosophy, the idea of an entity with these unique self-referential properties lies at the foundation of the accounts of the nature of the a priori and of the unique natures of philosophical systems and truth. Unfortunately, it is obviously beyond the scope of the present discussion to follow all the issues suggested here to their conclusion.

15. Fichte's notion of a science is not properly comparable with the contemporary notion(s) of an empirical science. Quite the contrary, in Fichte's view a science in the fullest sense is characterized by the self-contained, pre-suppositionless and holistic dimensions indicated in the preceding discussions. Fichte's whole point is that the sorts of systems which we now call sciences are only properly accorded that description, insofar as they are encompassed within the fundamental science—philosophy—in the manner sketched in footnote 12.

16. There are many possible examples of the new sorts of views which emerge in Wittgenstein's logicist transformation of the basic idealist views. One good example is indicated in the present book as early as Chapter II, section

6. It has often been felt that our certainty about the logical propositions, for example, must ultimately be subjective in nature. The mind must grasp the truth of the logical propositions, but from the fact that the logical propositions seem certain to the mind, it does not follow that they are certain themselves. That is, in this traditional model our certainty must have an essentially subjective dimension. It is my view that Wittgenstein's rejection of the notion of self-evidence at 5.4731 and 6.1271 is the rejection of the account of certainty which involves such a subjective dimension. By contrast, in the view of the *Tractatus,* the account of the certainty or a priority of the logical propositions is given without reference to any subjective act or intuition or subjective feeling of self-evidence. In Wittgenstein's view, the account of the certainty, the a priority, of the logical propositions is given in terms of the objective properties of the logical propositional symbol itself. The tautological symbol is a priori true by virtue of that which is presented with its symbol. Note that one of the remarks in which Wittgenstein rejects the notion of self-evidence is 6.1271, which is a comment on 6.127. Here Wittgenstein says that every tautology itself shows that it is a tautology. That remark is one of best indicators that Wittgenstein is opposing a new model of certainty to the old subjectivist one. As it is pointed out at II.5, Wittgenstein transfers the burden of the a priori, of certainty, and so forth, from the subjective self to the symbols themselves. The fundamental concepts out of which one can construct a genuine alternative to the traditional paradigm of a purely subjective certainty had not been clearly visualized prior to the *Tractatus.* One of the really significant additions of the *Tractatus* to the history of ideas is that it develops the fundamental concepts which underlie the notion of a purely *objective certainty.*

17. For example, one of the more systematic of contemporary philosophers is Hector-Neri Castañeda. Castañeda writes that "the method of philosophy is, like the method of the sciences: empirical, exegetical, hypothetical, deductive, iterative, and cumulative." [*On Philosophical Method* (Bloomington, Indiana: Nous Publishing, 1980), p. 27.]

In Castañeda's view, "data" is gathered and exegised, theoretical leaps are made, and so forth. Though a detailed discussion of Castañeda's method is impossible here, it is clear that his notion of a philosophical system is not at all comparable with the notion of a self-contained or presuppositionless system. His philosophical system is, in principle, open to revision every time new data are gathered. Castañeda's notion of a philosophical system is modeled on that of the lesser, empirical, sciences, but it is important to realize that there is a philosophical tradition which holds that the natures of philosophical systems and truth are fundamentally different, and more indifferent to change than empirical scientific systems and "truths".

18. A transcendental argument typically has a certain form, and though the explanation of why the argument of the *Tractatus* is not a transcendental argument in this sense is relatively lengthy, it is illuminating to recognize the difference between the argument of the *Tractatus* and a transcendental argument.

A transcendental argument of the standard type (1) has a certain characteristic form, (2) is based on certain kinds of presuppositions, and (3) is useful for certain kinds of purposes. Typically, such arguments are based on a description of certain phenomena, and the argument itself is an argument to the "necessary conditions for the possibility" of that particular phenomenon. To take an example which is directly relevant to the results of the present book, one might argue transcendentally from the existence of the phenomenon of linguistic meaning, to the necessary conditions for its possibility. In keeping with the results of Chapter VI, it might be argued that one of the necessary conditions for the possibility of linguistic meaning is that the propositional symbol involves a meaning locus. It is important to recognize that the premises in such a transcendental argument must not only state the existence of the relevant phenomenon, but they must also involve, whether explicitly or implicitly, a rather rich characterization of the relevant phenomenon. In the case of the phenomenon of linguistic meaning, the premise must include a characterization of the linguistic entities involved, the perceptible sentences, and of the sorts of things these perceptible sentences are about. Normally these characterizations are based on ordinary experience or conceptions, though this may not be true in all cases. Without some rich characterization of the relevant phenomenon, however, there is no basis on which to erect the argument leading to the conditions for the possibility of that phenomenon. The most important point for the present purposes is that such transcendental arguments are, therefore, arguments *from the less basic*, that is, the somewhat rich and diverse descriptions of certain phenomenon, *to the fewer and more basic* concepts and views which underlie it.

It is especially worthwhile to consider the possibility of such transcendental arguments in connection with the particular case of linguistic meaning. Russell's 1919 argument that the genuine propositional symbol involves a meaning locus can be viewed as a transcendental argument of this standard type. Russell characterizes both ordinary sorts of linguistic entities, his word-propositions, and the states of affairs which they are about. On the basis of these descriptions he argues that the perceptible word-proposition must "go through" a "mental intermediary". That is, he argues that such a mental intermediary is a condition of the possibility of the meaning connection between perceptible sentences and the world. It is important to recognize that the argument of the *Tractatus* is *not* a transcendental argument in this sense.

The conclusion of Russell's 1919 argument in "On Propositions," and one of the conclusions of the argument of the *Tractatus,* that is, that the propositional system involves a meaning locus, are indeed similar. But whereas Russell's argument is from the rich and less fundamental description of the phenomenon of linguistic meaning to the more fundamental concepts and views which underlie it, the argument of the *Tractatus* begins with concepts and views which are *even more fundamental still* than the notion of the mental and the meaning locus. The argument of the *Tractatus* is based on views about the tautologies and the nature of the logical constants, and these, it seems obvious, are more fundamental than the notions of the meaning locus and the mental. *The pattern of argument in the argument of the* Tractatus *is actually the reverse of that involved in transcendental arguments,* and it is important that this is so.

A transcendental argument of the standard type may result in the discovery of a set of fundamental concepts or views, but such an argument is not well suited to display the logical structure of the relevant nexus of concepts and views. That is, a transcendental argument might result in the discovery *that* such and such is a fundamental concept or view, but it does not normally result in a clear and precise view about (1) how that fundamental concept or view relates to other fundamental concepts and views, nor (2) how one is to comprehend fully the relevant concepts and views. Some of the flaws in Russell's account of the notion of the meaning locus are traceable to these two weaknesses which attend standard transcendental arguments.

On the first point, Russell countenances both logical notions and the notions which pertain to the meaning locus. If Wittgenstein's view (See VI.2d) is correct, however, then the notion of the meaning locus is a logical notion in a strict sense. On the second point, Russell imports the notion of private feelings into his account of the meaning locus without sufficient warrant. Since Russell's account is based on less than fundamental grounds, he must grope among whatever concepts and views which happen to be available in order to develop his account. An account which is based on less fundamental grounds than are possible is a logically disordered account in that (1) it contains an excess of concepts and views, (2) the relevant concepts and views are not developed in such a fashion that their real logical and/or ontological priority are clearly exhibited, and (3) the account may fail to contain concepts and views which are essential to the complete understanding of the relevant phenomenon.

The point is that transcendental arguments of the standard type are appropriate to the exploratory phase of a philosophical inquiry, not to the phase in which concepts and views are developed systematically from the most fundamental grounds which are possible in the case. The argument of the *Tractatus* is not a transcendental argument of the standard form, but it is an argument which belongs to the latter phase of philosophical inquiry.

19. Kant, *Critique of Pure Reason,* A11–12, B25.

20. The general idea that philosophy does not properly seek a point of view on the world is held by a number of philosophers. John Wisdom, for example, writes, "Philosophic progress does not consist in acquiring knowledge of new facts but in acquiring new knowledge of facts. . . ." ("Logical constructions," *Mind,* 1931, p. 195.) However, Wittgenstein's version of the view is unique.

21. In an earlier note to the present chapter, it is pointed out that the notion of an entity with self-referential properties is connected with Fichte's and Wittgenstein's accounts of the unique natures of philosophical systems and truth. The notion of self-reference has, however, been found to be problematic by many philosophers. It is interesting to recognize that in Wittgenstein's view, at least, there is in the final analysis *no* self-referential entity. Talk about the self-referential tautological symbol is only an oblique way of talking about the logical properties of those symbols—the genuine propositional symbols—which are not self-referential symbols. One must say of the genuine propositional symbol that it is true or false. It does not refer to, or show, its own truth or falsity, and this is because what it is about is external to its symbol. In short, in Wittgenstein's view the notion of the self-referential tautological symbol is only a convenient fiction which is useful for getting at the nature of genuine propositional symbols.

Chapter VIII

1. Katz, *Underlying Reality,* see Chapter 2. Though this work of Katz's is dated, and he has since published a much different view, a Platonist view of meanings, in his more recent *Language and Other Abstract Objects,* those portions of his view discussed here have not changed in his shift from mentalism to Platonism. The present discussion applies to Katz's present view.

2. Ibid., pp. 11 and 13.

3. Ibid., p. 21.

4. Ibid., p. 11.

5. Ibid., pp. 11 and 15. Katz's "logical body" of the sentence is, of course, a reified meaning, a meaning locus. Unfortunately, Katz does not display the same awareness which we find in Fodor of the remarkable nature of this "logical body," this meaning entity.

6. Ibid., p. 16.

7. Ibid., pp. 16–17.

8. Ibid., p. 10.

9. Ibid., p. 11.

10. Ibid., p. 15.

11. Ibid., p. 12.

12. For a sketch of the critique of the notion of the meaning locus, see Chapter VI of the present work, note 74.

13. Though the notion of a rule which can be *mechanically* applied is not normally considered worthy of serious reflection, it is a quite problematic one. Indeed, any such notion which implicitly compares what human beings do when they follow a rule with what, say, a word processer does when it types from a disc, ought to be accorded careful consideration. This sort of more searching treatment of ideas is what motivates much of the *Philosophical Investigations*. My own view is that the author of the *Investigations* was led to this more penetrating insight into such notions because of his own earlier view in the *Tractatus*. Here he had made the dependence of ordinary theories of meaning, communication and so forth, on these philosophical notions much clearer than it had been before.

14. Katz, *Underlying Reality*, pp. 16–17.

15. Dummett, "Theory of Meaning," p. 121.

16. Carnap writes:
    In the first place he seems to me to be inconsistent in what he does. He tells us that one cannot make philosophical statements, and that whereof one cannot speak thereof one must be silent, and then instead of keeping silent he writes a whole philosophical book. (See Carnap, "Philosophy and Logical Syntax," p. 435.)

Carnap's criticism, a very common sort of criticism, is *factually* wrong, and the factual error is connected with Carnap's failure to understand the personal dimension of Wittgenstein's concluding remark. Wittgenstein does not tell us to be silent, and *then* he writes a book. He writes his book, and *at its end* tells us to be silent. The fact that Wittgenstein tells us to be silent after he has written the book, after he has eludicated the structure of language to his own satisfaction, is itself because only then is he freed from the philosophical obsession. The philosopher is concerned with the elucidation of the structure of propositions, and for whatever reason, cannot rest until these questions are answered. But if that is true, then philosophy takes us away from concern with the world in which we live, and sinks us in a concern about our mode of representation of the world. Only after one has conquered one's obsession with symbols, can one cultivate one's concern for the world. Only then can one set about the real challenge of life, to live well. Carnap's criticism is really based on his confusing a personal statement by the philosopher who has already elucidated the structure of symbols, with a statement about the logical status of those elucidations themselves.

There is another dimension to this general question which has not even been touched upon in the present book, which stresses the "logical" as opposed to the "personal" dimension of Wittgenstein's views. As has been forceably pointed out to me by John N. Williams, Wittgenstein's view that the logical propositions are senseless does not mean that they are meaningless. See J.N. Williams, "Believing the Self-Contradictory," *American Philosophical Quarterly* (July 1982). This point is connected with the one stressed to me by Professor Fogelin, that although Wittgenstein holds that the logical constants are without a reference, in Frege's sense, they do have a meaning. These points by Fogelin and Williams are of the greatest importance. For if the logical propositions are meaningful then one can believe them, doubt them, perhaps even know them. The same point extends to the philosophical propositions which are elucidations of the logical propositions. Wittgenstein's views that the logical propositions are senseless, and the philosophical propositions nonsense, do not automatically preclude that one can have propositional, or as I prefer to call them, psychological attitudes toward them. Aside from the questions about the logical status of such propositions, there is the additional question of their *personal significance.* That they have such a personal significance, *that their role in human activities is the role of things believed, known, etc.,* is not precluded by Wittgenstein's views. Carnap's criticism, quite casually and on the basis of mere verbal points, mistakenly rules out of consideration a wholly new sort of philosophical account, a theory of belief and knowledge, wholly consistent with Wittgenstein's views, for logical and philosophical propositions.

Bibliography

Anscombe, G.E.M. *An Introduction to Wittgenstein's Tractatus.* Philadelphia: University of Pennsylvania Press, 1971.

Belnap, Nuel, and Anderson, Alan Ross. *Entailment.* Princeton: Princeton University Press, 1975.

Black, Max. *A Companion to Wittgenstein's 'Tractatus'.* Ithaca, New York: Cornell University Press, 1970.

Brentano, Franz. *Psychology From an Empirical Standpoint.* London: Routledge and Kegan Paul, Ltd., 1973.

Bursen, Howard. *Dismantling the Memory Machine.* Dordrecht: D. Reidel Publishing Company, 1978.

Carnap, Rudolph. "On the Character of Philosophical Problems." In *The Linguistic Turn,* ed. by Richard Rorty. Chicago: The University of Chicago Press, 1975.

————. "Philosophy and Logical Syntax." In *Readings in Twentieth Century Philosophy.* Edited by Warren Alston and George Nakhnikian. New York: The Free Press, 1969.

Castañeda, Hector-Neri. *On Philosophical Method.* Bloomington, Indiana: Nous Publications, 1980.

Chomsky, Noam. *Aspects of a Theory of Syntax.* Cambridge, Massachusetts: M.I.T. Press, 1970.

————. *Cartesian Linguistics.* New York: Harper and Row, 1966.

————. *Language and Mind.* New York: Harcourt Brace Johanovich, Inc., 1972.

Dummett, Michael. *Frege: Philosophy of Language.* London: Duckworth, 1981.

————. "What is a Theory of Meaning?" In *Mind and Language.* Edited by Samuel Guttenplan. New York: Oxford University Press, 1975.

Favrholdt, D. *An Interpretation and Critique of Wittgenstein's 'Tractatus'.* Copenhagen: Munksgaard, 1967.

Fichte, J.G. *Science of Knowledge.* Translated by A.E. Kroeger. London: Trubner, 1889.

Fodor, Jerry. *The Language of Thought.* Cambridge, Massachusetts: Harvard University Press, 1979.

Fogelin, Robert. *Wittgenstein.* Boston: Routledge and Kegan Paul, 1976.

Frege, G. "The Thought: A Logical Inquiry." In *Philosophical Logic.* Edited by Peter Strawson. ———: Oxford University Press, 1967.

Goldberg, Bruce. "The Correspondence Hypothesis." *Philosophical Review,* October 1968.

———. "Mechanism and Meaning." In *Knowledge and Mind.* Edited by Carl Ginet and Sydney Shoemaker. New York: Oxford University Press, 1983.

Hegel, G.F.W. *Phenomenology of Spirit.* Translated by A.V. Miller. New York: Oxford University Press, 1979.

Heil, John. "Does Cognitive Psychology Rest on a Mistake?" *Mind,* July 1981.

———. "Traces of Things Past." *Philosophy of Science,* March 1978.

Hume, David. *A Treatise of Human Nature.* London: Oxford University Press, 1973.

Husserl, Edmund. *Cartesian Meditations.* Translated by Dorion Cairns. The Netherlands: Martinus Nijhoff, 1970.

Kant, Immanuel. *Critique of Pure Reason.* London: Macmillan & Company Ltd., 1961.

Katz, Jerrold J. *Language and Other Abstract Objects.* Totowa, New Jersey: Rowman and Littlefield, 1981.

———. *The Underlying Reality of Language and Its Philosophical Import.* New York: Harper and Row, 1971.

Kripke, Saul. *Wittgenstein on Rules and Private Language.* London: Basil Blackwell, 1982.

Malcolm, Norman. *Memory and Mind.* Ithaca, New York: Cornell University Press, 1977.

McGinn, Colin. *Wittgenstein on Meaning.* Oxford: Basil Blackwell, 1984.

Nakhnikian, George. "Introduction to 'Logical Positivism'." In *Readings in Twentieth Century Philosophy.* Edited by Warren Alston and George Nakhnikian. New York: The Free Press, 1969.

Nozick, Robert. *Philosophical Explanations.* New York: Oxford University Press, 1981.

Plato. "Theaetetus." In *The Collected Dialogues of Plato.* Edited by Edith Hamilton and Huntington Cairns. Princeton: Princeton University Press, 1969.

Putnam, Hilary. *Mind, Language and Reality* Vol. 2. New York: Cambridge University Press, 1979.

Priest, Graham. "Sense Entailment and Modus Ponens." *Journal of Philosophical Logic,* 1980.

————. "Logic of Paradox." *Journal of Philosophical Logic,* 1979.

————. "Logic of Paradox Revisited." *Journal of Philosophical Logic,* 13, 1984.

————. "Semantic Closure." *Studia Logica,* 43, 1983.

Ramsey, F.P. "Review of Wittgenstein's 'Tractatus'." In *Essays on Wittgenstein's 'Tractatus'.* New York: The Macmillan Co., 1967.

Russell, Bertrand. *Analysis of Mind.* London: George Allen & Unwin Ltd., 1971.

————. *Introduction to 'Tractatus',* by Ludwig Wittgenstein. Routledge and Kegan Paul Ltd., 1966.

————. "Lectures on Logical Atomism." In *Readings in Twentieth Century Philosophy.* Edited by Warren Alston and George Nakhnikian. New York: The Free Press, 1964.

————. "On Propositions: What they are and how they mean." In *Logic and Knowledge.* Edited by Robert C. Marsh. New York: G.P. Putnam's Sons, 1971.

Stenius, Erik. *Wittgenstein's 'Tractatus'.* London: Basil Blackwell, 1960.

Urmson, J.O. *Philosophical Analysis: its development between the two world wars.* New York: Oxford University Press, 1969.

Von Wright, G.H., ed. *Letters to Russell, Keynes and Moore.* Ithaca, New York: Cornell University Press, 1974.

Williams, John N. "Believing the Self-Contradictory." *American Philosophical Quarterly,* July 1982.

Wisdom, John. "Logical Constructions." *Mind.* I:XL, 1931–33, in five parts.

Wittgenstein, Ludwig. *The Blue and Brown Books.* New York: Harper and Row, 1965.

————. *Notebooks, 1914–16.* Edited by G.H. Von Wright and G.E.M. Anscombe with an English translation by G.E.M. Anscombe. Harper and Row, 1969.

————. *On Certainty.* New York: Harper and Row, 1972.

————. *Philosophical Investigations.* Oxford: Basil Blackwell, 1958.

————. *Remarks on the Foundations of Mathematics.* Cambridge, Massachusetts: M.I.T. Press, 1972.

————. *Tractatus-logico-philosophicus.* London: Routledge and Kegan Paul, Ltd., 1966.

Index

301